Gander

Gander

Terrorism, Incompetence and the Rise of Islamic National Socialism

Saul M. Montes-Bradley II

Published by
TOBF Press
South Boston, Virginia, 2016

Printed in U.S.A.

This book is dedicated to the victims of Arrow Air flight 1285, in particular to

mayn gelibte

Stacey Michelle Cutler

A beautiful woman, a loyal friend and a sweet companion.

And to the memory of

mayn balibter zeyde

Yankel Kaplan

Peacemaker

מײן באליבטע זיידע

יאַנקעל קאַפלאַן

שלום ליבהאָבער

CONTENTS

Book I
The Crash at Gander

Book II
Jihad, the Arab Gotteskampf

ACKNOWLEDGMENTS

In no particular order, I would like to thank the following, who have at different times provided material or insight into the making of this book: Joanne Griffin Lawrie, Christine Vargo Linville, Maureen McMahon Muck, Janice Fried, Walter Jerusalinsky, Nemen Terc, David B. Mitchell, Esq., Charlotta Holmlund, Travis Clay, and my parents, Sara Kaplan and Nelson Montes-Bradley.

BOOK I

The Crash at Gander

1
Introduction

On the morning of December 12th, 1985, I was woken up by a phone call at about 7:00 AM. On the other side was a friend, Benay Cluff, who only said: "Are you watching TV? Turn on CNN." I did, and was immediately taken aback. An Arrow Air DC8 had just crashed in Gander. Over the course of the day, I learned that many of my closest friends—including the woman I loved and hoped to marry—had died in one of the worst air disasters to date.

Arrow Air DC-8
Similar to the one that crashed at Gander

The initial shock gave way to incredulity and the irrational hope that somehow survivors would be found. The images on the screen, of course, defied any such notion. As the day wore off, all kinds of idle speculations were aired by so-called reporters with a duty to fill airtime more than to elucidate facts.

Their carping turned onto the airline, suggesting a possible shoddy operation had been at fault; to the crew, suggesting the inexperience of "Florida crews" in the icy conditions of Newfoundland winters; and to the US Army, suggesting the possibility of illegal cargo such as live ordnance. Some even questioned the airline's practices in crew scheduling, insinuating that maybe the cockpit crew was too tired to perform their services efficiently. None of it was true, and none of these fantasies took into account the calls to France-Presse, Reuters, American diplomatic facilities in Europe and Africa—and to the CASB in Quebec—claiming responsibility in the name of *Islamic Jihad*.

A few days later, still dazed and confused friends and co-workers assisted a memorial service at the Chapel in the center of JFK international airport, and afterwards many of us went to the home of one of the flight attendants on Lefferts Boulevard near Grenfell St. in Kew Gardens, unwilling to part each other's company. I have had little contact with them since, except for a few years with Benay,[1] sporadically with my good friend Mo, and recently in the preparation of his book.

---

[1] Benay Alma Cluff, born in Wilmington, Los Angeles, on August 2nd, 1955, she left us all too soon on January 7th, 1991.

2

The Flight

Arrow Air flight R1285JW was chartered under contract with the Department of Defense to ferry troops from the *Multinational Force and Observers (MFO)*, established in 1982 to guarantee the peace treaty between Israel and Egypt and headquartered at Rome with two bases in the Sinai Peninsula. The South base at Sharm el-Sheik, a small town a little over 300 miles southeast of Cairo, and a North base at el-Arish, a hamlet near the Gaza strip. For nearly two years we had been doing flights to and from there, but this one would be different from the beginning.

MAC (Military Airlift Command) flights were an important part of Arrow Air's business, and we routinely carried soldiers and family members from military facilities in New York, Pennsylvania, Delaware, South Carolina, North Carolina, Nevada, Kansas, Arizona, Texas and California to military bases overseas such as Mildenhall, Aviano, Bodo, Rota, Singonella, Diego García, Rhein Main, Cologne, and Osaka. At one time or another, I had flown all of them, like most of Arrow's crews, including the one a few months earlier bringing the 101st airborne soldiers from Kentucky to el-Arish (el-Gorah Airport, a few miles from the Gaza strip) for the rotation they were now ending in time for Christmas.

For thirty years now, I have witnessed the botched investigations conducted by Canadian and US authorities, more an exercise in political posturing and ass-covering by an endless supply of pencil pushers and venal bureaucrats than any serious effort to discover the causes of the crash.

I have also seen, from the onset, an almost willful disregard for the airline's crews, always a footnote adding eight to the list of the dead and not much more. And, perhaps not surprisingly, I have seen an endless parade of conspiracy theories linking the fate of Arrow 1285 to anything from the Iran-Contra affair to some military-industrial complex foul-up, to the illegal use of tactical nuclear weapons, to the ever present CIA conspiracy to erase evidence of God-knows-what, to those "evil Jews" of the Mossad for reasons that are as difficult to imagine as impossible to comprehend.

These absurd—and often despicable—conspiracy theories notwithstanding, there is, to be sure, no reason for the Arrow Air disaster to remain unsolved so many years after the fact, except for the unwillingness or incapacity or both of those responsible then and now. I hope my recollections and observations might one day be useful, perhaps long before some of the documents are unsealed.

***

The regular route for the MFO flights was from el-Arish to Cairo—a refueling stop made necessary by the short runway at el-Gorah airport near el-Arish—then on to Cologne or Frankfurt, followed by another refueling stop at Gander, Newfoundland; and on to Ft. Campbell in Kentucky (sometimes Charlotte, Charleston or Philadelphia were used, depending on the troops being transported). El-

Gorah (HEGR) was a small airport in the middle of no-where,[2] surrounded by nothing but sand, some ten miles from the Israeli border, near the town of el-Arish and home to the North Base Camp of the MFO. We would park out of the way, under military surveillance, while all embarkation procedures were conducted at a small tent some 500 yards from the plane by two Egyptian officers and their American counterparts. The Arrow crew was not allowed to disembark except within a small radius around the plane, and we never got to see much at all.

El-Gorah, North Base Camp of the MFO in Sinai
Google satellite picture

After all passengers were onboard, we would depart for our short flight to Cairo, where the plane was always parked out of the way in a remote area of the tarmac, sur-rounded by Egyptian military forces forming a circle around it while the aircraft was refueled (I still remember

---

[2] It had been an Israeli Air Force base, Eitan, built during the occupation of the Sinai between 1967 and 1979, about 1½ hours from Tel Aviv, 5 hours from Cairo, and minutes from the Rafah border crossing into the Gaza strip.

the impression it caused upon me the sight of black-clad, German style helmeted troops surrounding us.) No one was allowed in or out of the perimeter—though they generally permitted us to open the doors to have some air circulation.

Approach to Cairo
The Giza Plateau to the left, Cairo airport in front.

The interior of the plane was extremely hot, and there were no APUs to provide for external air conditioning units. After the short refueling stop—which was done with all passengers and crew aboard—we would fly mostly to Rhein Main Air Force Base (adjacent to the Frankfurt airport)[3] or Cologne. There, new crews would board—as the leg to Gander would have exceeded permitted duty time. Contrary to some press reports, the accommodations for the layover were anything but shabby. In Frankfurt, we stayed at the Hotel *Maritim am Darmstadt*, a four star facility with an excellent restaurant and spa, across from *Platz der Deustchen Einheit*, that to this day receives rave reviews from travelers. The layover was usually for two to three days, de-

---

[3] Rhein Main AFB was closed in 2005. The last flight took off in September followed by a formal closing ceremony on October 10th, although the actual transfer to German authorities took place on December 30th. All operations were transferred to Ramstein (80mi southwest of Frankfurt) and Spangdahlem (about 100mi south of Cologne).

pending on the frequency of flights, and we would then continue on the America bound leg. Gander was but a short refueling stop made necessary by the range limitations of the DC-8s or 707s that were assigned to these routes. We were allowed to disembark there into a waiting area with minimal services and a gift shop with just about anything moose one can imagine, and the usual t-shirts and souvenirs. After forty-five minutes to an hour, the flight would resume to the appropriate home base of the troops.

***

But on that 11th day of December 1985, things were different. First, the flight did not depart from el-Gorah. This time, troops were being sent from the South base at Sharm-al-Sheik, and as the runway at Ras-Nasrani airport nearby was being lengthened, a shorter than usual run made it impossible for the DC-8 to land or take off from there. The troops were then ferried to Cairo in two chartered Egypt Air 737s out of Ras-Nasrani. Their luggage could not be carried in those small planes, so it was trucked to Cairo, some five hours away, arriving at the airport twenty-five hours before the flight. That luggage was kept in a storage facility with minimum security afforded by two Egyptian guards.

The soldiers of the 101st arrived on time, but as the Arrow flight was delayed nearly twelve hours, they were taken to the Cairo *Hyatt el Salaam* for some rest. When the Arrow plane arrived, the luggage was taken from the storage facility and loaded by an Egyptian *"commercial cargo handling crew,"* without military supervision.[4] Much has been

---

[4] When Congressman Hughes pressed Col. Carpenter on this subject, the response was as evasive as it was telling: *Was this standard procedure with all the MFO flights? — No, sir. Usually US Soldiers loaded US flights. — Did you physically observe the load-*

said about some discrepancies in the cargo, but perhaps not sufficient attention has been paid to the fact that the luggage was for many hours under the control of Egyptian civilian crews and to the obvious disorganization during the loading process that included a brawl among the handlers.

With no military oversight other than that afforded by a single Egyptian soldier; the Egyptian ground handlers loaded the cargo in virtual darkness. The auxiliary power that provided some lights broke down twice and during one of the blackouts a fight among the handlers started out near the tail of the plane—perhaps a diversionary maneuver, we will never know. In addition, only a portion of that luggage had ever been inspected—not that it would have made much difference given the lack of control. In fact, US Customs officers that were supposed to have cleared the cargo for importation into the US refused to do so.[5]

Simply put, in spite of the lack of control for many hours and the handling by unknown civilian employees, the luggage and additional cargo were not properly inspected. Based on reports, the cargo bins were so packed that a number of pieces had to be left behind, including, surprisingly, forty-four soldiers' packs. Captain Arthur Shoppaul, who commanded the flight from Cairo to Cologne, said in his report that there was **no security provided in Cairo for the luggage**, and that it was parked on the tarmac for

---

ing of the plane and the unloading of the truck? — Yes, sir, not continuously. And this upright citizen continued deflecting responsibility onto the Egyptian Government. [*Fatal Plane Crash in Gander, Newfoundland, December 12, 1995, Hearings Before the Subcommittee on Crime of the Committee on the Judiciary*, House of Representatives, One Hundred First Congress, Second Session, December 4 and 5, 1990, Serial No. 147, Printed for the use of the Committee on the Judiciary, US Government Printing Office, Washington, 1991, p. 182.]

[5] US Congress, *op. cit.*, p. 181-182. Capt. Deporter, the officer in charge of the Customs team was denied access to the airport. In consequence, there was no inspection of the cargo loaded onto the flight. Capt. Deporter notified headquarters and the officers on-site, but no action was taken.

five hours without any inspection being performed before loading it to the cargo hold. He also stated that there was no security check for the passengers prior to boarding: *"at no time was a baggage inspection carried out, neither in the barracks nor at the airport."* He also reported on the lack of security at Cologne, where various employees of multiple nationalities cleaned the aircraft's interior without any supervision. Capt. Shoppaul was to the point *"Ground security was* **very poor** *in Cairo and Cologne."*

The flight from Cairo to Cologne was quite uneventful, the cockpit and cabin crews were replaced there, a new preflight check was conducted—including a new passenger count—and the plane left Cologne at 02:50 GMT.[6]

***

Six hours and fourteen minutes later, the plane landed in Gander in a light drizzle.[7] Passengers deplaned to a sterile area where they could get some coffee and souvenirs while the plane was refueled. Ground crews removed trash, serviced the lavatories dumping waste water, and Mike Fowler, as was his habit, did his walk-around inspection of the plane, checking for ice or any kind of airworthiness issue. He was seen by ground workers as he checked the leading and trailing edges of the wing, the engines, the empennage and the nose section. Capt. John Griffin per-

---

[6] They had arrived in Cologne, from Gander, at 09:31 GMT on the 11th, almost 18 hours earlier. They were at the hotel from 11:00 AM local time on the 11th until 2:00 AM local time on the 12th. The hotel staff *"were of the opinion that that the crew did not leave the hotel during the crew rest period."*

[7] Ground observations in Gander at 06:00 GMT described a "measured ceiling 1,400 ft broken, 2,800 ft overcast, visibility 10 mi in light snow, barometric pressure 1011.6 mb, temperature 4 C, dew point -5 C, wind 330 T at 4 kt, altimeter setting 29.84 in. Hg, strato cumulus 6 tenths, strato cumulus 4 tenths."

formed his own check and, when both were satisfied, passengers were boarded and the plane taxied to its takeoff position. At 10:15 GMT, they began take-off at the intersection of runway 22 and runway 13. The weather was perhaps unusually mild for Gander winters.[8] No *"significant of unusual weather conditions were reported"* by the pilot of a Piper landing on runway 31 at the same time, nor twenty minutes later by the pilot of a 737, who could not recall encountering any icing conditions—other than a light precipitation below cloud—and described the weather on approach as *"smooth with light wind and no turbulence."*

Flight 1285 reached a speed of 172 knots before lift-off and, as it flew at low altitude over the trans-Canada Highway, witnesses described a bright orange glow underneath—bright enough to illuminate the interior of their truck cabs. It then made a sharp right bank and crashed into down sloping terrain 2,975 feet from the runway and 720 feet to the right of the runway's center line. It was 10:16 GMT. The entire flight lasted about a minute. Initial impact was a tree strike at 279 feet (ground elevation at this point was approximately 240 feet), and continued its descent hitting the ground 920 feet later. The wreckage trail was 1,300 feet long by 130 feet wide.

A full detail of the wreckage break-up is painfully described in the Investigation Report. But some things are worthy of notice. The fuselage was broken into several sections and *"substantially consumed by fire."*

---

[8] Ground observations at 10:00 GMT were "700 ft scattered, measured ceiling 1,200 ft overcast, visibility 12 mi in very light snow grains, barometric pressure 1011.8 mb, temperature -°C, dew point -5°C, wind 290°T at 4 kt, altimeter setting 29.86 in. Hg, stratus fractus 5 tenths, strato cumulus 5 tenths."

Smoldering portion of the fuselage
December 12th, 1985

Impact site
December 13th, 1985

The empennage was separated from the fuselage, and *"portions had been subjected to the post-crash fire."* There was no evidence, at the crash site or the runway, to suggest that the tail had struck the runway.

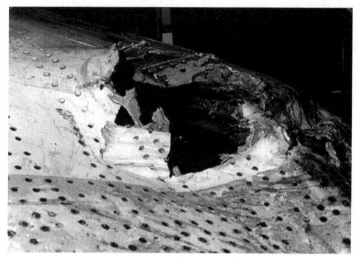

**Portion of the fuselage
with clear evidence of an explosion.**
CASB Dissenting Report.

Evidence was found of *"pre-impact explosive damage to the aircraft fuselage. The evidence consisted of a hole, roughly elliptical in shape, in a section of fuselage wall just aft of the right side forward door. The material that surrounded the hole exhibited an outward pucker, and the hole was assessed to be the result of an object striking the interior of the fuselage at high speed. A second hole was found in another unidentified section of fuselage. This hole was somewhat larger and also displayed outward deformation of the fuselage skin."*[9]

The RCMP Central Forensic Laboratory and the CASB Engineering Laboratory, however, disregarded this, as they found *"no evidence of foreign material or explosive residue"*—Semtex, we might as well note, would have left no

---

[9] *Pinkel Report*, discussed at length below.

such residue! [10] *"The hole in the fuselage wall section aft of the right side forward door was attributed to an object being forced through the fuselage during breakup...In the case of the second, larger hole, CASB investigators observed that the degree of curling at the edges of the hole was less than that of the other hole and that the edges were burned thin and were brittle, evidence of intense heat."* Of course, there is no question that an object was forced through the fuselage—there's the hole to prove that—but the RCMP report is silent as to what *propelled* the object and it determines, without the benefit of hard evidence, that whatever propelled it did so "during breakup." Evidence of intense heat along the edges precludes nothing—especially when one considers the fire that ensued—and the failure of the RCMP and the CASB to consider Semtex is one more instance of the incapacity born of inexperience displayed throughout the investigation.

---

[10] Semtex is a very pliable, odorless and practically untraceable plastic explosive. Terrorists obtained large quantities that were manufactured in Czechoslovakia and sold to Egypt and Libya—The Washington Post reported that Vaclav Havel, upon assuming the Presidency of Czechoslovakia, disclosed that his country had sold 1,000 tons of Semtex to Libya. Two years after the Arrow crash, Pan AM 103 was downed by a bomb made of only 400 grams of Semtex. Abdel Massed Ali al-Megrahi the Libyan intelligence officer who became the only person convicted for the Pan Am bombing had ties to al-Jihad operatives in Libya as early as 1984.

3
The Cockpit Crew

Captain **John Joseph Griffin, USAF,** was born in Steubenville, Ohio on March 26th, 1940, the son of John J. and Anna (Burke) Griffin. He married on December 28th, 1963 in Brooke Co., West Virginia, Teresa Ierise of Follansbee, West Virginia. They had three children, Jean,[11] Elizabeth and Patrick. Even as a student in Steubenville, he let everyone know that he would one day be a pilot. He graduated from Steubenville Catholic Central High in 1958 (ranked 10th among a Senior class of 180), earned a Bachelor's degree from the University of Steubenville in 1962,

---

[11] Jean died on 17 June 1968 in New York, just shy of her fourth birthday.

married his sweetheart in 1963 and joined the Air Force in Lubbock, Texas, serving a tour of duty as a pilot in Viet Nam. After retiring from the Air Force he joined Pan American Airways and, in January of 1982, Arrow Air. He was a check pilot on the DC8 and 707, and for some time Director of Operations. His last recurrent training on the DC8 had been completed in November of 1985, weeks before the incident. By December of 1985, he had been a pilot for 22 years.

By all accounts, John was a meticulous professional with a keen attention to detail. I remember his insistence on personally conducting walkabouts and performing thorough checks before every flight. I learned later that even when he was teaching his son how to drive he would perform "pre-drive checks." I also remember at least one occasion a year earlier when he had a 707 grounded before the flight over what turned out to be "an indication problem;" that is, there was no question over the airworthiness of the plane, but a fire warning light was malfunctioning. John would not sign on for departure until maintenance had taken care of it.

First Officer **Joseph Robert Connelly, USAF Lt. Col.,** was born on September 15th, 1940 in Washington, Pennsylvania (near Pittsburgh), the son of Davis Thomas and Frances (Silbaugh) Connelly. His family moved to Miami, Florida where he attended public schools graduating from North Miami Beach High and the University of Florida. He enlisted in the Air Force in 1959, and retired in 1985 as a Lt. Colonel in the Air Force Reserve. In 1963, he married Karen Ruth Chervenak, with whom he had three daughters and two sons. In 1981, while he was still active in the USAF Reserve, he joined Arrow as First Officer for the 707, and was later qualified for the DC-8 and DC-10. In

October of 1985, as Arrow reduced its DC-10 operations, he underwent recurring training in the DC-8. That was less than two months from the incident. At the time of the crash, he had 26 years of experience.

Flight Engineer **Arthur Michael "Mike" Fowler** was born on May 31ˢᵗ, 1937 in Tarpon Springs, Florida, the son of Arthur Hollis and Elizabeth Frances (Deyoreo) Fowler. He attended schools in Florida, and on December 20ᵗʰ, 1956 enlisted in the Air Force, remaining active until August 24ᵗʰ, 1976. In 1957, he married Patricia F. "Pat" Spratling. They had four children. Pat and their older daughter were Flight Attendants for Arrow Air. He was certainly not an inexperienced Floridian and he was not a cavalier airman who would risk his wife or daughter's lives—or anybody else's, for that matter—by taking an un-safe plane to the air. He was a thoughtful, capable man, who insisted on personally walking around the plane and checking every system before he signed on for takeoff. One of the first to join Arrow in 1981, he was qualified for 707, DC-8 and DC-10 aircraft. His last recurrent training on the DC-8 was in October of 1985.

Mike was not a young pilot keeping the third jump-seat warm while he waited for a promotion to First Officer. He was a Flight Engineer by choice, loved his work and had been on the third seat for over 20 years. In fact, at the time of the crash he had accumulated over 29 years of ex-perience.

***

Thus, the cockpit crew of Arrow Air 1285 was made of three highly capable Air Force veterans with more than

78 years combined experience. They were all highly regarded professionals, meticulous and thorough in their duties. Contrary to remarks by CASB and press reports, far from being a "Florida based crew" ill versed in the icy conditions at Gander, they were a thoroughly capable an experienced crew versed in the most extreme conditions around the world.

***

I was well acquainted with them, although perhaps a bit more with Mike Fowler, who was like a father to us. To know them was an honor and a privilege for which I am still grateful. The suggestion floated in the CASB Majority Report, the press, and the Senate hearing in 1986 that they were inexperienced pilots from a tropical area is ridiculous; that they would have been irresponsible enough to fly in less than perfect physical condition is ludicrous; and as their vast experience above demonstrates, the idea that they may have willingly or negligently compromised the safety of the flight to lower costs of for whatever other reason is not just absurd, it is an infamy.

4

The Cabin Crew

Flight Service Manager **Maia Matasovski** was born in Romania in 1957, the daughter of Michael and Bela (Kohane) Matasovski.[12] The family came to the US in 1965, and Maia grew up in North Miami Beach. She was an outgoing, no-nonsense girl, who had been flying for three years before being promoted to Flight Service Manager. As FSM, she would have been sitting on the jump-seat next to the forward left door just aft of the cockpit.

In spite of her difficult early childhood in Romania and as a newly arrived immigrant in Miami—or perhaps because of it—Maia was a fun loving, lively woman, always optimistic, always ready to cheer the crowd. Her boundless energy and determination to get the job done made it a pleasure not just to work with her, but to have her around as a joyful travel companion.

---

[12] Bela Kohane Matasovski was a Holocaust survivor from Poland. After the war, she emigrated to Israel, married Mike Matasovski and ended up in Romania.

Flight attendants

Jean Serafin was born Jeanne Eleanor Serafin on September 18th, 1948, in Hudson, Lenawee Co., Michigan, the daughter of Sgt. Joseph Francis "Frank" Serafin, US Army, and CPL Florence Amelia Coscarelli, USMC, both WWII veterans. Jean was originally based in Miami and had recently requested reassignment to New York. As the most senior FA she would have been seated to the left of Maia.

A wonderful woman who could not disguise her past as a teacher, she was always counseling and assisting new arrivals. I recall that in 1984, when I was temporarily reassigned to Miami to write Arrow's Flight Attendant Manual,[13] she found out that I was living at the Best Western on Lejeune Blvd. and without hesitation offered me to move to her place near Miracle Mile until the end of the assignment. She would not hear of payment, and was just glad to make my life better. A quintessentially Midwestern gal, her grandparents were immigrants from Poland, Russia and Ita-

---

[13] In September and October, 1984, I wrote the Flight Attendant Manual sections of the 707 and DC-8, including the service, safety and evacuation procedures.

ly. She was buried at Calvary Cemetery in Pittsford, Hillsdale Co., Michigan.

Ruthie Phillips was born Ruth Ann Vargo in 1959 in Bay Village, Cuyahoga Co., Ohio, the daughter of Paul G. and Ruth M. (DiCapua) Vargo. On June 1st, 1983, I met her on the Arrow 707 that took us from New York to Flight Attendant training in Miami. She was a sweetheart. With the mellow features of her father's Czech heritage and the amiability of her mother's Italian background, Ruthie was kind, generous and lively. Her sister, Chrissy, was already working for Arrow, and would come to the Marriott on Lejeune Blvd. to give us pointers and assist in whatever might be needed. During that training period she confided in me that she had joined Arrow because she wanted to meet and "marry a pilot". We flew together countless times, and she always proved to be capable, reliable and a lot of fun. In 1984 she began dating one of the pilots that we met in our earliest flights. They were to get married in April, 1986. Ruthie had already applied for a land job in anticipation of the wedding, and was to go into controller training four weeks after the flight. That was to be her last month as a Flight Attendant. Alas, on January 3rd, 1986, she was laid to rest at Holy Cross Cemetery in Brook Park, Cuyahoga Co., Ohio, near Cleveland.

Stacy Cutler was born Stacey Michelle Cutler on January 1st, 1961, in Miami, Florida, the daughter of Melvin Joseph and Frances Bertha (Rosen) Cutler. She grew up and attended schools in North Miami, where she lived with her mother and her older sister Andrea.

Stacey joined our class at the Marriott in June of 1983, a young woman who wanted to prove that she could live on her own. After training, she requested to be based in New York and moved there in July of that year. I helped her move into a small apartment in Manhattan, about two blocks from Bloomingdale's, on 60th Street between 3rd and 2nd Avenues. Her place was five stories up with no elevator, so she soon obtained a key for the building next door, and we would take the elevator there, get to her building through the rooftops and come down one flight to her place.

Having lived in New York for a few years, I became her guide, and in ways she probably never knew, she became mine. Her first flight was a few weeks later, a turnaround from JFK to—of all places— Miami on a DC8. She was working the aft galley and, much as I had experienced a couple of weeks earlier, was having an awful time of it. Unlike my previous experience, where I had the benefit of Charlotta Holmlund guiding me, she had a hellish time with a wench who did nothing but chide her. I took the time to assist her and reassure her that there was nothing wrong with her work. A few weeks later, she was the best worker on any crew that was lucky to have her and, over time, that is exactly what she became.

Off-duty, rather than lounge around waiting for the next flight she secured employment in Bloomingdale's. It was not unusual to find her behind a counter, or walking the aisles offering a taste of perfume. I frequently went to meet her there, and we would go for a movie at a small theatre on 3rd Avenue between 59th and 60th; followed by dinner, sometimes at her place just around the corner. During that time, my mother doubled her regular visits to Bloomingdale's to see her as often as she could, and would later tell me of their "chance encounters." Of course, there was no chance involved whatsoever, but she loved Stacey's company and made no effort to hide her approval of the *"sheine meideleh."*

I came to admire Stacey's tenacity, work ethic, optimism and courage; and while she thought I was helping her, she was indeed helping me become a better man. She was a strikingly beautiful woman whose modesty did not allow her to see herself as such. When she died she was in her prime, finally on her own, thriving in a city that tolerated no failure. The last time I saw her, we had spent the night at the Holliday Inn on Rockaway Boulevard by the cargo area of JFK. I was leaving on an early flight for Gatwick and she had just arrived a few hours earlier from Paris leaving us with no time to get back to the city.[14]

We were planning to take a few days off on our own for the holydays and travel to Miami to be with her family. As I left in the morning trying not to wake her up, I forgot my tie. When I turned around wondering whether to wake her up or not, there she was, smiling, looking radiant, holding the tie out the door. That is my last image of her, beau-

---

[14] It was not uncommon for Arrow's scheduling department to authorize a hotel room at the airport when the schedule was tight, even when we were at our base city. As I had just been assigned an unscheduled trip and had to ferry to London only ten hours later, they approved the hotel, and our scheduled dinner in New York turned into a late evening at the airport.

tiful, loving and happy. It took me thirty years to gather the courage to place a pebble on her grave.

Desiree McKay was born in Georgetown, Guyana, about 1960. Her father was Arrow's representative in Georgetown, and she had come to us when the airline assumed the operations of Guyana Airways. This included scheduled flights from Miami and New York to Georgetown, with Guyanese crews and one US based Manager. When I became In-flight Services Supervisor in New York, she asked me to help her to get transferred to the New York base, as she wanted to fly to other destinations and escape the dreariness of Georgetown-New York turnarounds. I managed to secure Arrow's sponsorship for a work visa, and in October of 1985 she called me to tell me that her paperwork had finally been approved and she would finally be able to fly to Europe. Arrow 1285 was her second such flight.

5
The Canadians

CASB

The Canadian Aviation Safety Board was established in 1984, replacing the Aircraft Accident Investigation Branch of Transport Canada, with the express object of making the investigation process independent of Transport Canada. In 1990, after the debacle of the Arrow Air investigation, the CASB was unceremoniously disbanded and replaced with the Transportation Safety Board of Canada, still the agency of the Canadian government in charge of investigations of aviation, rail, marine and pipeline accidents.

The first chairman of the CASB was Bernard M. Deschênes, a Montreal attorney with strong links to the Liberal Party co-Chairman of the Constitution and Legal Affairs Commission (he was appointed in February 1984, eight months before the CASB begun formal operations). His second in command was Ken Johnson, formerly a senior official in the Transport Department. The director of investigations was Tom Hinton, another bureaucrat from Transport Canada appointed by Johnson.

Also under Johnson was Peter Boag, a chap with a degree in Urban and Regional Planning who, after two tours of duty in the RCAF had managed to obtain his brevet as pilot of twin engine turboprops and, after joining Transport Canada in 1982, had successfully completed a three-week course in accident investigation, just before being transferred to the CASB with Johnson and the rest of his staff. He later completed a two-week course in Stockholm. He must indeed have excelled in the pencil-pusher craft to have been appointed the head investigator in Canada's worst air disaster with such lean resume![15] As Les Filotas said of him: *"More seasoned investigators describe him as inexperienced and arrogant."*[16]

Other Board members included Dave Mussallem, Norman Bobbitt, and Les Filotas, all aeronautical engineers; Ross Stevenson, a former DC8 pilot for Air Canada (all four subscribed to the Minority Report); Arthur Porterlance, a Liberal MP from Montreal with some interests in aviation matters; Roger Lacroix, a former combat pilot and member of the RCMP who resigned in disgust before the final vote without disguising his contempt for the icing theory; William MacEahern[17]; Bruce Leslie Pultz, a pilot who retired from the RCAF in 1959 and became the owner of Pultz Aviation Training and Aircraft Sales Company in Saskatchewan (who became a full member in 1986); and Frank Thurston *"a wily old bureaucrat"*, according to Filotas, who was appointed to a one-year term in June

---

[15] If the original intent of the CASB was to create an agency independent of Transport Canada as was declared at the time, we can be forgiven for stating that the execution of the law was a most abject failure.

[16] Les Filotas, *Improbable Cause*, Booksurge, 2006.

[17] He was quoted on the Chicago Tribune in April 22nd, 1990, while still defending the already debunked icing-on-the-wings theory: *"To be responsible and reasonable, you have to come up with more than speculation and conjecture"*. Why he consistently failed to follow his own advice remains a mystery.

1984, mostly through the efforts of Deschênes to counter-act the obvious patronage appointments of Porterlance and MacEachern.

By the time of the Arrow crash, Thurston's appointment had expired, but he continued to participate in and, indeed, on occasion preside over the meetings of the Board and vote on its resolutions. His is one of the five votes for the Majority report, in spite of his initial opposition to the icing theory.[18]

RCMP

The Mounties, best known around the world for the affable if not too bright cartoon character of the 1960s Rocky and Bullwinkle Show, had control of the crash site and any criminal investigation that might ensue, at least within Canadian borders.

---

[18] Considering Thurston's peculiar status as a non-member of the Board, one would think that any decisions taken while he presided and, indeed, cast a decisive vote would abate. Alas, that was not the case, and the icing theory survived.

Heady Gill, a rental car attendant recalled his encounter with the investigators:

"So that's where I was going, to meet the passengers. I was on my way to the airport and I had just parked my car in our parking lot in front of the terminal. I saw the aircraft taxiing out from the terminal, and then I saw an explosion at the end of the runway. She had just lifted off the runway and—bang! You could have seen it anywhere in town. It wasn't quite light out and it was this big ball of fire.

When I saw it, I ran into the airport. The only person there was a commissionaire, and I said, 'Did an aircraft just leave here?' and he said, 'Yes, b'y. Military.'

And I said, 'Well b'y, I think she's blowed up at the end of the runway.'

At around 8 p.m., two RCMP officers from St. John's in civilian clothes came to my house to talk to me...They asked me if I saw the plane explode. They asked me if I thought there was a bomb aboard, and I said I didn't know."[19]

And apparently, based on this expert opinion, the RCMP shelved the bomb theory. Or so it seems.

Certainly, other than the inconclusive and incomplete analysis of wreckage—and that only at the request of the CASB and owed almost exclusively to the insistence of the four members that would in the end produce a Minori-

---

[19] The Telegram, 4 Dec 2010, *In Gander, the Scars Remain.* He also recalls that *"the crash had an effect on his whole family. His son [Kelly] was part of the airport's crash crew, and it was only his second day on the job. 'He was four days out on the site picking up bodies, pieces of bodies. He lost his appetite; didn't eat for four days'. 'One of the things that amazed me was how little of the airplane appeared to be left after the crash,' Kelly said. 'I've seen pictures of lots of crashes and there was large amounts of airplane left, but this one, there was very little which indicated the ferociousness of the crash. Normally, they can put the plane back together piece by piece until they find the cause, especially in the case of an explosion—like the one that exploded over New York in 1976. That couldn't happen with this one, so there was a whole lot of mystery surrounding the crash for years later."*

28

ty Report—no criminal investigation was conducted. No serious investigation followed the calls of *Islamic Jihad* to the CASB on December 13th, 1985, and no report from the RCMP was ever made public. Or at It appears that, as the FBI left the field in the hands of their capable neighbors to the north and did nothing, the capable neighbors to the north did nothing more than post guards around the wreckage and talk to a few locals. Mission accomplished.

Justice Willard Estey

In March of 1989, Transportation Minister Benoit Bouchard appointed Justice Willard Estey[20] to review the findings of the CASB. Justice Estey concluded that ice contamination was not a cause, *"or even a probable cause of this accident,"* nullifying the CASB report in a single sentence. He also found that there was not enough evidence to support a fire or bomb theory.

Since he constructed his mandate narrowly and adamantly refused to consider any additional evidence to that which was included in the CASB report, and since the CASB had either ignored or refused to investigate evidence of fire or bomb, it was no surprise Justice Estey could not find sufficient evidence. Had he included Dr. Richard Shepperd's pathological analysis—among the many submissions that the CASB had ignored—he may have come to a different conclusion. Even if hard evidence of an explosion contained in Irving Pinkel's report is thrust aside, Dr. Shepperd, based on pathological reports on the victims, concluded unequivocally that a pre-impact fire had indeed engulfed the aircraft.

---

[20] Justice Willard Zebedee Estey (1919-2002) was a respected jurist and former member of the Canadian Supreme Court (1977-1988).

Once Justice Estey debunked the CASB report, calls for a full enquiry were rejected with the facetious argument that such an investigation would not further elucidate the facts and cause undue anguish to the relatives of the victims.

How could Justice Estey anticipate the results of an inquiry that would not be limited to the CASB report information he did not say. And by what rationale he came to the conclusion that shoving the whole affair under the carpet was preferable for the families of the victims is yet another unsolved mystery.[21]

Canadian Forces

The folks at the Canadian Forces Base in Gander are a sterling exemption to the collection of incompetents that landed on Gander on December 12th, 1985. At about 7:00 AM local time, a Base recall went out, and by 8:00 AM the Command Post had been established, and the 60 or so personnel of the Base Defense Force of the CFB Gander were ready to assist the RCMP, already at the scene. Among the first to arrive at the crash site was Capt. T.C. Badcock: *"I could see that the further down I went, more was missing from the tops of the trees. Pieces of material were hanging rather ominously from the broken trees, and, despite the fact that their tops were missing, none of the broken parts were at the base of the trees...Suddenly, the road divided and the scene that met my eyes is one I will never forget. There*

---

[21] Associated Press, *Canada Judge Rejects New Gander Crash Probe*, July 22nd, 1989. *"A judge who reviewed the official investigation of the 1985 air crash in Newfoundland that killed 256 Americans said Friday that the probe did not find the cause, but reopening it would produce 'the same lonely result.' Willard Estey, a retired Supreme Court justice, said the evidence does not support the conclusions in the report of the Canadian Aviation Safety Board about what caused the disaster."*

were firemen, civilians, RCMP officers and others I know not who, hurrying around with no apparent goal."[22]

A gruesome depiction of the site follows this remark, but I see no point in repeating it. On December 14th, at 19:30 GMT, the CF military personnel were no longer required, and received the order to stand down. In two days, they had assisted in the removal of the bodies to the makeshift morgue in Hangar 21, provided logistical assistance to the other forces on the ground, and collected all of the weaponry from the crash, consisting of mangled personal weapons from the soldiers and three training duds. Capt. George Atkinson, the ranking officer on site, produced the final report:

> *Report of CFB Gander Assistance—12 DEC 85—Arrow Air Disaster.*
>
> *Part I—Introduction*
>
> 1. *At approximately 0645L on 12 December, 1985, an Arrow Airways DC-8 crashed on departure from Gander International Airport. The aircraft impacted between the end of runway 22 and Gander Lake. The site is rough, heavily wooded, steeply sloped towards the lake. The passengers were 248 soldiers of the US Army, 101 Airborne Division. They, and the eight crew, were killed instantly as the crash was catastrophic.*
>
> 2. *A gravel road run through the idle of the crash site and provided relatively quick access from the Trans Canada Highway. This facilitated response by all agencies. Two small creeks run through the site. At the time of the crash, there was no snow on the ground. Light snow began to fall on the afternoon of the 13th, somewhat hampering search efforts at the site.*

---

[22] T. C. Badcock, *A Broken Arrow*, St. John's, Newfoundland, 1988, p. 21

3. *CFB Gander was alerted at 0650L by airport authorities. Duty personnel immediately contacted the Base Commander at home. A full base recall was ordered. From that point on, CFB Gander response was in accordance with the Base Disaster Plan.*

4. *Airport authorities operated an Emergency Control Centre (ECC) at the airport terminal. The Base Commander was located there, as were senior representatives of the RCMP and other agencies. The base Command Post was manned and received its orders by telephone from the Base Commander. Operations monitoring and routine direction of base resources were provided by the Command Post Staff. At the crash site, an RCMP Inspector was in charge. A military On Scene Commander (OSC) was co-located with the RCMP site Commander during intense operations. The Base Defense Force (BDF) command and control structure were used to direct military assistance at the site and coordinate/control committed personnel resources while at rest. When site activities were reduced to cordon duties at night, a BDF officer acted as OSC. Duty at the site ended for CFB Gander Personnel at 1600L on the 14th.*

5. *A greatly augmented BDF was the key requirement. All base elements were required to provide these personnel and to undertake the significant support activities that were necessary. Base Supply, Food Services and Transportation were the most heavily tasked support groups. Over 300 Gander personnel, military and civilian, participated in the operation or in support of it. Routine base activity was largely curtailed during operations. 103 Rescue Unit maintenance ceased for a period, as did all routine maintenance at 226 Radar Squadron and 770 Communications Research Squadron. Operation Shifts at both squadrons were also altered to make more augmentees available to the BDF.*

6. *A number of other, lesser support and assistance activities were carried out by the base in the aftermath of the crash. They will be further described in Part II below.*

Part II—Details of CFB Gander Assistance

7. *Command and Control. The military chain of command was preserved and utilized throughout. Tasks were accepted by the Base Commander and relayed to the Command Post for execution. The various base elements received their tasking from the appropriate officer in the Command Post. The BDF command structure was also tasked by the Command Post. OSC's represented the Base Commander/Command Post at the disaster scene during intense operations. OSC's, BDF officers and Command Post staff showed initiative and foresight in making decisions within their scope of duties. At the same time, officers referred decisions and reported information to senior levels as necessary. All base officers, all unit commanding officers and a number of unit officers were involved. Similarly, at the senior NCO level, most base personnel and many from the units filled C and C functions.*

8. *Base Support Function. Virtually every support element of CFB Gander was involved. Food services operated around the clock. Supply and Transport were heavily tasked to support the BDF and its augmentees. In addition, Transport was asked to provide vehicles for several protocol occasions and various other specialized tasks.*

9. *BDF. In less than two hours after first notification from the airport, over 50 BDF personnel were organized and deployed at the crash site. All personnel were in winter environmental clothing. No weapons were carried. During daylight hours, BDF strength was maintained at approximately 50, with personnel providing cordon security and*

body recovery teams. BDF members worked directly with RCMP officers[23]. On cordon, when potential intruders were seen, a number of individuals, mostly press, tried, this was reported either to directly or by radio to the RCMP, who intercepted and dealt with them.[24] Each body recovery team was headed by a RCMP specialist who documented the remains and marked the location before team members placed them in body bags for transport to the morgue. Approximately 140 individuals served at the site during the operation. Shift rotation, especially over the daylight hours, was relatively frequent, with each on-going shift fed a hot meal before duty. Personnel coming off shift were given refreshments and bedded down in the gym (BDF HQ). Once shift rotations were established, some personnel were allowed to return to their residences for rest. At the site, supervisors were careful to rotate personnel very frequently between cordon and body recovery duties. This was necessary due to the physical and mental strain involved in the latter task. Significantly, there are no reports of any personnel being unable to carry out their share of this most unpleasant duty. Although some snow did fall, temperatures were mercifully moderate throughout the operation. There were no weather related health problems and the issue of environmental clothing was adequate for the task. BDF personnel and augmentees performed their duties in an exemplary manner and earned justifiable praise from the RCMP, US Army and other agencies at the scene. The BDF command and control structure proved sound, flexible and effective. Leadership and initiative were evident at all levels of supervision.

---

[23] Capt. Badcock remembers that the RCMP officers only assisted in the body recovery process *"when their supervisors were watching."* I guess there is no surprise there.

[24] This was apparently not enough to avoid the disappearance of personal items, especially photo cameras, that both disgusted and angered Capt. Badcock.

10. *Pollution Control. Shortly after the crash, concern was raised over the safety of the town water supply. The pumping station is located on the shore of the lake, approximately ½ km west of the crash site. Fuel from the aircraft was being carried into the lake by the two small brooks that run through the crash site. CFB Gander provided a second OSC, technical expertise and communications to a team which monitored the situation at the pump house. SAR technicians from 103 Rescue Unit also assisted in the installation of a floating boom to contain the fuel spill. In the event, no contamination of the water supply actually occurred.[25]*

11. *Assistance to the Accident Investigation Board (AIB). On Friday afternoon, in the face of forecast snow, the AIB requested assistance from CFB Gander to conduct a sweep search from the end of the runway to the crash site. Haste was required since, at the time of the request, only two hours of daylight remained. Fifty BDF personnel, off-duty from the crash site, were employed. It was not possible to complete the sweep before dark, but since only a dusting of snow fell during the night, it was reinstated and completed on Saturday. No additional personnel were brought out to carry these searches.*

12. *A number of minor requests from the AIB were met. The provision of some packaging material and the loan of several maps and display boards are representative of this assistance.*

13. *EOD. The badly damaged personal weapons of the victims were scattered through the site. After some initial discussion, they were released to the US Army by the RCMP. A number of suspected mortar rounds were*

---

[25] Indeed, the 100,000 lbs of fuel consumed themselves in the explosion and post-crash fire.

found. While it was fairly certain that these were training dummies, the CFB Gander Weapons Technician (Air) was dispatched to provide concrete identification. He confirmed that the items were harmless training aids.[26]

14. *Assistance to US Forces. Capt. (N) Joseph Payne, the commander of USN Argentia, arrived in Gander at 1200L on the 12th. He was accompanied by approximately 40 US Navy personnel. After meeting with RCMP and airport authorities, Capt. Payne established his headquarters in the Base Commander's office at CFB Gander. The USN personnel from the Argentia were not used at the crash site, but their USN public relations personnel did provide excellent assistance to the Transport Canada public affairs staff in the early hectic hours of the operation. Capt. Payne acted as the senior US military representative until the arrival of MGen John Crosby, the Assistant Deputy Chief of Staff (Personnel) from the US Army Headquarters in Washington. MGen Crosby, accompanied by a number of experts, arrived at 1645L on the 12th. MGen Crosby was introduced to all agencies and was given the Base Commander's office as a temporary headquarters. Over the remainder of the operation, the number of US Army personnel varied considerably. Most were quartered in local motels; however, MGen Crosby and some groups were housed on base. Likewise, while most US Army personnel ate in town or at the airport, town or at the airport, a number of meals were served to them by CFB Gander. Capt. Payne and his USN personnel returned to Argentia on the 13th. By Saturday, the 14th, MGen Crosby and his staff were given office space at the airport and their headquarters was shifted to that location. Other than rations and quarters, the most useful ser-*

---

[26] And these represent the totality of the weapons found at the crash site. So much for the weapons-aboard conspiracy theories.

vice provided by CFB Gander to the US Army was access to the AUTOVON system, including valuable operator assistance from the 226 Radar Squadron switchboard operators.

15. *Protocol Assistance. In the aftermath of the disaster, a number of senior officers (both US and Canadian) visited Gander. Also, on Sunday the 15th, the Town of Gander held a moving memorial service which included provincial and federal government representation plus the US Ambassador to Canada. CFB Gander, provided protocol help including transport, rations, administrative arrangements and assistance for these activities.*

Part III—Assistance Clarification

16. *Although Chapter 3, Section 2 of the DNDP 55 does not list air crashes as a civil disaster, there is no question but that Arrow Air Crash was a disaster of overwhelming proportion to the local community. Only through the application of all available resources was the situation kept under control. The RCMP brought in reinforcements from throughout the island.*

17. *When the implication surrounding the accident became clear, it was immediately evident that the correct approach for CFB Gander was to render all possible assistance. The fact the passengers were Allied Military personnel reinforced that obvious conclusion. The circumstances demanded immediate action and the Base Commander, CFB Gander, elected to commit all useful resources to the operation. At an early opportunity, Atlantic Region Headquarters, Halifax, and functional commands were appraised of the steps taken. Atlantic Region staff were advised verbally that written agreements had not been sought in view of the urgency, obvious need and simple correctness*

of what was being done. Cost recovery implications were not considered a vital matter while operations were underway.

Part IV—Concluding Material

20. *Lessons Learned.*[27] *For CFB Gander, response to the disaster was virtually a text-book application of the Base Disaster Plan. AS a result of the operation, there will be a fine tuning in a number of areas. However, the existing plan is basically sound. What is necessary to recognize is that both the Base Disaster Plan and the airport inter-agency command and control arrangements had been extensively exercised during the preceding months. During spring and early fall of 1985, CFB Gander prepared for and underwent its Operational Evaluation. The Base Disaster Plan and BDF operations were areas of particular emphasis during that process. Also, during 1985, the airport emergency procedures had been activated during several aircraft diversions due to bomb threats, a wheels-up landing emergency and a crash exercise. Each of these instances provided an opportunity for airport, police, hospital, fire department, military and other agencies to become familiar with the procedures and interrelationships necessary in handling emergencies. These also provided opportunities to establish reliable communications and "command post" procedures. When handling the Arrow Air disaster, there was virtually no confusion or lost effort. Calm efficiency was evident. The lesson in all this is simple, yet often lost due to the pressure of other demands on time and resources—emergency procedures must be frequently exercised in a realistic manner if they are to function well when needed.*

---

[27] 18 and 19 are missing in the copy of reference.

21. Conclusion. CFB Gander con tribute in a significant way to the operations required in the aftermath of the Arrow Air crash. This disaster was subject of extensive media and public attention. The fact that passengers were US Army personnel created a unique situation which placed additional obligations on CFB Gander. It is considered that this base reacted in a manner consistent with the wishes of the Department of National Defense and the Government of Canada.

For the duration of the operation we had provided 1416 breakfasts, 1445 lunches, 1452 dinners and an immeasurable amount of coffee. We had used 18 vehicles which logged a total of 4217 kilometers in 792 hours. Over 300 military and civilian personnel from CFB Gander provided whatever equipment and support was asked for during the operation.

On Monday, we rested."[28]

We have reproduced the final report of CFB Gander nearly in full because these brave 300 men and the officers who led them for the scarce two days that they assisted in the aftermath of the crash represent the only efficient and selfless group of people of any agency US or Canadian that had anything to do with the disaster, with the single exception of the sailors of Argentia. Their service, in the most God-awful circumstances imaginable was compassionate and honorable. They did not limit themselves to follow procedure, but acted according to the *"urgency, obvious need and simple correctness of what was being done."* Comparing Capt. Babcock's objective yet inevitably impassioned account of the aftermath of the crash to the answers given to US Congress from representatives of US agencies or to the CASB

---

[28] T.C. Badcock, *op. cit.*, pp. 58-66

report is heart-wrenching, but a necessary step in understanding the scope of the tragedy.

6

The Americans

Several US Agencies participated—or not—in the investigation that followed the crash:

FBI

A few FBI agents were dispatched to Gander on December 12th. They sat at a hotel near the airport for thirty-six hours, where denied access to the site—then under the jurisdiction of the Mounties—and left back with a report that the RCMP determined that no sabotage had occurred, all while the plane's remains were still smoldering. Surely a finding for the record books. While in other instances, such as the case of Pan Am's flight 103 two years almost to the day later, the FBI used its resources to conduct a worldwide investigation as to the possibility of a terrorist attack, no such investigation was conducted in this case in spite of the known claims of responsibility by proven terrorist organizations. Or so it appeared.

Arrow Air's attorneys suspected that the FBI was, nonetheless, conducting some type of investigation when its agents interviewed three of the company's pilots. We know that some interviews were conducted in San Diego and others in Ft. Lauderdale and Miami, and we presume that it was done at the request of the RCMP. In the 1990 Congressional hearings, we learned further that the Justice Department had obtained a copy of an FBI file. It included 78 documents comprised of letters, memorandums, tele-type communications and reports. However, 239 pages of the 289 page file had been deleted by the Access to Infor-mation section of the Justice Department. The few copies obtained through Freedom of Information requests of the remaining pages were so heavily redacted that no infor-mation of any importance could be found. One can, never-theless, conclude that there was some kind of activity for four months following the crash, involving field offices in Miami, San Francisco and Washington. Although the heavi-ly redacted file that made it to the Congressional hearing in 1990 does not allow us to discern much.

Some of the questions asked of the pilots might give us a clue. Capt. Stephen Saunders was asked *"If an explosion occurred in the B pit, what areas would be most adversely effected structurally and if hydraulic and flight control systems were adjacent would irretrievable or catastrophic failure occur? What seat row occu-pants adjacent to these cargo areas would be most likely to be struck by shrapnel from these explosions?"* One cannot imagine, how-ever, that the only source the FBI would have is a Captain in the affected airline. Surely there were all kinds of experts in the FAA, the NTSB and McDonnell Douglas that would have been able to offer a complete technical review. We have found no evidence that any of them were asked any questions.

NTSB

Absent without cause. They accepted every report of the Canadian CASB, despite their obvious flaws. After sharp criticism from the Congressional Hearings in 1990,

Ronald Schleede, who supervised the chief NTSB investigator at the crash, George Seidlein, clung to the icing theory—already debunked in a series of reviews—only to be told by Representative Larry Smith: *"You're nuts."* Criticism was not limited to these two outstanding public servants. Confronted with the fact that the NTSB had not conducted any scientific tests to determine whether a pre-crash fire or explosion had occurred, subcommittee Chairman Bill Hughes said: *"I find the whole thing appalling, if not frightening, that your agency could be so derelict in its responsibility."*[29] Mr. Seidlein went as far as to surprise his supervisor stating unequivocally that he did not believe icing to have been a cause, but went on to affirm his belief that pilot error had been at fault, though he acknowledged that he had never conducted any tests to corroborate his theory.

**Pan Am 103 reconstruction,
Lockerbie, Scotland**
No such efforts were ever undertaken with Arrow 1285

[29] Ken Cummings, *NTSB Inquiry Blaster US Investigator of Crash Shut Out*, The Sun Sentinel, Fort Lauderdale, December 6th, 1990.

GAO

In 1986, the GAO asserted that two charter airlines had flown military flights in violation of FAA rules.[30] Those were South Pacific Island Airways of Honolulu, and Air Resorts, of Carlsbad, CA. They found no issues with Arrow Air.

US Army

A team of some forty-three odd members arrived in Gander on December 12th, under the command of then two-star General John S. Crosby, Deputy Chief of Staff for Personnel—and a former commander of the 101st. Their duties consisted primarily in the retrieval of the bodies for shipment to Dover AFB. While Gen. Crosby denied the reports that he had suggested the plowing of the site as early as that afternoon, it was done less than three months later. Unlike other investigations, no efforts were made to secure the aircraft parts for later reconstruction, and most of the wreckage ended up in a landfill or plowed under at the crash site.

On December 13th, 1985, a day after the crash, a US military spokesman issued an interesting statement: *"Attempts will be made to learn if unauthorized persons had access to the plane at its previous refueling stop in Cologne."*[31] Nothing was ever heard of this again. Giving Capt. Shoppauls' report mentioned earlier, there is absolutely no question that unauthorized personnel had every opportunity to access the plane in Cologne while cleaning and service crews were roaming

---

[30] Chicago Tribune, 2 Charter Airlines Defied FAA to Transport GIs, Report Says, March 13th, 1986.

[31] Damien Comerford, *Cover up*, North Charleston, NC, 2014.

about without supervision. What—if anything—the Army did to find out remains a mystery.

The autopsies were performed at Dover AFB, at the Institute of Forensic Pathology. The decision to rule out terrorism and ship the bodies to Dover was made barely 48 hours after the crash. One of the major difficulties was that the medical records of the military personnel aboard were on the plane, and were completely destroyed. Also, about 100 victims were in a section of the plane that burned uncontrollably for 20 hours after the crash. Seventy-six of the victims had only torsos left. Yet, by December 20th, all remains had been flown to Dover. As we have seen elsewhere, there seems to be a contradiction between the cause of death and the presence of *lethal doses* of carbon monoxide and hydrogen cyanide.

There is also the question of the passenger roster. The manifests at Cairo, Cologne and gander list 250 passengers onboard, and the reported casualties initially listed 258 people aboard.[32] So did the early reports from the CFB Gander. Soon, however, the Army revised this number down to 248 passengers. I have had problems with this. The first duty of the Flight Service Manager was to count the passengers aboard. This was done with a mechanical counter—I still have mine—and with the assistance of at least one additional crewmember. The Captain and the FSM would sign the manifest only after the count by the two cabin crewmembers and ground agent had agreed.

Further, Arrow 1285 carried a full load, and soldiers were left behind. I know that at least in Cairo there would have been a visual check of the cabin once everyone was seated to ensure that no empty seats remained. The procedure was repeated in the stopovers to ensure that no pas-

---

[32] Chicago Tribune, Army Charter Crash Kills 258, December 13th, 1985.

senger was inadvertently left behind. I therefore trust the original count, confirmed by Donna Ogelsby, Maia Matasovsky, Capt. Shoppaul, Capt. Griffin and at least two ground agents. I have no explanation for the discrepancy, and the Army has provided none. There is also the question of the pathology report by Dr. David Elcombe included in the CASB report, *"Estimated Time Interval from Moment of Injury to Death,"* curiously lists 250 soldiers, not 248.

As if to remind us of the general incompetence shown by most of the officers whose responsibility it was to protect the soldiers under their charge, Lt. Col. Ronald W. Carpenter Jr., US Army, Assistant Chief of Staff for Personnel at Wiessbaden and the man in charge of security at Cairo said to the Congressional hearing in 1990: *"Sir, there was, to my knowledge, no direct, specific threat against the Arrow Air flight on the 11th of December...But, again, the responsibility [for security] was the Egyptian Government's"*. In the space of a few seconds, the good colonel transferred what was clearly his responsibility to a foreign government, and protested that the terrorists—if it indeed was a terrorist attack—had not sent him a memo detailing the threat. I have heard the same kind of specious *"lack of direct, specific threat"* nonsense a million times since. A word to the wise: Seldom, if ever, will there be a specific threat. The nature of terrorism is to attack by surprise, creating the most damage where it hurts most and where nobody expects it. If we can ever say that there was any such *"direct threat"* it probably means they've already failed.

US Navy

Forty-five sailors from the US Naval Station at Argentia under the command of Capt. Joseph Payne which arrived at the scene at noon on the 12th, and a smaller contingent embedded with the 770 Communications Research

Division at Canadian Forces Base Gander rendered valuable assistance during the immediate aftermath of the crash—they were the first Americans to arrive at the site—assisting airport officials in maintaining security at the airport until relieved by the RCMP. US Naval Station Argentia was a small base at Plasentia Bay in Newfoundland, some 200 miles from Gander, that begun operations during WWII (July 15th, 1941). Commissioned on August 28th, 1941, it operated mostly as a refueling station. In 1959 it became a US NavFac, part of the Ocean Systems Atlantic (Submarine Force Atlantic Fleet), continuing as a joint Canadian-US facility after 1972, with powerful arrays keeping an eye on Russian submarines—SOSUS (Sound Surveillance System), an installation of a 1,000 foot-long line array of 40 hydrophone elements. NavFac Argentia was decommissioned in 1994.

Capt. Payne and his men were used mostly for public relations assistance at the airport, and were dispatched back to their base the following morning.

Defense Intelligence Agency (DIA)

Not much here either. In Congressional hearings in May of 1990, William J. Allard, Esq., General Counsel for the DIA (accompanied by James S. Van Wagenen, Assistant Deputy Director for External Affairs) was grilled on the failure of the Agency to pursue the matter of the Arrow Air crash, his answers were quite unbelievable: *"we have no reason to believe that the Canadians were withholding information or, in fact, that they had in any way mishandled the investigation."* And he could say this with a straight face in spite of the fact that half the board of the CASB and ultimately independent judicial enquiries in Canada were precisely pointing to a gross mishandling of the investigation. Questioned further about the apparent lack of curiosity in not challenging the Canadians as to the reasons for discarding terrorism as a possible cause (let's remember that such a possibility was, in fact, discarded on December 14th, 1985, before an investigation had actually begun), his answer was: *"I would say we are prepared to accept what the Canadians were concluding also, that they could find no terrorist connection, and therefore there would be no motivation to go back and challenge them; we had nothing to..."* Subcommittee Chairman, Mr. Hughes, interjected: *"Well, that's poppycock. I happen to believe that if you had said to your counterpart in Canada, 'We'd like to know the basis for your conclusion,' they would have provided it for you. You can't tell us what the response would be, because you never asked that very simple question, and that's where I fault your agency; they didn't ask the question."* Mr. Hughes concluded: *"You had 248 servicemen that were killed in this crash and 8 crewmembers, and nobody asked them for any evidence that suggested that sabotage or terrorism wasn't involved. I find that reprehensible, I'm sorry."*[33]

We are not sorry to say that the inactivity followed by the evasiveness of the DIA throughout this affair was, indeed, reprehensible.

The DIA's *raison d'etre*, in their own words, is to provide *"the nation's most authoritative assessments of foreign military intentions and capabilities. The agency's four core competencies — human intelligence, all-source analysis, counterintelligence and technical intelligence — enable military operations while also informing policy-makers at the defense and national levels. DIA's mission is unique and no other agency matches its military expertise across such a broad range of intelligence disciplines."* I can understand that they missed the threat faced by US military personnel in the world, even after such singular wake-up calls as the Beirut

---

[33] *Fatal Plane Crash in Gander, Newfoundland, December 12, 1995, Hearings Before the Subcommittee on Crime of the Committee on the Judiciary,* House of Representatives, One Hundred First Congress, Second Session, December 4 and 5, 1990, Serial No. 147, Printed for the use of the Committee on the Judiciary, US Government Printing Office, Washington, 1991, p. 192-193

Marine barracks attack. But their lack of interest in identifying the threat—if any—after the Arrow disaster is not just reprehensible. It is appalling.

State Department

Nothing at all. According to the State Department, it was *"a total Canadian matter."* And that was that.

The US House of Representatives

On the 4th and 5th of December, 1990, owing to pressure from families of the victims, the Subcommittee on Crime of the 101st Congress held hearings. Yes, it is no typo. The Subcommittee on Crime of the Committee on the Judiciary. I guess one has to be content with any action, however ridiculous it may appear although unfortunately, even today, terrorism is treated as a crime as if it were some sort of shop-lifting.

The beginning was not auspicious at all. It started with an apology from the Chairman, Mr. William J. Hughes of New Jersey, as they were waiting for one more member to have a quorum. Only five of the nine members eventually showed up. The more than 900 pages of their report (including the appendices) make for some difficult reading. In his opening statement, Mr. Hughes was quite clear:

"Our examination of the Gander tragedy reveals similarities, as well as some differences, from the Pakistan experience.[34] *One nota-*

---

[34] He was referring to the downing of a US C-130 plane in Pakistan on August 17th, 1988, killing Pakistani President Zia-ul-Haq and the US ambassador to Pakistan, Arnold Raphel, among 31 other high ranking US and Pakistani officials. The FBI attempted to investigate but was prevented by the State Department. True to form, the US Army investigation concluded that the probable cause was mechanical failure, while the Pakistani investigators determined it was

*ble difference, and a regrettable one, is found in the level of official in-
terest displayed by agencies of our Government. In the case of the Pakistani incident, the FBI, to its credit, very aggressively sought approval within our own Government to be allowed to do its job and investigate the killing of two Americans who died in that particular
tragedy. Gander differs from this in that, incredibly, no U.S. Government agency, or at least none with official responsibility, demonstrated any determination to find out just what caused this particular
crash.*

    *During the 4 years following the Gander disaster, our lead
agency, the National Transportation Safety Board, and other agencies
of the U.S. Government chose to sit back and watch as the Canadian
efforts became embroiled in controversy and dissension which drew into
question the effectiveness of the investigation. Despite this controversy,
the National Transportation Safety Board routinely rubber-stamped
the Canadian findings, without comment, when it was given the report
for its review. A subsequent review of the report by a Cabinet-level
agency of the Canadian Government found serious flaws in the investigation, concluding that 'Data appears to have been gathered to prove a
preconceived concept of why the accident occurred, not to investigate and
evaluate all possibilities.' The 'preconceived concept' referred to its conclusion that icing on the wings caused the crash. In fact, within hours
that seemed to be the preconceived notion.*

    *Similarly, still another Canadian review of the investigation
by Justice Estey found fundamental shortcomings. Yet, apparently,
none of these developments caught the interest of the US Government.
As a result, the families and loved ones of the 256 Americans who
died in that particular crash not only have had to endure the loss of
their loved ones, but also to struggle with a feeling that their Government is not concerned with learning why this Americans died."*

---

sabotage, citing that chemicals that could be used in small explosives were detected in mango seeds and a piece of rope found on the aircraft.

The first statement following the Chairman's was that of the Hon. Robin Tallon, Representative from South Carolina. His words are still relevant today:

"I have been shocked and dismayed at the responses I get from the various US agencies. Are they lying, incompetent, lazy or just insensitive? Many times, I don't receive the same answer. Agencies have different answers to the same questions, and sometimes the answers seem like they are intentionally misleading...At this point, we need to hold all U.S. agencies which were or should have been involved in the investigation accountable. The Army, which had the primary responsibility for its soldiers, has yet to be thoroughly questioned. As the overseer of the entire Multinational Force, the State Department should have and perhaps did play a key role in the investigation of terrorism. The highly questionable autopsy work of the Armed Forces Institute of Pathology is a serious matter which needs to be looked into further. The cloistered files of the NSC, the CIA, and the NSA have not been scrutinized...for the past 18 months...and investigation that has led me to believe that this must be the most incredible case of U.S. Government ineptness in the history of the Republic, or at best is the best contrived cover up."

And so the statements continued, sometimes poignant, nearly always hurtful.

Capt. Lee Levenson, former Chairman of the Airline Pilots Association and a personal friend of John Griffin, who led an independent team; Dr. Les Filotas, author of the Minority Report of the CASB; Dr. J. Douglas Phillips, a renowned pathologist in his own right, and his wife, Zona, founders of Families for the Truth About Gander, and parents of Sgt. James D. Phillips Jr., one of the victims; Col. Lewis Millet, father of one of the victims, and recipient of the Congressional Medal of Honor (and the Silver Star, three Bronze Stars for Valor, four Purple Hearts and the Distinguished Service Cross in a career that span from

WWII to Vietnam). Their statements, to the point and factual, are part of the public record.

After a protracted hearing at the Rayburn House Office Building, once the interested parties had read their statements and a few hapless Army and DOD representatives were drilled, the honorable gentlemen called it a day, pat each other in the back, produced a 200 page report with some 700 additional pages with 48 appendices, filed it, and went home.[35] In spite of the sometimes explosive admissions that one may find in this report, no action was ever pursued, except for a failed attempt to create a Commission several years later.

The LA Times was not amused: *"The congressional report says that no U.S. official had enough detailed information to assess whether terrorism was involved because American officials relied too heavily on the Canadians. There was a 'near total absence' of U.S. government participation in the investigation, according to the report, a copy of which was made available to The Times.*

Both the report's criticism of the U.S. government and its suggestion that the cause of the disaster will remain a mystery are likely to add to the controversy surrounding the crash of the chartered aircraft on Dec. 12, 1985, as it was leaving Gander, Newfoundland."

And thus, with a lengthy report after a cathartic if unproductive event, ended the first official attempt to investigate into the causes of the crash.

On August 3rd, 1993, various congressmen introduced to the 103rd Congress House Resolution 2838, *"to establish a [bicameral] Commission on the Airplane Crash at Gander, Newfoundland."* The commission was to have sixty days to figure out the cause of the crash. The bill was referred to the Committees on Public Works and Transporta-

---

[35] *Fatal Plane Crash in Gander, Newfoundland, December 12, 1995, op. cit.*

tion and Foreign Affairs. HR 2838 died in committee and no roll call vote was ever taken on it,[36] and we never heard from them again.

The US Senate

Two days after the crash, Senators Albert Gore Jr. and James Sasser of Tennessee, called for a congressional investigation into the crash in a letter to Charles Bowsher, Comptroller General of the General Accounting Office. Al Gore—the same one who gave us phony pictures of stranded polar bears some years later—questioned whether the plane had followed *"proper flying procedures"*, and whether the Air Force's safety review for charters was adequate.[37] In March 6th, 1986, hearings were held by the Senate Investigations Subcommittee. After two pilots testified about alleged long hours and unsafe conditions at the airline to the point that pilots were *"falling asleep in the cockpit"* (although they claimed they themselves had never been involved in any such incident nor could they name anyone who had),[38]

---

[36] A similar bill was introduced in the Senate, discussed in the next section.

[37] LA Times, *Military Aircraft to Bring Sinai Soldiers Home: Two Senators Seek Probe of Charter Policy in Wake of Crash That Killed 256*, December 15th, 1985.

[38] The two pilots were Captains Daniel Hood and Michael Sanjenis. While Arrow Air did not officially comment on these two, the Arrow Air Pilots Association called them *"former...disgruntled employees that have left the company in less than ideal circumstances."* [Senate hearing report, *op. cit.*, p. 103]. It is a sad commentary that all of the press reports at the time and since that questioned Arrow's practices were based solely on the unsubstantiated allegations of these two, ignoring the hundreds of other Arrow pilots that professed a different, indeed, diametrically opposed version of events. Capt. Hood exploited his supposed bereavement over the loss of his fiancée, but his actions following the crash speak far louder than his words. There are plenty of sources to aid in elucidating his character, and his self-centered, unclear recollections' penchant for distorting facts to his benefit. He peddled his 15-minutes of fame into a class B movie about his heroics in Vietnam, though his wife and son have different memories. None of the allegations of Hood and Sanjenis were ever proven and, in fact, the only time anyone attempted to use them in a court of law, the Court threw the case for lack of merit. On Appeal, that dismissal was reversed as *"There is evidence which refutes the testimony given by the appellant's witnesses*

and a declaration of the Arrow Air Pilots Association was entered into the record vehemently defending the airline and its crews and denouncing their detractors, Arrow Chairman George E. Batchelor testified that it was *"ludicrous"* to say that his airline pilots were so overworked that they fell asleep in the cockpit, and that if he knew of any they would be immediately fired.

"It sounds as though the chairman is asleep in the boardroom and the whole company is on automatic pilot," interjected Sen. Albert Gore Jr., of Tennessee, though the honorable gentleman did not care to elaborate on the source for such bombastic innuendo. Those of us who knew Mr. Batchelor could not imagine the man taking a nap anywhere, let alone at the boardroom. Mr. Batchelor continued that *"...To suggest that economic considerations superseded the proper performance of airline operation and maintenance at Arrow Air is absurd."* And so it was. Unfortunately, Mr. Gore's ambitions got ahead of the one opportunity before the Senate to attempt to elucidate some facts.[39]

---

as to Arrow's operational practices. That evidence, however, merely creates issues of fact. It is not the role of the trial judge, in ruling on a summary judgment motion, to weigh the evidence for the purpose of resolving the conflict." The dissenting opinion expressed that *"In my view, the entry of summary judgment in favor of Arrow Air was proper. '[I]n order for an employer's action to constitute an intentional tort, the employer must either exhibit a deliberate intent to injure or engage in conduct which is substantially certain to result in injury or death. This standard requires more than a strong probability of injury. It requires virtual certainty'... As a matter of law, however, I believe that the facts adduced in discovery do not give rise to a finding that Arrow Air's conduct was virtually certain to result in death or injury...On the authority of Lawton, I would hold that the action is barred by the exclusivity provisions of Florida's worker's compensation statute and affirm the order on appeal"* [District Court of Appeal of Florida, Third District, Connelly v. Arrow Air, Inc., No. 89-806., 568 So.2d 448 (1990)]

[39] Mr. Gore, as many of his colleagues, received substantial contributions for his political campaigns from large airlines and unions that opposed de-regulation. He seems to have been particularly inclined to cast doubt on the safety of smaller airlines in general—and Arrow's crash afforded a golden opportunity—although careful reading of his interventions will yield no substance to his claims.

The hearing was not about the crash in Gander but about airline safety in general during the early years of deregulation, and Democrats were busy attempting to cast doubt on the whole process citing exaggerated when not wholly fabricated safety concerns. Railing for the breakup of monopolies in an industry that provided millions to their campaigns, both from corporate headquarters and unions, they purposely obfuscated comingling routing and safety regulations, as if Arrow Air, Air Florida, People Express or Jet 24 or, for that matter, any other small airline at the time, did not have the same stringent requirements—and sometimes much closer scrutiny—than behemoths like Pan American Airways, TWA, Eastern or Braniff. If these dedicated public servants had had their way, air travel would still be a privilege of the few.

Still, in the absence of any other enquiry, it was a golden opportunity to try and discern some facts and perhaps plant the seed on a future investigation. But Senator Gore chose to abuse his perch to lambast Mr. Batchelor for imaginary naps, four year old safety reports and not much more. And the opportunity was irretrievably lost.

While Senator Gore was looking for scapegoats in 1982 FAA reports, the Air Force spokesman had no problem affirming just a few days before the hearings that *"As far as we know, there is no reason to believe at this juncture that Arrow is an unsafe airline."* [40]

On June 24th, 1993, seven years after the fiasco at the Investigations Subcommittee hearings, Senator Shelby of Alabama introduced Senate Bill 1157, identical to HR 2838 discussed above, and with the same results. It died an ignominious death at the Commerce, Science and Transpor-

---

[40] Los Angeles Times, *Air Force Defends Charter Use, Arrow Air Safety*, December 18th, 1985. The spokesman also confirmed that Arrow was continuing to operate charter flights at that time.

tation Committee without ever reaching the floor. Apparently, the 103rd Congress had no more interest in finding the causes of the crash than its predecessors or, for that matter, its successors.

8760/624

S. HRG. 100-25

OVERSIGHT OF AVIATION SAFETY

HEARINGS

BEFORE THE

SUBCOMMITTEE ON AVIATION

OF THE

COMMITTEE ON COMMERCE, SCIENCE, AND TRANSPORTATION UNITED STATES SENATE

ONE HUNDREDTH CONGRESS

FIRST SESSION

ON

OVERSIGHT OF AVIATION SAFETY

JANUARY 29 AND 30, 1987

Printed for the use of the Committee on Commerce, Science, and Transportation

Y 4. C 73/7
: S. hrg. 100-25

U.S. GOVERNMENT PRINTING OFFICE
70-326   WASHINGTON : 1987   06 13 847

For sale by the Superintendent of Documents, Congressional Sales Office
U.S. Government Printing Office, Washington, DC 20402

7
The Investigation

As the remains of Arrow's DC-8 smoldered over an improbably large area, some investigators of the CASB (Canadian Aviation Safety Board) were already floating the idea of icing on the wing as probable cause, while the US Army representative, Major General John S. Crosby, US Army deputy chief of staff for personnel, was suggesting the *"immediate bulldozing of the crash site"*, allegedly to avoid the *"taking of souvenirs."* Denials notwithstanding, only ten days after the crash General Crosby was coordinating the site's cleanup with Canadian officials in Gander and in Ottawa, with the proviso that *"a representative of the Army [be] present at all times."* [41] The FBI agents sent to investigate,

---

[41] Report of the Union of Canadian Transport Employees, 7 May 1988:

"Major General John S. Crosby of the U.S. Army calls for the bulldozing of the crash site the day after the tragedy:

In an internal memo from Michael Mendez Director of maintenance for Arrow Air to Betty Batchelor an executive with Arrow Air reporting on the events that took place in Gander on December 13, 1985, Mr. Mendez says: *"It was after this that N.T.S.B. (National Transportation Safety Board — U.S.) representative, George Seidlein, mentioned that Major General John Crosby wanted to bulldoze over the crash site immediately to prevent pilferage".* Mendez then added; *"This was also understood by the claims adjuster for AAU, (Associated Aviation Underwriters) Bruce Mally."*

meanwhile, cooled their heels at a local hotel and thirty-six hours later left without having had access to the site, which was also denied to airline representatives and insurance investigators. While the FBI claimed that the Canadian authorities did not allow them access to investigate the crash site, it never conducted any investigation anywhere else in the world as to the possibility that the *Islamic Jihad* claims may have been true.

Almost at the same time, White House Spokesman Larry Speaks, as quoted by Time magazine, was quick to assure the world that there was *"no evidence of sabotage or an explosion in flight"*. Robert Sims, chief spokesman for the Pentagon was not going to be outdone: *"We have no indications of explosions prior to the crash or of hostile action."* Of course, there was at the time no evidence of an alien invasion, mechanical failure, or, for that matter, of any cause at all, as the investigation had not even begun. But as we have sadly come to see all too often, the knee-jerk reaction of second-rate bureaucrats and third rate politicians is to deny the obvious as a first attempt to control the narrative,[42] even in the presence of evidence of terrorism.[43]

Whatever the Major General's intentions might have been, no such bulldozing took place. The on-site investigation went on well into February. This does not however explain what motivated or pressured General Crosby to utter his demands. The only thing we do know is that *"Crosby did not have the authority to see his command through."*

Major general Crosby had been the commanding officer at Ft. Sill, Oklahoma, a major field artillery and air defense post, receiving at the end the first Commander-in-Chief's award for Installation Excellence, his third star and command over all Army training (TRADOC).

[42] As I am writing this (September 18th, 2016), Mayor di Blasio of New York is carping to assembled journalists that a pressure cooker bomb that exploded earlier today on 23rd Street in Manhattan is *"no evidence of terrorism."* Surely it is no evidence of a theatrical promotion either.

[43] A few months before the Arrow tragedy—on February 14th, 1985—Leamon Hunt, Director General of the Multinational Force and Observers based in the

Indeed, from the onset the investigation concentrated on the hypothesis that icing on the wings was at fault and dismissed any evidence to the contrary, however compelling. In some cases, their report seems like a haphazardly arranged string of contradictions. The four dissenting members of the board—the only ones with any relevant experience—destroyed those assumptions in a rational, matter-of-fact way to the point that the only criticism leveled at them was their inability to prove their thesis. No surprise there, since their objections and observations went unheeded and the CASB flatly refused to pursue those leads. In other words, under the leadership of Deschênes first and Thorneycroft later, every obstacle was placed before those who wanted to expand the investigation, only to be faulted later for not having an investigation to back their thesis! As Orwellian as it gets.

Some of the most glaring contradictions involve the most important aspects of the investigation:

1- **Stall:** Perhaps the only honest statement in the original report is the opening line: *"The Canadian Aviation Safety Board was unable to determine the exact sequence of events."* And yet, they proceed to elucidate a sequence of events out of thin air, leading inescapably to their pre-ordained conclusion: *"The most probable cause of the stall was determined to be ice contamination on the leading edge and upper surface of the wing."*

   There was, of course, no evidence of a stall either. As Les Filotas wrote on the Minority Report: *"The conclusion that the aircraft did not stall can be drawn from evidence of a number of witnesses about the*

Sinai was gunned down in the streets of Rome by a terrorist group. There should have been no question that the MFO was a terrorist target.

level attitude of the aircraft as it crossed the TransCanada Highway. ("It was a normal departure... but that leveling-off effect was abnormal"; "The aircraft's attitude appeared to be level as it crossed the Trans-Canada Highway"; "The plane was leveled off. The plane wasn't nose up or nose down. It was level"; "It looked very flat. Just two or three degrees"; "The nose was not pointed up": "The aircraft was pretty level... Very level.") In conclusion, the Arrow Air DC-8 did not stall before it crashed."

2- **Icing on the wings:** While dedicating numerous paragraphs to sustain that theory, including endless repetition of generic studies underscoring the real danger of ice formation on the wings, the fact remains that icing conditions were not present, that ground crews—including fuel operators—saw no indication of ice, that the cockpit crew was observed checking the aircraft, and that nothing in the behavior of the plane in-flight suggests icing. In fact, the dissenters were unambiguous: *"The witness testimony and the detailed meteorological evidence (as presented at the Board's public inquiry and discussed in our previously cited paper) establish that the wing of the Arrow Air DC-8 could not have been contaminated with ice during the take-off run at Gander on 12 December 1985."* The CFB Gander forces that arrived at the scene shortly after the crash noticed *"no snow on the ground"* and *"moderate weather."*

3- **Crew fatigue:** One of the longest segments, full of innuendo and irrelevant information, in the face of testimony and facts that make it impossible for fatigue to have been a factor. In fact, as the Minority Report stated: *"We found no basis for supposing that the crew's performance could have been af-*

fected by fatigue. In the absence of evidence of abnormal behaviour and in consequence of testimonials to the crew's professional competence, we conclude that no act or failure to act by any member of the crew contributed to this accident."

4- **Take-off weight:** According to the Majority report, *"There was considerable evidence to suggest that the crew-calculated take-off weight (330,625 pounds) at Gander was less than the actual take-off weight."* What that considerable evidence was, they do not say. In fact, it would be quite impossible to determine the weight of passengers and cargo based on what was recovered. The CASB majority based their assumptions on some kind of magical calculation of the "actual take-off weight" and in that *"The post-accident position of the internal bug on the co-pilot's airspeed indicator was eight knots lower than the corresponding V_2 speed predicated by the actual take-off weight. If the lower V_2 speed is used as a reference, the 18-knot stall margin that would be available under normal conditions would be reduced by eight knots. If, for whatever reason, the stall speed was increased, the stall margin could be reduced to zero if lower than normal reference speeds were selected and flown."*

The post-accident position of the bug is, in fact, quite irrelevant, as it is common for these sliding plastic devices to move as a consequence of the violence of impact. Be that as it may, the crew followed standard calculations for take-off weight and the speed at rotation was sufficient even at the levels guesstimated by the CASB. The level of speculation in this section is mind-boggling. If, for whatever reason, the CASB had stuck to the facts, we would not be having this argument.

5- **Mechanical failure:** The Majority report spends page after page in baseless lucubration's on the possible failure—or not—of myriad mechanical and hydraulic parts and systems, without reaching a definitive conclusion on any of them. Of course, an explosive device in the forward cargo hold would create precisely that massive malfunctions, cutting off the cockpit controls and causing the kind of generalized catastrophic failure implied in their explanations. The minority report is less convoluted: *"We believe it unlikely that the contradictory evidence about flaps, spoilers, EPR gauges, N1 tachometers, and other systems can let explained separately through unrelated hypotheses. To us, the extent of the contradictory evidence suggests* **simultaneous multiple system failures due to a common cause."**

That common cause, it seems evident, was an explosive device in the cargo hold, just forward of the wings, as more evidence will indicate. If the Majority had listened to their own investigators, perhaps they would have had a clue. John Garstang, an engineer in the CASB laboratory was the only member of the investigation team with any forensic experience. In June of 1985, Air India Flight 182 was destroyed in-flight over the North Atlantic,[44] and Garland was *"immersed in the*

---

[44] On Jun 23rd, 1985, an Air India 747 was blown out of the sky as it flew over Irish waters en-route from Montreal to London. The group responsible was *Babbar Khalsa*, a Sikh militant organization, allegedly in retaliation for the attack on the Golden Temple at Amristar in June of 1984, ordered by the government of Indira Ghandi—herself murdered by the same group on October 31st, 1984. Only one person was ever convicted, a Canadian of Sikh extraction. Ironically, the final report of a commission appointed in 2006 to review the case under the direction of Justice John Major concluded on June 17, 2010—twenty-five

arcane arts of detecting traces of explosives and…formed close professional relationships with the world's foremost specialists. Later, he would be invited to join American explosives experts Walter Korsgaard and Tom Thurman to search for traces of an explosion in the wreckage of Pan Am flight 103 at Lockerbie, Scotland."[45]

Of his work at Lockerbie, Garstang loved to describe the difficulty of detecting *"the very subtle differences between soot from an explosion and post-crash fire,"* and that *"fracture damage typical of explosives is not much different than break-up and can only be differentiated through minute examination. Detecting evidence of an aircraft bombing is very difficult even when you know what you are looking for."*[46] Just imagine how difficult it can be when nobody is looking. Alas, they were not looking at all. Garstang's job at the Gander site was barely to provide for *"site survey and security."* When asked by Les Filotas who, then, was looking for subtle differences between soot from explosion and post-crash fires, he laconically answered *"You would have to refer to the RCMP for that."* [47]

6- **On-board fire:** The Official report concluded that there had not been a fire onboard prior to impact. This is contradicted by eyewitness reports, wreckage and toxicological analysis. As the Minority Report states regarding eyewitness re-

---

years after the attack—that a *"cascading series of errors"* by the Government of Canada, the RCMP and the CSIS (Canadian Security Intelligence Service) had allowed the terrorist attack to happen in the first place.

[45] Les Filotas, *op. cit.*, p. 86.

[46] Ibidem.

[47] Idem, p. 87.

ports: *"Both witnesses who observed the 'orange/yellow glow' from directly under the flight path believed that the engines were not running.* Witness 1: *"The airplane passed right over my truck. When it passed right over us, the engines were not running. I did not hear any whine from the engines. I had gone by there hundreds of times when planes were taking off and you could hear the engines. But I could not hear the engines yesterday. There was no whine but there was some type of rumble... I'm certain that when the aircraft passed over us the engines were not working."* Witness 2: *"I heard the noise. I looked. I could see the plane coming over. It didn't sound like engine noise... I live fairly close to the Sydney Airport and I've heard planes taking off before. This one didn't sound right.... There was no roar from him at all".*

This *"ear witness"* testimony is all the more striking since the engines would sound louder than normal as the aircraft flew lower than usual over the trucks. Ann Hurley, a local resident, declared: *"We were driving to work when we saw this big explosion...and it **dived down** very quickly."* Lastly, John Pittman, the airport manager at Gander who saw the "accident," when asked if he thought there had been a fire on board before the crash he answered with a laconic *"yes."*

That the wreckage evidence and toxicological analysis were ignored by the Majority and only included in their report as an afterthought is quite significant, as it necessarily leads to the conclusion of a fire aboard before the crash.

7- **Cause of death:** After autopsies were performed at Dover AFB with the not unexpected result of attributing the death of crew and passengers to *"traumatic injuries"* causing *"instant death,"* toxicological reports were buried under pages of irrelevant gobbledygook—the Captain and co-pilot were found to have had caffeine and aspirin in their bloodstreams, and so did at least two flight attendants—were some surprising and, indeed, telling results.

Two Flight Attendants[48] and 158 of the 187 passengers for whom measures were available, exhibited high levels of carbon monoxide (CO) and hydrogen cyanide (HCN). That is, fully 85% of the passengers and crew tested in the passenger cabin revealed high levels of compounds that show the presence of fire and can only be present in the bloodstream when inhaled.

To add to the confusion, the CASB commissioned tests that allowed them to estimate survival times after the crash based on the concentration of said compounds in their bodies. This is nonsense in more than one way. First, because *"the percentages may be underestimates, as cyanide is quickly eliminated in blood also after death,"*[49] second, because the presence of CO and HCN combined *"in blood would suggest that the victim was alive and inhaled smoke from a fire...No fatality under non-fire accidents was found in which the levels of both gases were determined to be at or above the stated levels."*[50] And,

---

[48] Maya Matasovsky and Stacey Cutler, at their families request, were exempted from the autopsy.

[49] K. Stamyr, G. Thelander, L. Ernstgård, J. Ahlner, G. Johanson, *Swedish forensic data 1992-2009 suggest hydrogen cyanide as an important cause of death in fire victims*, Work Environment Toxicology, Institute of Environmental Medicine, Karolinska Institutet, Stockholm, Sweden, 24 February 2012.

[50] A.K. Chaturvedi, D.R. Smith, D.V. Canfield, *Blood Carbon Monoxide and Hydrogen Cyanide Concentrations in the Fatalities of Fire and Non-Fire Associated Civil Aviation Accidents, 1991-1998*, FAA Civil Aeromedical Institute, Oklahoma City, Oklahoma

more to the point, *"the presence of COHb and CN in elevated concentrations in the blood of victims found by autopsy to have died on impact would indicate an in-flight fire."*[51]

In fact, the autopsies did reveal lethal doses of hydrogen cyanide: *"the highest levels appear to have been confined to passengers in one section of the passenger cabin...while the pilot and flight engineer were unaffected."* It goes on to say: *"the cyanide was also found in bodies which were dismembered or decapitated on impact."* At the same time, crash analysis used to determine the cause of death in the death certificates suggests that all victims died *"on impact or seconds later from being engulfed in flames."* The CASB received the toxicology report on February 20th, 1986, and immediately proceeded to bury it and ignore it.

Of course, there is only one explanation that reconciles the fact that no person survived the crash but perhaps for a few moments, that high levels of CO and HCN were found in a cluster of passengers, and that even those who were decapitated on impact would have been able to inhale lethal doses of these gases. And that single explanation is that they inhaled the toxic fumes **before impact.**[52]

8- **Voice Recorder:** The so-called black boxes—they are, in fact, bright orange—contain vital in-

---

[51] D. V. Canfield, A. K. Chaturvedi, K.M. Dubowski, *Carboxy-hemoglobin and blood cyanide concentrations in relation to aviation accidents*, Civil Aerospace Medical Institute, Federal Aviation Administration, Oklahoma City, Oklahoa

[52] Capt. T. C. Badcock, of the CFB Gander, relates that, on the morning of the 13th, as they began recovery efforts, "There had only been two or three badly burnt bodies, and the rest had been killed as they struck the trees as it neared the ground." T. C. Badcock, *op. cit.*, p. 41

formation of the last moments of the flight. There are two of them. One, the VDR (Voice Data Recorder), registers what is said in the cockpit; the second one, the FDR (Flight Data Recorder), registers technical data that provides information on how systems were operating, if they were operating at all. Both were recovered soon after the crash and were delivered to NRC Playback Center of the CASB at 20:50 of the 12th.

On December 13th, only one day later, Christiane Beaullieu, spokesman for the CASB, was pleased to inform the public that *"Both tapes are readable..."* But on January 10th, on an interview in the Globe and Mail, Peter Boag, the pencil pusher that was in fact chief investigator, put it differently: *"That* [the failure of the voice recorder] *means accident investigators have none of the conversation between the pilot and co-pilot from the time the plane started its takeoff roll until the crash."* What happened between December 12th and January 10th, we do not know.[53] The only conversations discernible according to the CASB were those between the pilot and the tower before takeoff, which contained no information of value. Needless to say, actual failure of the device to record is extremely rare, and turning on the cockpit mi-

---

[53] We do know that there was a kind of evolution between the two statements, on December 14th, the LA Times reported: *"No useful information has been obtained from the recorders...Both recorders suffered extensive internal damage in the crash...I can't say at this time if any useful information can be obtained, although technicians are still working in Ottawa laboratories to decipher the fire-damaged material...Analysts were able to listen to the tapes."* In other words, the recorders were damaged by fire—it was not a maintenance failure, after all—and the technicians listened to the tapes but could not listen to the tapes and were still working on listening to the tapes. Clear as a whistle.

crophone is standard procedure during the pre-flight check.

9- **Fire Warning Light:** A finding of the report, against toxicological and eyewitness evidence, as we have already seen, was that there was no fire aboard until after the crash. Again, the Systems Group report finds otherwise. Their conclusion was that Capt. Griffin activated an engine fire extinguisher before the crash. The actual finding states: *"The second container did not have the raised areas. When the valves were disassembled it was found that one explosive cartridge had been fired but that this had occurred while there was still agent in the container to dampen the force of the impact on the exterior surface."* For the uninitiated, that means that in that extremely short flight, Capt. Griffin had deliberately discharged the extinguisher, and that it was not a consequence of the impact forces.

The Systems Group's report further states: *"The Master Fire Warning Light located on the instrument panel glare shield was recovered with one of the two bulbs intact. Initial laboratory examination has indicated that the light was on at the time of impact."* The warning system in question is activated by the pilot. So now we have toxicological reports, eyewitness accounts and equipment evidence that the pilot activated the fire warning system and triggered at least one fire extinguisher. Yet the bureaucrats at the CASB saw no evidence of fire before the crash, and the NTSB did not figure something was wrong in their interpretations.

10-**Flight Data Recorder:** he FDR analysis concludes that there was a sudden deceleration. One minute and thirty-five seconds after initiating takeoff, the plane was travelling at 140 knots. Two seconds later, the speed had dropped to 30 knots. Just imagine yourself in a car at 110 miles per hour, coming to a complete stop in two seconds. That is the kind of deceleration suffered by the Arrow Air DC-8 seconds after take-off.[54]

Finally, there is the question of the *Pinkel Report*. Dispatched to the crash site by Associated Insurance Underwriters, Arrow's insurance company, Irving Pinkel was no run of the mill investigator. In a biography published by NASA, he is described as *"an authoritative voice of aerospace safety not only at the laboratory that today is the NASA Glenn Research Center, but across the Agency and industry. Although he was involved in a wide array of aircraft operational issues, it was the massive Crash Fire Test program from 1948 to 1957 that made Pinkel a preeminent figure in aircraft accident investigations. The program determined how fires spread and how loads were distributed in crashes, and it led to Pinkel's patents for an extinguishing system and a crash-resistant seat. Pinkel's expertise was repeatedly called upon over the years, including for investigations into the Apollo 1 fire and the Apollo 13 accident. He remained active with aerospace safety issues long after his retirement in 1974...NASA called upon Pinkel's crash fire experience following the deadly Apollo 204 (renamed Apollo 1) fire in January 1967. Within days Pinkel arrived at the NASA Kennedy Space Center to help inspect the damaged capsule, develop a timeline of events, and offer insight into the origin and propagation of the fire. Pinkel spent over a year helping with the redesign of the Apollo capsule and spacesuits. Following the investigation, NASA Administrator James Webb asked Pinkel to serve as Director of the new*

---

[54] Spooling of all the engines due to some catastrophic failure can explain this unbelievable deceleration in ways that drag cause by a thin layer of ice on the wings never will. And that is assuming there was any ice, in spite of massive evidence to the contrary.

NASA Aerospace Safety Research and Data Institute (ASRDI) being established at the NASA Lewis Research Center in Cleveland. ASRDI collected information regarding all of NASA's safety problems into a single dynamic database accessible to the entire Agency. Pinkel authored papers on safety issues for engineers to consider while designing the space shuttle, and he led an investigation into the crash of the Center's F–8 Crusader in July 1969. While in this position, Pinkel was summoned as an official observer to the review board for the Apollo 13 incident in April 1970. Board Chairman Edgar Cortright thanked Pinkel afterwards, 'It was a long and concentrated effort and required a considerable personal sacrifice on your part to be so long away from home and office. However, your dedicated participation was instrumental in bringing our work to a satisfactory conclusion in a relatively brief time span'."

I will resist the temptation to compare the credentials of Mr. Pinkel to those of, say, Deschênes or Boag. Any comparison would be offensive to the memory of Irving Pinkel. Let us only say that the fellows who wrote the majority report were no rocket scientists. Mr. Pinkel was.[55]

Mr. Pinkel was allowed to the crash site in May of 1986, nearly five months after the incident, when the CASB turned over the crash site to Arrow Air. In spite of the time lapsed and the inevitable destruction of evidence that had taken place by both exposure to the elements and the incompetence of the CASB and the RCMP, Mr. Pinkel found two pieces of the fuselage of about 30 sq ft each, with a pronounced *"outward pucker,"* suggesting that these panels had been *"punched out"* by some object propelled from the inside of the plane at high speed.[56]

---

[55] Irving Pinkel passed away on March 13th, 2008. He was 95 years old.

[56] Similar scorch marks and parts bent and buckled outward were found on pieces of Pan Am flight 103, downed over Lockerbie in December 1988.

One of the sections displayed no inside damage attributable to the crash, making it unlikely that anything other than a pre-impact event had caused this damage.

Inside image of the explosive hole shown on page 12.
CASB Dissenting Report.

Explosive fracture in the fuselage.
CASB Dissenting Report.

Mr. Boag, the great investigator, citing the report already mentioned that the RCMP lab had found no evidence of explosive residue, discarded Mr. Pinkel's findings in a letter dated November 6th, 1986: *"it was concluded that the damage occurred during break-up of the aircraft and subsequent post-impact fire."* He must as well have said that he had no intention of allowing some trifle like real evidence interfere with his prejudices.

Another suspicious hole in the fuselage.
CASB Dissenting Report.

We have already stated that Semtex leaves no discernible residue. But even if a more common explosive had been used, there is no way that any residue can survive a 20-hour fire, as was the case with the wreckage of the Arrow plane. At most, if one wanted to disagree with the findings of the most renowned expert in the field anywhere in the world, there is always the option of claiming the evidence is inconclusive. To dismiss it out of hand on such feeble grounds is not just irresponsible. It is plain stupidity.

Pinkel also found evidence that the engine No 3 had ingested explosion fragments, thus explaining a marked bank to the right before the crash. He based his observation on the study of that engine's inlet guide vanes. According to Pinkel, such ingestion would cause a compressor stall that is *"usually accompanied by flames torching from either the engine inlet or tailpipe of both."* That, of course, explains the orange/yellow glow observed by witnesses, and what appeared to be Capt. Griffin's frantic attempts in the last moments of his life to trigger the fire suppression system. The CASB, this time, simply chose to ignore Mr. Pinkel's observations and did not pursue that line of investigation. From his home in San Diego in 1990, Mr. Pinkel insisted that *"I don't know if it was a device...**All I can say is that there was an explosion, and in all probability it happened while the airplane was in flight.**"*[57]

Irving A. Pinkel (1914-2008)
Photo: NASA

---

[57] Chicago Tribune, *Air of Mystery*, April 22nd, 1990

We must return at this point to John Garstang. Despite the limited role assigned to him—as described in point 5 above—he found a 6 x 3 ft piece of *"composite material cargo liner exhibiting soot and burn marks and small punctures,"* which he marked with stake 29, and noted in his log that the piece in question was found in an area **"where ground not burned"** [58] at the extreme right side of the crash site. He turned his notes to Peter Boag, but when this finding was mentioned in the final report, it had inexplicably been abbreviated to *"Composite material from cargo liner"* [59] without any of Garstang's observations. The RCMP lab did not find anything significant, and essentially dismissed the liner. [60] No explanation was attempted as to the cause of the holes or how come there were burns where no fire had occurred on the ground around this particular piece.

***

As early as April 10th, 1986, Peter Boag was advertising his prejudices, which came in the form of *"conclusions"* advanced on the first day of public hearings by the CASB. He first mentioned that the plane was fatigued from 51,000 of flying, and that he was considering several factors whose combination could prove significant. First, that the plane was carrying 1,700 pounds more weight than the flight crew had calculated, which may have decreased takeoff

---

[58] Les Filotas, Op. cit., p. 87.

[59] Item number 39.1.

[60] RCMP Forensic Laboratory Report, File No 85-OL01597, Report TWO, submitted by B. W. Richardson, July 2nd, 1986: *"Ex. 1,000,683 was examined visually. It was crumpled out of shape and had several holes punctured in it. The fiberglass was charred in the areas around the puncture holes. The areas surrounding the puncture holes were examined microscopically for foreign material, with negative results. Spot tests for explosive residue were applied to areas surrounding the holes, with negative results."*

speed.[61] Second, that there was possibly ice formation on the wings, though he was quick to add, accurately for once, that *"there is no evidence that there was or was not ice on the wings."* Third, that the No 4 engine may have been running *"at an extremely low speed;"* and, true to form, that *"this engine had been used so long that it was scheduled to be retired at the end of that trip."*[62] Fourth, that an elevator control *"may have been defective."* He added a list as ridiculous as irrelevant, such as *"flight attendants complained in Cologne that the washroom floors were unusually soft or squishy,"* that *"passengers complained that windows...were sealed with duct tape, cold air was leaking through the front passenger door..."* And then he ended that there was *"no evidence of structural failure...no fire or explosion before the crash, and no sign of multiple engine failure."*[63] Of course, the former commentaries are irrelevant at best—ridiculous at worst[64]—, and the latter was proved to be false.

At the memorial ceremony at Fort Campbell, President Reagan, visibly shaken, said *"We wonder how this could be, how it could have happened and why."* Thirty years later, we are no closer to finding an official answer than we were then.

---

[61] How he arrived at that figure is known but to him and his *Ouija Board.* Nevertheless, even if by some unexplained procedure the figure is correct, differences of that magnitude are well within margins and quite inconsequential. The figure, of course, changed numerous times, all with the same unknown origin.

[62] One is compelled to note that ALL engines will be eventually replaced after reaching a stipulated number of hours. That this engine was scheduled to be replaced well within its life cycle means absolutely nothing.

[63] Chicago Tribune, *Clues Told in Crash of GI Charter,* April 10th, 1986.

[64] I cannot imagine a plane surviving the flight across the Atlantic with "duct taped windows" without any mishap, nor can I imagine any way in which cold air can filter through a gap in a door into a pressurized cabin. Whatever somebody though they saw was probably of a more benign nature, like tape over some plastic panel near a window or a vent blowing cold air. Either way, discussing these matters in a public hearing investigating the causes of the crash as preliminary conclusions shows Mr. Boag's bad faith, prejudice, or both.

President Ronald Reagan
Dover Air Force base, December 16th, 1985
Screenshot, The Ronald Reagan Presidential Library

Dover Air Force Base
December 16th, 1985
Photo: DoD media image # DA-ST-87-05196, SGT Vincent R. Kitts

8
The Airline

George Edward Batchelor
USA Major WWII
(1920-2002)

Anthony Kijek, the FAA's principal operations inspector of Arrow Air, praised the company at the CASB inquiry in April 1986, and said that Arrow had recently developed a system of keeping training records that was *"the model of the industry."* He added that any violations were not done deliberately by the company but were a result of *"human error."*[65]

So much for the early reports that irresponsibly targeted the airline's allegedly shoddy maintenance practices.

---

[65] Chicago Tribune, *Death Jet Owners Get FAA Praise*, April 17th, 1986.

But what kind of company was Arrow Air, then, and where did it come from?

George Edward Batchelor was born in Shawnee, Oklahoma, on December 20th, 1920, he learned to fly when he was sixteen years old and throughout his life remained passionately committed to aviation. During WWII, he became a mechanic for North American Aviation (NAA),[66] where he helped re-design the P-51 Mustang fighter plane[67] and on November 4th, 1942, enlisted in the US Army as a pilot in the Air Corps for the remainder of the war. He flew DC-4s in Europe, rising to the rank of Major, and was released on February 7th, 1946. The following year, he purchased a surplus DC-3 in Honolulu,[68] flew it solo to California and sold it there for a profit.

P-51 Mustang

---

[66] NAA, founded in 1928, was an aerospace manufacturing division of General Motors (1933-1948) that eventually merged into Rockwell International and later Boeing Integrated Defense Systems. During WWII, they were responsible for the P-51 Mustang fighter and the B-25 Mitchell Bomber.

[67] Originally designed for the British as a medium altitude fighter, it was redesigned by NAA in the US. The American prototype, the NA-73X, was first flown on October 25th, 1940, and soon became the first American fighter to fly over Europe after the fall of France. In 1944, it was recognized as the *"most aerodynamically perfect pursuit plane in existence"*.

[68] Batchelor was in California, and a stock DC-3 did not have the range to make the flight from Honolulu to the continent, so he went to Hawaii, modified the fuel system and flew the plane back for the 18 hour trip to Santa Monica, where he sold it for U$S 25,000.

Soon he launched *California Arrow Airways,*[69] a small carrier run out of an engine crate at the Lomita Airstrip in Orange Co.[70] His business model was simple: *"Fly Whatever, Whenever, Wherever."* Started as an intrastate air carrier, it began scheduled services between Burbank, Oakland and Sacramento.

A little known fact that received no attention in the press coverage that followed the crash in Gander—or the congressional hearings held later—was that on December 7th, 1949, a California Arrow DC-3 left Burbank for a routine trip to Oakland, Sacramento and back to Burbank where the airline was headquartered. After the stopover in Oakland and routine cleaning and maintenance, six passengers boarded for the flight to Sacramento and Burbank. They never made it. Because of poor weather over the Sacramento area, the crew was advised that they needed to file for a flight plan under instrument flight rules (IFR), they did so, were then assigned a route at 4,000 ft— well clear of any terrain obstacles—and departed Oakland at 4:46 pm. Twenty-six minutes later, they reported from their first checkpoint over Richmond, still at 4,000 ft. The next checkpoint was to be Fairfield, but the call never came. At 8:33 pm, an hour after they would have run out of gas, the plane was reported overdue and a search began. Hampered by the rain and clouds that had forced an IFR flight plan, Coast Guard seaplanes and helicopters checked a wide area from Franklin Canyon, near Martinez, to Napa and Fairfield. The following morning, a search plane spotted the burning wreckage in the hills north of Benicia.

Among the six passengers that departed from Oakland were Lorraine B. Batchelor (26), George Batchelor's

---

[69] August 12th, 1949.

[70] The predecessor to Torrance Municipal Airport, Orange Co., California.

wife, and their two year old son George Patrick. George Batchelor arrived at the crash site in Benicia in time to see the bodies of his young wife and infant son removed for the smoldering wreck.

The cause of the accident—giving the scant resources available at the time—was never determined. Instrument malfunction was a distinct possibility, but it was not uncommon in those early days for pilots to become disoriented in bad weather with avionics that look to us like the middle ages. The Civil Aeronautics Board speculated that either the altimeter malfunctioned or the pilot was trying to fly by visual at a much lower altitude than had been assigned. In spite of the loss of his family, Batchelor continued the airline's operations until 1953, when a highly regulated commercial environment made it nearly impossible for smaller airlines to survive.[71]

California Arrow DC-3
December 7th, 1949
near Benicia, Solano Co., California

---

[71] Arrow continued as a non-scheduled carrier until the industry's de-regulation in 1981.

That year, on November 14th, he married in Los Angeles New Yorker Myrna Tarshis, who gave him two sons, George Falcon (1954) and Douglas E. (1957).[72] One year after the birth of Douglas, he married his third wife, Bettina Laverne (Pearson) Stewart.

N707ME, 1983
One of the first Arrow Air 707s, still with the livery of Surinam Airways,
To which was added the big A on the tail and the company name on the side. Ruthie Phillips and I took our first flight on Arrow Air on this plane on June 1st, 1983, from JFK to MIA.

In 1964, Mr. Batchelor and his family moved to Miami, Florida, where he launched Batch Air, a maintenance facility that grew to become the leading independent FAA approved maintenance station in Miami, eventually servicing over 70 clients, including the US Air Force, NASA, Air Canada, Braniff, Continental Airlines, Alaska Airlines and a

---

[72] Falcon suffered from cystic fibrosis, and through treatment at the University of Miami survived twenty years. His father's gratitude toward the Pediatric Center was expressed in numerous donations throughout his life. At the dedication of the Batchelor Children's Research Institute of the University of Miami School of Medicine in 2001, Mr. Batchelor (who had donated 15 million dollars for its construction) said that *"The 20 quality years we had with Falcon after his visit to the campus were a gift from the University of Miami that we will never be able to repay."*

Doug, after a somewhat troubled youth became a minister, is now the senior Pastor of Granite Bay Church in Rocklin, California, and lives in nearby Sacramento with his wife Karen and five children.

host of major international carriers. Soon after, he consolidated his aircraft trading business into International Air Leases (IAL), for decades one of the most important sources of aircraft for hundreds of customers across the globe.

In 1981, sensing a better regulatory environment,[73] Arrow Air started charter and scheduled passenger services. When I joined the company in 1983, there were a few scheduled routes, including service from Miami to New York, San Juan and Georgetown and New York to Georgetown and San Juan. During 1983, further scheduled services extended the system to Denver, London, Tampa, Aguadilla, Orlando, Baltimore, Montreal, Toronto and others, with hubs in Miami and San Juan, operating 707s, DC-10s, DC-8s and 727s.

In 1983, Arrow carried more than one million passengers to 228 cities in 55 countries, including scheduled, chartered and military flights under the direction of Byron G. Ellison.[74] The expansion did not come without growing pains, and despite the favorable arrangements with Batch Air and IAL, Arrow lost money. Mr. Batchelor, who was mostly dedicated to Batch Air and IAL, took the reins of Arrow in January of 1984, and in June of that year appointed Grant G. Murray, after an intense search for a suitable man to lead the company. In early 1985, Richard Skully, one of the most capable men I ever found in the airline business, was appointed President and began a restructur-

---

[73] Again, the regulatory environment to which I refer in these instances has nothing to do with safety. Rather, it refers to economic authorities that for decades had favored major carriers granting them monopolies on profitable routes and essentially impeding the entrance of new airlines into the marketplace. That began to change in 1981 under President Reagan's initiative to de-regulate the airline industry.

[74] The New York Times, Business People, *Arrow Air Appoints Chief Operating Officer*, August 28th, 1984.

ing that consolidated the most profitable routes, reduced the type of aircraft in the fleet concentrating on DC-8s and DC-10s, jettisoned some money losing city pairs and overhauled the maintenance procedures and record keeping bringing the standards of Arrow to lead the FAA inspector assigned to supervise Arrow's operations to declared them *"an industry standard."*

ARROW AIR
POINTS THE WAY

WHEN YOU TAKE THE A-PLANE...

Miami-based Arrow Air is a U.S. flag carrier with offices and operations worldwide. Our scheduled flights link key cities and countries throughout the world. And our people are strictly pros—from million-mile pilots to mile-a-minute reservations experts. Led by innovative management that points to better service all the way.

There are hundreds of Arrow employees worldwide—all dedicated to the comfort and convenience of our passengers. We offer these passengers low fares and a high standard of service, on the ground and in the air. As a full service airline, we really know how to take people under our wing.

Wherever we fly throughout the world, Arrow employs only the most experienced personnel. Our facilities and equipment are always the most modern. Our record is one of consistent reliability. Our quality of service constitutes a definite customer value.

And our continued growth seems to show that Arrow's operating philosophy is right on target.

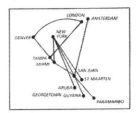

*A*RROW AIR
Go straight for the value.

World Headquarters
7955 N.W. 12th Street
Miami, Florida 33126-1899
305-594-8080   Toll Free 800-872-8000

Advertising Flyer
Showing the schedule system as of June 1984, and pictures of New York base crewmembers.

Just as Arrow was beginning to turn a profit, the Gander incident occurred, and in February of 1986, the company was forced to file for reorganization under Chapter 11, laying off 400 employees. It was slated to begin scheduled services from Miami to Cancun, Caracas, Cozumel and Merida and resume services to Tampa on December 13th, 1985. That never happened. It did, however, survive as a mostly cargo airline. In 1987, George Batchelor sold Batch Air and IAL,[75] and appointed Richard Haberly to lead Arrow. In the following years, arrow returned to passenger service offering non-scheduled services and some regular flights as a lessor to LOT, the Polish carrier (Warsaw-New York-Chicago), and Air Marshall Airlines.

N8969U, 1983
One of the first two Arrow Air DC-8s,
still sporting the red and blue livery of United Airlines.

---

[75] In 1997, he launched Aerospace Finance Corp., which continued to operate until 2012. It is perhaps ironic that while many derided Arrow as a tax write-off for the other businesses, Batchelor stubbornly held on to it in the face of seemingly insurmountable odds. Alas. Arrow survived him just shy of a decade. There is no question that his commitment to the airline went beyond the accounting books and was more of a personal dream.

The flights were operated as LOT or AMI, but the aircraft and crews were Arrow's. In 1991, Arrow was back in the military charter business, carrying troops to the Persian Gulf. The recession that followed the Gulf War affected Arrows revenues, and in 1994 Jonathan D. "Jon" Batchelor, son of the Chairman and Founder, assumed the reigns.[76] By this time, Arrow was operating 18 aircraft, and wet charters to other airlines represented half of it business. In 1995, Arrow was carrying more freight out of Miami International than any other airline. Jon presided over Arrow for all but a few months until 1998, when he relinquished direction to Guillermo Cabeza, who had been Arrow's vice-president of operations.

N902JW, 1984, Satellite Terminal, Gatwick, 1983
Home away from home for nearly two years, it was one of the first two Arrow Air DC-10-10s, originally from Laker Airways, it sported the first version of Arrow's livery, light blue and red.

However, the company struggled under Cabeza, and in 1999 was sold to Fine Air Services, its long-time compet-

---

[76] In many references, Jon is referred to as the "stepson" of George Batchelor. While it is true that he was a son by a previous marriage of Betty Batchelor, his name, and the relationship that I witnessed makes me state that he was George's son as much as if he had been his biological child.

itor in the cargo arena, for 115 million dollars.[77] Frank Fine and his son, Barry, planned to keep the livery and restart scheduled passenger services.

Alas, many adverse circumstances combined to thwart Fine's plans. A downturn in the Latin American market—Arrow's and Fine Air's main source of revenue—rising fuel costs, a recession and the servicing of the acquisition debt led Fine Air to lose 108 million on revenues of 152 million in 2000, and while the market improved a little the following year, Fine Air lost 36 million on revenues of 148 million. By then, Fine Air had filed for bankruptcy (September 27th, 2000,) and by the time it emerged from the courts the Fines no longer controlled it, Fine Air had relinquished its name and the new Arrow Air was controlled by a holding group from Connecticut. After some mixed results over the following years, it briefly re-entered bankruptcy in 2004 (January to June), and in 2008 entered into an agreement with Mattlin Patterson Global Holdings, a private investment firm that controlled Varig Logística (a Brazilian cargo airline) and ATA Airlines. The renamed Global Aviation Holdings scuttled Arrow Cargo on June 30th, 2010, nearly 61 years after its founding, and 8 after the death of its founder.

When George Batchelor died in 2002,[78] he left most of his considerable fortune to charity, including the University of Miami, the Community Partnership for the Homeless, Miami Children's Hospital, Miami Metro Zoo, Audubon, Aviation scholarships through the Greater Miami Aviation Association (Batchelor Aviation Scholarship Fund), and his own The Batchelor Foundation. The Foundation continues George Batchelor's charitable legacy under the

---

[77] The purchase included 13 DC-8s, 4 L-1011s, 130 jet engines, and spare parts for all planes.

[78] George Batchelor passed away at his home in Miami Beach on July 29th, 2002.

co-chairmanship of his son Jon and daughter-in-law Nancy Batchelor, and *"supports food banks and organizations involved with arts and culture, education, the environment, animals and wildlife, health, human services, and economically disadvantaged people. Special emphasis is directed toward programs designed to engage in medical research and provide care for childhood diseases; and promote study, preservation, and public awareness of the natural environment."* In 2008, the Foundation had assets of 316 million dollars, and had distributed nearly 12 million.[79] At the time of George Batchelor's death, Donna Shalala, President of Miami University, said that *"Mr. Batchelor improved the quality of life for our most vulnerable citizens. He was shrewd, smart, fun, and had a huge heart."* We could not say it better.

In the years I worked at Arrow, I got to know some of its officers quite well. When I joined the company in 1983, it was still a small operation run out of a trailer at Miami International Airport, not so removed perhaps, from the engine crate at Torrance Municipal Airport some 34 years earlier. Maintenance, of course, was run by Batch Air out of their own facilities, but scheduling, in-flight services and administration were run out of that modest trailer near the tarmac on the East side of the airport. Some months later, it moved to an office building on 12th Street NW near 82nd Avenue. It was a spartan facility, with sections for accounting, administration, scheduling, in-flight services and sales barely inches from each other. I had met Jon Batchelor on my first flight—he was the Flight Engineer on that 707, and his fiancée the Flight Service Manager—and at the offices on 12th Street I met George Batchelor and his third wife, Betty.[80] George was a stocky, energetic man, sporting

---

[79] Among the many gifts, in 2014 the Foundation gave 7.5 million to fund a new building and exhibition center for the Patricia and Phillip Frost Museum of Science at Florida International University.

[80] Bettina Laverne "Betty" Pearson was born on October 31st, 1927 in Scottsville, Kentucky, the daughter of Willie Orval "Orville "and Mary Beth (Rector)

a signature pony tail, comfortable in his shirtsleeves, always active yet always attentive to all. Within a couple of days he would greet me by name, although I was a Flight Attendant who would rarely go to the office. I learned later that this personal attention was a trademark of his dealings with everyone throughout his companies.

Left to right:
**Capt. Al Wells, George Batchelor,
Betti Batchelor and Capt. Vito LaForgia, c. 1983**

Betti was a class act. A former Miss Kentucky who still showed the beauty and grace that had made her a career in modeling;[81] she was also an energetic, charming

---

Pearson; she died on March 22nd, 2007 in Miami Beach, Florida. Betti married George Batchelor in Los Angeles in 1958, her second.

[81] Besides the title of Miss Kentucky, she had become the icon of the Virginia Slims ads in the 60s (though she never smoked), and was an actress in the TV series 77 Sunset Strip and The Big Payoff. Her first husband was NBC's Johnny Andrews, and the couple was notorious in the New York social scene, entertaining the likes of Nat King Cole, Frank Sinatra, Tony Bennett and Liberace, among many. After her divorce, she had a brief romance with Joe DiMaggio,

woman with such an easygoing manner that one could not help but feel at ease in her presence. She was at the time putting together the crew's uniforms. Her sense of style was remarkable, and soon the results were obvious. I could not believe, however, that the charming, vivacious and friendly woman working side by side with us was Arrow's Vice-President, interior designer and the Chairman's wife.

Soon, however, it became obvious that Arrow was more of a family enterprise than I had imagined. It was common for the daughters and wives of cockpit crew-members to be flight attendants or airport agents.[82] When they were not working on a plane, they were travelling for a variety of reasons. Arrow's policy on interline travel was one of the most generous I have ever seen in the industry. When maintenance workers from Batch Air run checks on Arrow's planes, they knew their families would be onboard. The same can be said of Captains, Engineers, schedulers and, indeed, everyone from the Chairman down.[83]

That is not to say there were never any issues. Of course there were. Airplanes are incredibly complex ma-

---

and later moved from New York to Los Angeles with her young son, Jonathan D. McAndrews, where she met George Batchelor.

[82] Capt. Vito LaForgia, pictured above, was not only one of the most proficient airmen I ever met, but also an old school gentleman who made any encounters with him a pleasurable experience. He was one of the first DC-8 pilots I met at Arrow, and later transitioned to the DC-10. As was all too common at Arrow, his daughter Lisa was also a Flight Attendant with us. After Arrow, Vito launched his own company, Aero Services (right next door to Aeroposta, on 36th St NW); a simulator facility that soon became a world class training center. In 2011, he launched his latest venture, VLF Consultants. Among the many well-wishers at the gala to celebrate VLF's launch was Jon Batchelor.

[83] During the Senate hearings in 1986, Mr. Batchelor stated: *"I think it is everyone's responsibility to maintain safety at all times, and I feel probably more strongly than most people. I am a pilot. I've been a pilot for some 45 years. My son's a pilot [Jon] and has flown for this airline and continues to do so. My daughter-in-law [Charlota Holmlund] is a cabin attendant who has flown for this airline for the last—since its beginning, almost 5 years, until just a few months ago. My wife and my other sons ride it."* [op.cit., p. 70]

chines and things can and do go wrong. It is the nature of the beast. However, the attention to detail and serious maintenance had ensured a sterling safety record since that day in 1949 when George Batchelor lost his family on a DC-3.

Many complaints were printed in every newspaper after the crash at Gander, over what in retrospect seems like minutiae. Coffee makers that did not work, condensation leaking on landing, a lavatory that overflowed. Well, having spent a good many years in the industry I must say that even in brand new planes these things can and frequently do happen. But Arrow enjoyed a unique position among independent airlines: the readily available resources of Batch Air gave it the best possible access to ensure the airworthiness of its aircraft. And it showed. While the incredible growth of the first two years did create some problems, particularly in record-keeping, by early 1985 Arrow's performance had become one of the best in the industry.

After the crash, a handful of former employees surfaced with a slew of complaints. That an engine had backfired, that Arrow was sloppy in its maintenance, that the company pressured pilots to ignore maintenance issues. These complaints range from the ridiculous to the slanderous. But try as one may to research these issues, the complainants remain the same handful. In all but one case I have come to the conclusion that they were unscrupulous individuals vying for their 15 minutes of fame. Their history in subsequent years seems to prove that fact.

After the crash, there was a memorial at Kennedy Airport. Jon Batchelor and his fiancée Charlotta Holmslund were there. They knew, as we did, that they could have been the ones on that plane. We had all flown on it in the weeks preceding the crash. But for pure chance, Jon could have been the engineer that day and Charlotta the Flight Service Manager. The crewmembers were their friends. How could anyone believe that the company had in any way been negligent without assuming that everybody from the Vice-President down had suicidal tendencies? We did not discuss these matters, though. In fact, we did not say much at all. We did not have to. We filed out of the church in silence, hugged each other, and that was the last day I saw most of them.[84]

***

After a couple of years as General Manager for AER Airlines in New York, I left for Argentina to try a completely different industry. But in 1989, unable to stay away from the smell of the tarmac, I helped Miguel Angel Conde and Jorge Igarzábal launch *Aeroposta* in Buenos Aires—the first privately run major airline in that country since the Fascist dictatorship of general Perón had nationalized the industry. In 1991, Jorge Igarzábal sold his share of the airline, and I replaced him in the three-member Board. Soon after, I returned to Miami as Aeroposta's Director and General Manager for North America. We were under contract with GE Capital to take delivery of two 747s to fly from Miami to Buenos Aires and other South American destinations.[85] While the economic authority was from Argentina, I had insisted that we obtain FAA certification and maintained our aircraft under FAR part 121. Somehow, Ar-

---

[84] We now keep in touch through Facebook, but we say very little. It is just enough to know how we are doing.

[85] In the meantime, we had already started operations under a wet-lease contract with Rich International Airways. Jeanne Rich, the owner, was a long time friend of George Batchelor's and the L-1011 and DC-8 that we used were both from IAL and maintained by Batch Air. In 1986, I had represented her in Montevideo, in a bid to acquire Pluna, the national airlines of Uruguay.

row's obsession to detail had been engrained in my mind, and I could not sign on to the project unless the planes were maintained in Miami under FAA supervision.

As General Manager and Director for Aeroposta, I returned to familiar grounds and established our North American headquarters at Miami International, at an old Pan Am building on 36th St. NW known affectionately as the *Taj Mahal*, though luxury was assuredly not one of its characteristics. I proceeded to hire a slew of other Arrow graduates: James Lee Kaplan as Director of Operations;[86] Rhoda Landis as Interline Manager; Hector Orr as Catering Manager; and Mario Yedo as Cargo manager, among many more. They were the best at what they did, and they proved as valuable to me as they had for Arrow in the past.

At Rhoda Landi's insistence, I went to the IAL offices to meet with George Batchelor for the first time since the crash. Very little had changed, except that now a sign at the lobby greeted me by name in full color. George knew how to make one feel welcome. Either he recognized me or Rhoda put him up to it, but the greeting soon veered into my status as an Arrow *alumnus*. I told him that indeed I was, but that I had had no contact with anyone since leaving the company right after Gander.

I do not have the words to express the pain I saw in his face. Six years had passed, but Gander was still raw for him. We left the meeting room and the people who were there and he took me to a small break-room where we sat down, had some coffee and talked for a long time. He told

---

[86] Jimmy, Arrow's Director of Operations in New York when I was In-flight Services Supervisor there, was a wonderful man. A Vietnam veteran (Maine Air National Guard) who had flown countless missions for Air America and had then been a pilot for Braniff and Varig Airlines. He was a friend, a mentor and an endless source of mirth. He passed away on November 24th, 2012, after a long battle with cancer.

me everything about the investigations to that point, the Congressional hearings, a 20/20 program that had recently aired, and his own ideas on the subject. I still did not know about the 1949 crash, nor did he ever mention it. But when I found out about it I knew exactly the kind of pain I saw in his eyes that day. The following morning I received by messenger a VHS tape with his library label with the 20/20 production. I no longer have a VCR, but still conserve the tape as a reminder.

Over the following two years, George—no longer Mr. Batchelor—proved to be as valuable a friend as one could ever hope for. His knowledge of the industry was encyclopedic, his advice always to the point and always useful and his door always open. Sometimes I'd meet him at a restaurant on E. Okeechobee Rd. behind the Office Depot, as unassuming as the man himself, where he used to go nearly every day for lunch from his office on 12th St. He was always available, and always ready to share his vast knowledge.

In September of 1993, the Argentine government granted Iberia a monopoly on Aeroposta's routes—we had refused to pay the "tribute" that would have kept us in the air. We were soon left without routes, without planes and without friends, except for George Batchelor and Frank Fine. Frank leased me a DC-8 for $1.00 per month, to ensure that I maintained an aircraft in my certificate so that the Argentine government could not revoke it, and George gave me the most generous terms to fly our stranded passengers back to Buenos Aires on an Arrow DC-10. For those familiar with these matters, he offered to wet lease the aircraft to me for a deposit of 5,000 dollars. Neither he nor I knew at the time if I would ever be able to pay him the balance.

Many people in the industry did not have kind words for George Batchelor. There is a simple explanation for that. He was a shrewd businessman, indeed. He knew the industry like no other man I ever met and he was relentless in the fulfillment of contracts. Sometimes he would act on a handshake, but whether there was a contract or an oral agreement followed by a handshake he expected and demanded that each part, including himself, honor it. Those who did not honor their agreements with him saw his most ruthless side. Some of those became his enemies and detractors. Perhaps what they did not realize, whatever the real or perceived harm they faulted him with, was that all they had to do was to be honest and straightforward and, most importantly, honor their word to see the most loyal and generous side of George Batchelor.

I did not know in 1983 that I would ever say this, but I miss George. I grew to admire and appreciate his tenacity, his fortitude and his generosity. I saw it applied to hundreds of causes and scores of people. The notion that this man may have at any time, under any circumstance, placed profits over the safety of one of his airlines' flights is preposterous. Those who suggested it at the time, like then Senator Albert Gore Jr. from Tennessee,[87] will live in infa-

---

[87] United States Senate, *Airline safety: hearings before the Permanent Subcommittee on Investigations of the Committee on Governmental Affairs,* Ninety-ninth Congress, second session, March 6, 13, 1986, Washington, U.S.G.P.O., 1987. Senator, then Vice President and ultimately one of the sorest losers in the history of Presidential elections, Albert Gore questioned George Batchelor at large during the March, 1986, Hearings on Airline Safety before the Permanent Subcommittee on Investigations of the Committee on Governmental Affairs of the United State's Senate. Senator Gore's often insolent questioning and sarcastic interruptions start on page 81 of the printed report. None of his questions were relevant to the crash, but there is enough innuendo to go around. On the same report, starting on page 103, the statement of the Arrow Pilots Association clears many of the issues regarding crew rest and the maintenance stance of the company.

my. As the Arrow Air Pilots Association made clear in its submission to the Congressional committee:

"The public deserves both sides of the story which to this point has been one-sided. The story has been twisted by the media from a tragic plane crash and its cause into a witch hunt by Congress and the FAA to divert attention and pressure away from them and onto Arrow Air. As of today, there is still no answer as to why our airplane crashed not even a probable cause. Yet the FAA, pressured by Congress and the media, has acted irresponsibly and incompetently in bringing out action against Arrow to force it to drastically alter the way it operates.

Nothing to date has been said about the dedicated professionals that continue to fly for Arrow amid all this controversy.

1- Is the public aware that many of Arrow's pilots are furloughed from other airlines such as Pan Am, Flying Tigers, and United?

2- Is the public aware that Arrow's pilots must operate under the same Federal regulations that every major carrier must follow?

3- Is the public aware that Arrow's pilots use the same training aids and flight simulators caused by a major carrier?

4- Does the public know that Arrow's Captains have the final authority given them by law to say whether an airplane is safe for flight and that no company official can force him to take an unsafe airplane?

The pilots flying for Arrow are dedicated professionals with many years experience. Unfortunately for us, we also have to answer for a few former disgruntled employees who have left Arrow under less than ideal circumstances. The public should know who these people are and why they no longer work for Arrow."

To this day, the questions of Arrow's pilots in 1986 remain unanswered. The public did not know then, nor—I am afraid—know until now how professional, dedicated and well trained were our crews, especially the one flying the MFO troops on December 12ᵗʰ, 1985.

Arrow Air planes at Miami International Airport, c. 1993

9

The Conspiracies

Inevitably, as the Canadian investigation spiraled down in acrimonious controversy and eventual failure, some began to raise the specter of some sort of conspiracy or another. Most were just responding naturally to the void created by the incompetence of the CASB. Others were after their own—sometimes obvious—motives.

It is a fact that our mind abhors a vacuum. We instinctively need to find a cause-effect relationship to what happens around us. A good example of this phenomenon can be observed every day as the financial pornography networks dissect the closing of financial markets. On any given day, myriad individual decisions will cause these market to go up, down or sideways. Sometimes, these moves can be quite substantial, and immediately the need arises to explain why. A variety of talking heads will then proceed to venture that, say, a 1% variation in the price of a commodity (whatever caused it), is responsible for an unrelated index to rise (or fall) substantially, say, 5%. Of course, the events may, and usually are, completely unrelated, except for a rather fortuitous coincidence in the timing of their occurrence. More seasoned analysts, who seldom have any time for the TV commentary circuit, now much better: Just because two events happen at the same time, it does not follow that they are in any other way related.

This need to establish the cause of the effect may well be an evolutionary trait. If we were not able to correctly define patterns in the world around us, humanity might well have become extinct thousands of years ago. It is that impulse that leads us to find refuge when lightning strikes around us, or to look before we cross a street. But not all patterns we see—much less those we search for—have a basis other than happenstance. Most superstitions are born of such mistaken relationships. If one falls down the stairs after crossing the path of a cat, it does not mean that the cat had anything to do with the fall.

The same happens when a tragedy like the loss of Arrow 1285 shakes the foundations not just of our beliefs, but of our ability to function in modern society. How could we maintain the ability to travel that characterizes our times if we have no confidence that the plane we are stepping into will reach its destination? The inability of our government institutions to provide a rationale for the event creates the need to fill the void by whatever will allow us to accept it and move on. Thus, all sorts of theories take hold of people's imaginations, regardless of their actual worth. Some are easily identified. Others not so. But by and large, we can apply a rational process to determine their worth as viable constructions.

The second, almost inevitable process is that of exploiting the event for personal gain. That can be in the form of pecuniary gains, or of political advantage. Those who opposed the de-regulation of the airline industry saw in the Arrow Air crash a poster child of the evils of a lax regulatory environment. The fact that de-regulation was an economic phenomenon and that flight safety continued to be highly regulated—perhaps more so than before—

escaped the understanding of most people, but I find it hard to believe that some of our legislators were so obtuse as to confound the two. Others, given the fact that the flight was a military charter, saw government conspiracies of every color and shape. We should review some of them if for no other reason than to clear the air.

On *Improbable Cause*, after successfully punching holes in the CASB report and establishing that sabotage or a terrorist act were more likely culprits, Dr. Leslie Filotas advances the notion that a possible cause for the tragedy had to do with Iran sponsoring some sort of pay-back attack for perceived bad dealings from the Oliver North chumps during what came to be known as the Iran-Contra affair. Dr. J. Douglas Phillips, father of one of the victims, during the Congressional hearing in December, 1990, made the theory his own: *"If we assume that the Iran/Contra disgrace is, indeed, a fact, it did happen, and I think that we were stonewalled and met with callous disregard and indifference by our governmental agencies and others that we attempted to contact because there was something terrible politically embarrassing that could be brought out relative to the Gander crash, that being, if the Iran Contra affair had been found out in 1985, as opposed to 1986, a terribly embarrassing situation for our President and our country at the time…if you will please and the subcommitteemen, read the Tower report, if you want to know where the motivation lies for the Gander crash…[on] November 25th, 1985, [Lt. Col. Oliver North] delivered to the Iranians some missiles, which they had paid some $18 million for and they were the wrong ones and they were extremely upset with this situation. If one then looks at the Tower report, December 9th, 1985, there is a quote by Col. North that states—not the exact quote—that a dire emergency had arisen, a highly explosive dangerous situation exists relative to the botched arms deal. We must do something immediately or the Iranians have promised to retaliate in American lives. That* *was December 9ᵗʰ, 1985. As we all know sitting here what happened December 12ᵗʰ, 1985, it is more than just a coincidence."*[88]

I will be the last person to ever question the intention or the character of Dr. Phillips. I cannot imagine his pain and anguish, nor do I dare to attempt it. I believe he was sincere, and I believe that he fell prey to his own necessity to find an explanation where none was forthcoming.

There is no doubt that we were all lied to and stonewalled from the moment the news of the Arrow disaster hit the wires. There is no doubt that US Government agencies acted with callous disregard to their duties, if not worse. There is no doubt that the criminally insane shenanigans of the Iran/Contra crowd would have been just as much of an embarrassment to the Administration in 1985 as they in fact were just a few months later. There is no doubt; finally, that the delivery of the wrong missiles to the Iranians must have pissed them off and that in that particularly state of being they were more dangerous than under their already abnormal natural disposition. But was all of that a coincidence? Yes, it was.

First, *Islamic Jihad*—the group that claimed responsibility—was a *salafi* Sunni group from Egypt, and was not sponsored by Iran. We will discuss this further.

Second, the Iranians were more interested in getting the correct missiles they had bought and paid for, which they eventually did. The wrong ones were returned, the correct ones were delivered, and under their predicament—the war with Iraq—the *mullahs* would have not cut off the supply of badly needed weapons blowing up an American plane. Crazy as they were—and still are—that was not their favorite negotiating technique.

---

[88] *Fatal Plane Crash in Gander, Newfoundland, December 12, 1995,* p. 127.

Third, a terrorist attack is not a spur-of-the-moment kind of thing. The two days between Oliver North's memo and the Arrow Air crash are but an expression of *ex-post facto* causality. Find a large enough field of search, and sure enough there will be something that *seems* related. If the Arrow Air crash was caused by a terrorist attack—and I believe there is no other logical explanation— it would have taken months to plan and execute it. The positioning of assets, the procurement of the necessary elements and the laying in wait for the opportunity are not a 48 hour proposition. This would have been in motion long before the Ayatollahs had a run-in with Ollie and his friends. In fact, this is one of the reasons I believe that if there was indeed an explosive device, it was planted in Cologne, not in Cairo.

$$***$$

Another widely publicized conspiracy was based on a letter sent to the Hon. Porter Goss, Chairman of the House Intelligence Oversight Committee on February 14th, 1998, by a fellow named Charles M. Byers, President of Accuracy Systems Ordnance Corp.,[89] claiming that at the company's munitions factory in New River, Arizona, they had developed *"a device"* sold exclusively to the CIA, that according to his friend, LAPD Sergeant Arleigh McCree, *"was the device responsible for blowing up the US Army chartered Arrow Air DC-8."* He then elaborates further, stating the there was a *"nuclear accident"* following the crash, involving a *"grapefruit sized"* object glowing *"white-hot"* that was in reality the *"sub-critical core of a nuclear bomb."* For good measure, he

---

[89] Incorporated in Scottsdale, Arizona in 1989, it became inactive in 1994. It is known that they developed a low-lethality anti-terrorist family of munitions named SPLLAT (Special Purpose Low Lethality Anti-Terrorist) shells, and hold patents for a High Impact-Low Penetration round to be used as shotgun ammunition. They are generally known for non-lethal alternatives.

claims a small group of Special Ops personnel boarded the plane at the last minute, smuggling aboard a *"nuclear back-pack bomb"* because *"they had discovered the true nature of their recently cancelled hostage rescue mission."* Apparently, this hostage rescue involved detonating a nuclear bomb in an Iraqi nuclear facility to make it look like an accident. Of course, the whole thing was directed by Oliver North, and only the alertness of these brave soldiers prevented a catastrophe by disobeying an illegal order, trotting through the desert to Cairo and getting themselves into the MFO charter plane without anybody noticing. After a few more ramblings, including a Government conspiracy to implicate him in an attempt to assassinate Corazon Aquino, Mr. Byers claimed to have photographs of the detonator used in Pan Am 103, manufactured in Florida and sold to the CIA. More specifically, he claims that *"A bomb was planted during a stop at Gander and remotely detonated shortly after the landing gear retracted upon takeoff."*

How can anybody read this letter and not conclude that the poor fellow rightfully belonged in a loony bin is beyond me. I'll leave the diagnosis to the doctors; but I smell the sulphuric vapors of paranoia in pathological doses and a serious detachment from reality. In any case, his delirium must have been related to some other flight, for the Arrow Air landing gear never retracted.

Yet, this is the origin of numerous conspiracy theories involving the CIA, nuclear weapons and imaginary Special Operations foul-ups that fill the collective consciousness. One that is priceless in its stupidity is that somebody in the Pentagon decided to do away with the remainder of a Special Operations team that had failed in a hostage rescue operation in Lebanon. According to this theory, the six *"boxes"* loaded in Cairo were not filing cabinets but coffins; the two missing passengers between the passenger manifest count and the bodies recovered where special ops guys; and some nuclear backpacks (essential in a hostage rescue mission, I guess), where expedited through the wilderness in Israel, Jordan and the Sinai—and through the streets of Cairo—to be placed on the plane so they could be blown up in Canada to eliminate the evidence of the fracas. It takes a singular mind to come up with this one. It takes a very small one to believe it.

***

I will not discuss at length the theories about the mysterious contents a few wooden crates seen in some pictures of the crash site that range from clandestine ordnance—including in some claims nuclear weapons—because their absurdity is palpable. Surely those crates were made of wood from another planet, capable of withstanding the post-crash fiery inferno without a scratch.

But this does lead me to the claims that the plane carried missiles or some other type of illegal weaponry. Of course, any such cargo would have been in violation not only of every US Army or FAA rules, but also of the Camp David accords. Incompetent and negligent to the point of dereliction as many of the actors in this tragedy seem to have been, a willful violation of the Camp David accords does not seem to be a reasonable assumption. It is one thing for an Army officer to lower his guard and later find excuses for his negligence, but to deliberately design a course of action that endangers the lives of his troops and the very peace process they are tasked with enforcing is more than I can imagine. Further, no evidence of any kind was found to indicate the presence of any live ordnance onboard, nor was there any indication that would lead one to conclude any were present. In fact, only a *"small quantity of small arms and ammunition,"*[90]—the mangled remains of the soldiers' personal weapons and their empty magazines—and three rocket duds used in training were found by the Canadian Forces after an exhaustive search of the crash site.

The fireball explosion when the plane hit the ground, as witnessed by many, was but the logical consequence of the 100,000 pounds of jet fuel that had just been loaded before takeoff. The difficulties faced by firemen putting it out was—far from a singular circumstance—the inevitable result of fighting a fuel fire with water. One does not need to be an expert to realize that such fire would continue to burn until the fuel was consumed. And that is precisely what happened, almost on schedule. Fears of the Canadian Forces that fuel might contaminate the water supply at Gander proved to be no more than an alarm. A single floating boom was enough. Most of the fuel just burned itself out.

In the absence of any positive proof—or of any circumstantial or even remotely plausible scenario—I have to consider the claims of nuclear or explosive materials onboard as no more valuable than the ranting of the Arizona lunatic above. The fact that Capt. T.C. Badcock, who I have extensively quoted, was the Nuclear Defense officer at CFB Gander, that he allowed his personnel and civilian volunteers, not to mention US Navy personnel from the *Argentia,* US Army troops, journalists, RCMP personnel and just about anybody who could give a hand without any reservations and without any kind of protective gear—bringing the number of people accessing the site to well over a thousand—should be enough to discard any theory of nuclear material at the crash site. If that were not

---

[90] T. C. Badcock, *op. cit.,* pp. 21-23

enough, the fact that after 30 years not a single case of radiation poisoning has surfaced seals the deal.

***

In the end, if there was a conspiracy at all, one is tempted to call it a *Conspiracy of Dunces*. Pusillanimous officers and bureaucrats in the US Army, the DoD, the DoS, and the White House, fearful of the prospect of a repeat of the foul-up that ensued after the Marine barracks and US embassy bombings in Beirut just a few months earlier, and conscious as few could have ever been of the security lapses at Cairo and Cologne, were perfectly happy to lay back and enjoy the spectacle of inexperienced Canadian pencil-pushers embroiling themselves in a four-year exercise in absurdity while the prospect of their taking a drubbing in the press moved further into the sunset. The heroic efforts of a few knowledgeable technicians and professionals in the CASB were not nearly enough to overcome the willful apathy of those who just wanted the whole affair to go away, and the Challenger disaster on January 19th, 1986, causing the press to move on to the next calamity.

By the time pressure from the families of the victims, led by Zona and Douglas Phillips and their *Families for Truth About Gander* got anyone in Congress to pay attention five years had passed and the hearings led nowhere. A futile attempt in 1993 to establish a Congressional Committee to investigate the crash died without fanfare, never making it to the floor and, by 2005, even the most ardent supporters of an investigation were giving up.

On June 7th, 2013, Dr. James Douglas Phillips, father of Sgt. James D. Phillips Jr. and co-founder of *Families for Truth About Gander* passed away in Inverness, Florida, without ever hearing the truth about his son's death. A Diplomate of the American Board of Clinical Pathologists, Emeritus Fellow of The College of American Pathologists and of the College of Clinical Pathologists, however, he knew it all too well. Unlike most, he was able to study his son's pathology reports before the Army locked them up, and his conclusion was clear: *"The airplane exploded in mid-air and then went down and hit the ground with a gigantic fireball when the fuel ignited. But there's no doubt in my mind that there was a fire or explosion, while the plane was still in flight."*

It would appear that the *Conspiracy of Dunces* succeeded in delaying the inevitable and no more.

***

Unfortunately, the same callousness exhibited by those responsible for the obfuscations and delays in the investigation of the Arrow Air disaster, continues to be the norm. Rather than face the mounting casualties of their incompetence, so-called public servants continue to fabricate stories and deny the obvious facts.

The murder of 13 soldiers at Fort Hood, Texas, on November 9th, 2009, was called *"workplace violence;"*[91] the Al-Qa'ida[92] attack on the US diplomatic facility in Benghazi on September 11th, 2012, was a *"spontaneous demonstration,"* as was the attack the same day on the US Embassy Cairo, only

---

[91] It took six years and an act of Congress to change the Pentagon's classification to secure a Purple Star and benefits for the victims, yet the administration still maintains that Maj. Nidal Hasan, the gunman who acted under direction of al-Qa'ida cleric Anwar al-Awlaki, *"has been charged with criminal ativity, but has not been adjudicated a terrorist."* And so the fallacy lives on.

[92] Ansar al Shari'a (Defenders of Sharia) was the main group of Al Qa'ida in Eastern Libya, an offspring of Zarkawi's Ansar al Islam thrown out of Iraq during the Anbar Awakening.

thwarted by the providential intervention of the Egyptian Army.[93] The massacre of dozens at an Orlando night club on June 12th, 2016, was a *"hate crime"* or a grievous example of *"gun violence,"* the murder of two Marines in Chattanooga, according to President Obama, no more than *"what appears to be a lone gunman,"* even though the FBI was investigating the same event as a *"terrorist attack."*[94] And as the list goes on indefinitely, the dunces continue to hide behind euphemisms in an ultimately futile attempt to shove the consequences of their incompetence under the rug.

However, there are always those that continue to search for the truth. We lost in Gander eight beautiful people and at least 248 soldiers—peacemakers—who by any rational interpretation of events died in the service of their country. The fact that their sacrifice is not recognized as such is a mountain of insults over the injury. Even though there were never efforts to reconstruct the plane and seriously study the causes of the crash. Even though the site was eventually bulldozed—just as MGen Crosby had recommended only forty-eight hours after the crash—we still have enough information to arrive at a more rational and accurate conclusion.

What could have happened if what happened had not happened is always an exercise in futility, yet I cannot help but wonder: Had our officials done their job on December 12th, 1985, would they have been more vigilant on December 21st, 1988, when an eerily similar attack took

---

[93] Led, among others, by Mohammed Rabee al-Zawahiri—brother of Ayman al-Zawahiri, the leader of Al-Qa'ida—and a renowned terrorist in his own right since his days as a student in Cairo University in 1974. We will discuss him further in the second part.

[94] The Washington Post, *Obama's Disturbing Pattern of Playing Down Islamic Terror,* Washington DC, July 20th, 2015.

down Pan Am 103? Would security at Cologne have taken notice of the threat and been more vigilant?

Since 1984, Islamic National Socialist groups have caused over 15,000 deaths in terrorist attacks on the West, and hundreds of thousands in the Middle East. The numbers are numbing, and yet, the same feeble excuses keep coming up. The same efforts to cover up the events under a mantle of nonsense, with no other apparent reason that the fear of our bureaucrats *du jour* that their inadequacies may come to light; that their abject failure to act and face our common threat is littering our streets with the bodies of innocents. Better blame it on icing on the wings.

10
Probable Cause

In the previous pages we have gone through multiple scenarios and potential causes for the crash that were considered by the CASB investigation, and more than a few that they did not. We know that, against all logic and before the investigation had even begun, the CASB settled on *icing on the wings* as a primary cause, a finding that was resisted by half the CASB's Board and later thoroughly debunked by the Estey judicial enquiry. The CASB does list a few other aspects in their report, sometimes coaxed with caveats as if they were attempting to deflect the accusations of bias that were—justifiably—leveled on them in subsequent enquiries:

1- The CASB was *"unable to identify any physical evidence of* [pre-impact] *failure or malfunction.*

2- *No conclusive evidence of* [binding or jamming of the elevator] *was found in examinations of the wreckage, nor was the source of the* [previously] *reported binding identified…The position of the elevator thus suggests that full-up movement was available to the pilots.*

3- *Examination of the aircraft wreckage did not reveal any evidence of a hydraulic system failure.*

4- *EGT indications of the number four engine were approximately 40 degrees hotter than the other three engines. As a result, the Cologne/Cairo sector crew was retarding the throttle slightly on take-off to keep the temperature under limiting values. It is reasonable to assume that the accident crew was doing the same. Information supplied by the engine manufacturer demonstrated that such an action would reduce total engine thrust by about 2.5 per cent. Such an event would have an* **insignificant** *effect on take-off performance...Engines one, two, and three were determined to be operating at high-power settings at ground impact...Metallization in the transition duct provided positive evidence that the engine was operating at tree impact and had not flamed out...In conclusion, although the possibility of the number four engine operating at less than full power cannot be eliminated, such an event, on its own, should not have caused the accident.*

5- *There was evidence to indicate that the potable water system was leaking...There are no aircraft control systems in the lower portion of the cargo pits which would be affected by water leakage, nor could water accumulate in a quantity sufficient to cause significant changes in the aircraft weight or centre of gravity.*

6- *There was no evidence found during the examination of the wreckage to suggest that the aircraft configuration was abnormal at impact.*

7- *The stabilizer angle determined from the wreckage was close to that applicable to the take-off weight and centre of gravity position calculated by the crew and the corresponding V2 speed. It was within the flight-deck indicator's 1 ANU margin of error. Because of indications that the flight crew had underestimated the take-off weight and may have inadvertently used a V2 speed applicable to 310,000 pounds, the corresponding take-off stabilizer an-*

gle was calculated. This value (5.8 ANU) was also close to the value determined from the wreckage. It too was within the flight-deck indicator's 1 ANU margin of error. Thus, the Board concludes that an inappropriate stabilizer setting did not contribute to this accident.

8- Examination of the recovered wing slot hydraulic actuators suggested that the wing slot doors were in the appropriate (open) position at impact. This conclusion was supported by the determination that the wing slot door light was not illuminated at impact.

9- There was no evidence to suggest that an inadvertent extension of the ground spoilers had occurred. Examination of the ground spoiler system hydraulic actuator determined that it was in the extended position at impact, consistent with spoilers retracted.

10- The landing gear was extended at impact. Normally, retraction of the landing gear is initiated within three seconds of lift-off, once a positive climb rate has been established... Tests in the simulator confirmed that, when faced with a situation involving degraded climb performance, a gear-up selection was rarely completed.

11- Initial examination of the number four thrust reverser at the accident site raised the possibility that the reverser had deployed in flight...No pre-impact faults with the reversers were identified...Therefore, when the position of all four reverser assembly translating rings is considered, uncommanded deployment of a thrust reverser could not have occurred...The evidence did not support the occurrence of an uncommanded deployment of a thrust reverser.

12- There was considerable speculation that the accident occurred as a result of the detonation, either accidental or through sabotage, of some explosive device...Detailed examination of the wreckage with the assistance of forensic experts of the RCMP, including examinations at the RCMP Central Forensic Laboratory, revealed no evidence of an explosion or pre-impact fire.

13- There was no evidence found of any ammunition or military ordnance in the wreckage. A thorough inspection of personal baggage loaded on board the aircraft had been carried out prior to departure from Cairo. No explosive materials or otherwise hazardous items were discovered. The Board noted no significant difference between the weapons recovered and those reported to have been on board.

14- Although there was some level of HCN detected in the remains of the majority of aircraft occupants, it was the conclusion of all pathologists involved in the assessment of the pathological and toxicological findings that the HCN values were unreliable as an indicator of pre-impact fire and, at best, only indicative of exposure to fire.[!?][95]

15- There was considerable evidence to suggest that the crew-calculated take-off weight (330,625 pounds) at Gander was less than the actual take-off weight. Determination of the actual weight was difficult due to inconsistent load documentation and, in some cases, an absence of adequate load documentation. Nevertheless, the Board estimates that the actual take-off weight exceeded that calculated by the crew by about 14,000 pounds...According to information provided by Douglas Aircraft Co., the use of these lower speeds **would have had little effect** on the take-off performance of the aircraft. Early rotation would

---

[95] We know through extensive studies cited in this work that the opposite is true; that even small quantities of CO combined with HCN are sufficient to cause death in a short period, that it can only be present when inhaled, and that many of the passengers had anything but small quantities in the samples studied. It appears this is but an 11th hour effort to justify the CASB's decision not to consider the pathological results in arriving at their conclusions.

have resulted in a slight increase in take-off distance and time to take off. A slight decrease in initial climb rate would have also occurred. The stall margin would have been reduced by three knots if the 330,625-pound V$_2$ value was used as a reference speed by the crew.[96]

16- *The Board found no reason to conclude that the accident was the result of an aircraft unserviceability or malfunction.*

17- *An analysis of what was known of the flight crew's behaviour while in Cologne, during the flight, and while on the ground in Gander indicated no clear behavioural pattern that could be associated with fatigue.*

18- *The normal ongoing surveillance of Arrow Air by the FAA did not identify any deficiencies in Arrow Air's ability to comply with applicable FARs or established FAA procedures. Both assigned principal inspectors testified at the Board's public inquiry that, during their surveillance, they noted no significant discrepancies in Arrow Air's methods of operation.*

19- *The aircraft stalled at a higher than normal airspeed after leaving ground effect.*[97]

20- *The flight crew was certified and qualified for the flight in accordance with existing regulations*

21- *The aircraft was certified in accordance with existing regulations.*

22- *The take-off weight and centre of gravity position were within prescribed limits.*

---

[96] Maximum take-off weight for the DC-8-62 was 355,000 lbs, fuel capacity 24,260 gal, and the structural limit payoff (MZFW/OEW) 111,782 lbs.

[97] It actually did not stall, as clearly shown on the CASB's Minority Report.

The Minority Report agreed with nearly all findings except two crucial points:

1- *Members of the cockpit crew performed their duties without apparent fault.*

2- *Weight and balance considerations were not factors in this accident.*

3- **Ice contamination was not a factor in this accident.**

4- *The right outboard engine (the number four engine) was operating at low power before contacting trees.*

5- *All four thrust reversers may have been deployed prior to impact.*

6- **Fire broke out on board while the aircraft was in flight, possibly due to a detonation in a cargo compartment.**

7- *The determination of the causes and factors that led to this occurrence was severely hampered by the lack of information that could have been provided by a thorough effort to analyze and reconstruct the wreckage.*

Two subsequent inquiries agreed with the Minority Report both in their dismissal of icing on the wings and in their consideration that a fire indeed broke out onboard before the crash and stating, in fact, that icing on the wings was *not even a probable cause.*

Thus we get to the inevitable conclusion that maintenance failures, thrust reversers, crew qualifications or fatigue, airplane airworthiness, hydraulic system performance, engine performance, weight and balance, jamming of the elevators, or any other single mechanical failure can be discarded as a cause of the accident. On the other hand, there is clear and compelling evidence, visual, medical and through examination of the wreckage that there was:

1- A fire aboard before the crash; and

2- A catastrophic failure of major systems not attributable to their condition before takeoff.

Then, the inescapable outcome is that some kind of IED (Improvised Explosive Device) was necessarily present. But it is difficult to assert apodictically what kind of IED and where it was located, given the scant information. We have, however, sufficient evidence and the unfortunate event of Pan Am 103 two years later to venture a likely scenario.

The nervous system of the DC-8, indeed, of just about any airliner, is located below the cockpit, separated from the forward cargo hold by a bulkhead, sometimes no more than a composite material divider. All of the aircraft controls go through this section.

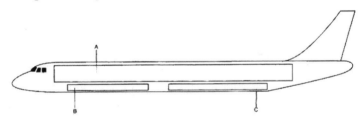

A: Passenger cabin; B: Forward cargo hold; C: Aft cargo hold.

A small explosion in the forward cargo hold or, as the FBI put it in their questioning of Capt. Sounders, in the *B pit*, would instantly compromise all hydraulic and flight control systems, essentially decapitating the plane and rendering the pilots helpless to control the inevitable massive, irretrievable and catastrophic failure that would ensue.

As the investigation on Pan Am 103 revealed, while such explosion may puncture a hole no larger than 20 inches in the fuselage, structural damage would occur almost instantly, producing fractures on fuselage panels immediately aft of the site of the original explosion. From the investigation report on Pan Am 103, we read:

"An explosive detonation within a fuselage, in reasonably close proximity to the skin, will produce a high intensity spherically propagating shock wave which will expand outwards from the centre of detonation. On reaching the inner surface of the fuselage skin, energy will partially be absorbed in shattering, deforming and accelerating the skin and stringer material in its path. Much of the remaining energy will be transmitted, as a shock wave, through the skin and into the atmosphere but a significant amount of energy will be returned as a reflected shock wave, which will travel back into the fuselage interior where it will interact with the incident shock to produce Mach stem shocks re-combination shock waves which can have pressures and velocities of propagation greater than the incident shock.

The Mach stem phenomenon is significant because it gives rise (for relatively small charge sizes) to a geometric limitation on the area of skin material which the incident shock wave can shatter, irrespective of charge size, thus providing a means of calculating the standoff distance of the explosive charge from the fuselage skin. Calculations suggest that a charge standoff distance of approximately 25 inches would result in a shattered region approximately 18 to 20 inches in diameter, comparable to the size of the shattered region evident in the wreckage." [98]

Depending on the altitude, these fractures can propagate away from the original explosion due to the effects of the release of cabin pressure, holding only by the window belt. At lower altitudes—when the cabin is not yet fully

---

[98] UK Air Accidents Investigation Branch. http://www.aaib.dft.gov.uk/formal/n739pa/n739pa.htm (34 of 57).

pressurized and the exterior atmosphere is not yet as thin as it would be at higher altitudes—the fractures would not propagate as far, and one would expect to find perhaps no more than a hole or two in the fuselage and a few fractures below the window belt.

Depending on the position of the explosive, there would also be damage to the bulkhead of the cargo hold, precisely like the a 6 x 3 ft piece of *"composite material cargo liner exhibiting soot and burn marks and small punctures"* found by John Garstang at the crash site, again consistent with the Pan Am 103 investigation findings: *"Clear evidence of soot and small impact craters were apparent on the internal surfaces of all fragments of container and structure from the shatter zone, confirming that the this material had not had time to move before it was hit by the cloud of shrapnel, unburnt explosive residues and sooty combustion products generated at the seat of the explosion."*

In the Arrow Air plane, that area looked like this:

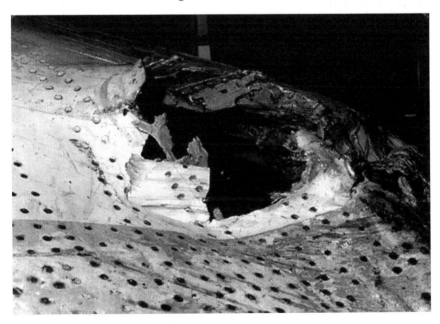

That initial explosion would have been followed by *"a secondary high pressure wave—partly caused by reflections off the baggage behind the explosive material but mainly by the general pressure rise caused by the chemical conversion of solid explosive material to high temperature gas emerged from the container. The effect of this second pressure front, which would have been more sustained and spread over a much larger area, was to cause the fuselage skin to stretch and blister outwards before bursting and petalling back in a star-burst pattern, with rapidly running tear fractures propagating away from a focus at the shatter zone."*

The secondary high pressure wave would have also ruptured the floor immediately above the explosion area as a result of explosive overpressure as gases emerged from the cargo hold loading the floor panels. Tests conducted by the UK Accidents Investigation Branch following the Pan Am disaster leave no doubt that such pressures would far exceed the failure load of the floor beams of a Boeing 747 by a large margin, and the same conclusion must apply to the floor beams of a McDonnell Douglas DC-8.

N950JW landing at Prestwick, Scotland c. 1984
The window with the O above, over the forward cargo area,
and the emergency exit clearly visible over the wings.
Photo: Mark Piacentini, Glasgow, Scotland

Thus, the fire started by such an explosion would inevitably extend to the passenger cabin above, and those passengers sitting on the rows forward of the wings would be most affected. Those sitting around rows 5 to 15 might be struck by shrapnel, and those in the forward section of the passenger cabin would immediately be exposed to smoke with high levels of carbon monoxide and hydrogen cyanide. Contrary to the Majority Report's off-hand dismissal of the results of carbon oxide and hydrogen cyanide inhalation, death would occur quite rapidly.[99] The cockpit crew, separated by the passenger cabin by a bulkhead and a door that even in those days remained closed during take-off, would also eventually be affected by smoke, but the evidence suggests that the sequence of events was so rapid that smoke had not yet travelled to the cockpit before the crash.

The images on page sixty-seven show precisely the kind of damage to be expected from an explosion and, sadly, almost identical to the damage found on Pan Am 103. Other pieces show clear evidence of a fire aboard before the crash. Besides the cargo liner mentioned above and significantly found in an area where there had been no fire on

---

[99]K. Stamyr, G. Thelander, L. Ernstgård, J. Ahlner, G. Johanson, *Swedish forensic data 1992-2009 suggest hydrogen cyanide as an important cause of death in fire victims.* "*Data on carboxyhemoglobin (COHb) and blood cyanide from deceased fire victims in the period 1992-2009 were collected from two Swedish nationwide forensic databases (ToxBase and RättsBase). The databases contain data on COHb and/or cyanide from 2303 fire victims, whereof 816 on both COHb and cyanide. Nonparametric statistical tests were used. Seventeen percent of the victims had lethal or life-threatening blood cyanide levels (>1 μg/g) and 32% had lethal COHb levels (>50% COHb). Over 31% had cyanide levels above 0.5 μg/g, an indication of significant HCN exposure. The percentages may be underestimates, as cyanide is quickly eliminated in blood also after death. Our results support the notion that HCN contributes more to the cause of death among fire victims than previously thought.*"

Also, Chaturvedi et al, *op. cit.*: "*If an accident victim was alive and inhaled smoke, then these gases should be present in the victim's system; whereas, if an individual was dead because of injuries prior to a post-crash fire, then the combustion gases should not be present in blood...Since carbon monoxide and hydrogen cyanide affect neurologic functions and have interactive effects (Gossel & Bricker, 1994; Baselt & Cravey, 1995; Chaturvedi et al., 1995; Hartzell, 1996), both gases, jointly, have a potential to hasten the onset of neurotoxic effects, including performance impairment or incapacitation, leading to death.*"

the ground, other pieces lead us to the same inescapable conclusion.

In the picture below one can see soot surrounding a window on an otherwise un-burnt section of the fuselage. That window was located right under the O of the Arrow Air legend. On the DC-8 at Gander, that would have been the 6th window aft of the front door, corresponding to the 8th to 10th row of seats, right above the forward cargo area and precisely where one would expect fire in the cabin after an explosion in the forward cargo bin.

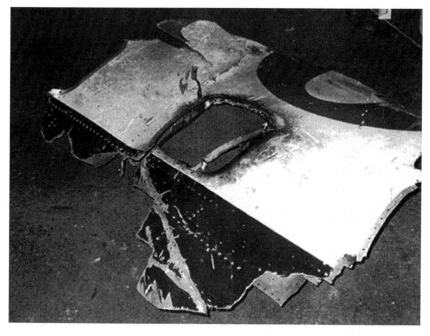

Just aft of this section, the 9th window would have been an emergency exit just above the leading edge of the wing. Not surprisingly, this emergency exit also shows soot on the inside:

As can be expected, one of the forward doors also shows soot and signs of fire damage on the inside:

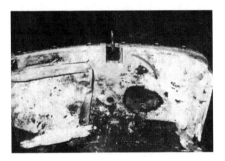

But not on the outside:

There is, of course, the testimony upon which all witnesses agree. Namely, that upon crossing the Trans-

Canada Highway seconds after takeoff there was an intense orange-yellow glow underneath the plane (one refers to flames coming out of the front wheel housing), that the aircraft's engines uncharacteristically made little or no noise, and that there was a big explosion as it hit the ground. Again, all consistent with our hypothesis. The UK report continues its analysis of the sequence of events following an explosion in the forward cargo hold:

"The design of the air-conditioning/depressurization-venting systems on [most commercial aircraft] *is seen as a significant factor in the transmission of explosive energy, as it provides a direct connection between the main passenger cabin and the lower hull at the confluence of the lower hull cavities below the crease beam. The floor level air conditioning vents along the length of the cabin provided a series of apertures through which explosive shock waves, propagating through the sub floor cavities, would have radiated into the main cabin.*

Once the shock waves entered the cabin space, the form of propagation would have been significantly different from that which occurred in the cavities in the lower hull. Again, the precise form of such radiation cannot be predicted, but it is clear that the energy would potentially have been high and there would also (potentially) have been a large number of shock waves radiating into the cabin, both from individual vents and in total, with further potential to recombine additively or to 'follow one another up' producing, in effect, sustained shock overpressures.

Within the cabin, the presence of hard, reflective, surfaces are likely to have been significant. Again, the precise way in which the shock waves interacted is vastly beyond the scope of current analytical methods and computing power, but there clearly was considerable potential for additive recombination of the many different shock waves entering at different points along the cabin and the reflected shock waves off hard surfaces in the cabin space, such as the toilet and galley compartments and overhead lockers. These recombination effects, though not understood, are known phenomena."

The forces at play would have had an enormous impact on the plane and on its passengers. While we were unable to obtain autopsy reports, the gleanings we can infer from other available sources support the idea that passengers in the area immediately above the explosion inhaled a toxic mix of CO and HCN, found in their specimens in quantities that today we know are sufficient to cause death in a very short period. Further, many revealed injuries that would have been consistent with the forces endured during the secondary wave. Indeed, it is likely that many of those unfortunate souls perished almost instantly and *before* the plane hit the ground, seconds from the initial explosion.

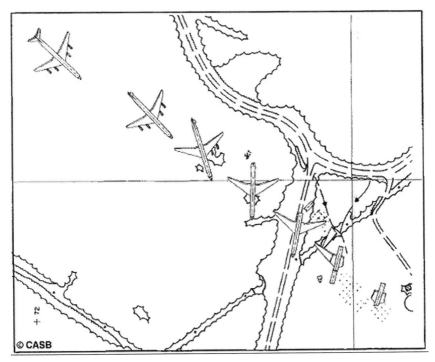

Aircraft breakup sequence.
CASB Report

Many were expelled from the plane as it broke up, *"being picked by the trees;"* others, still in their seats, were massed into a hellish pit of bodies, metal and fire where the parts of the aircraft folded over each other like an accordi-on. [100] In the scarcely minute and seventeen seconds of flight, the cockpit crew frantically attempted to do what they could—triggering at least one fire extinguisher—but they were doomed the moment the IED exploded not much further than 25 inches from the right side of the plane in the forward area of the forward cargo hold, cutting off their controls from the rest of the plane.

Upon hitting the ground, a massive explosion caused by thousands of gallons of aviation fuel ensured the de-struction of nearly every part of the aircraft. Again, the Pan Am crash site was not much different, even allowing for the 18,000 feet that separated the flight paths.

Left: **Crater cause by the explosion of Pan Am 103's wing.**
Right: **Crater caused by the explosion of Arrow 1285.**

We can, therefore, review the findings based on the cumulative evidence of the Canadian investigation, such as it was, with the information gleaned from later reports, in-cluding the Congressional hearings, the CFB Gander report and science on carboxihemoglobin published in the last twenty years:

---

[100] T.C. Badcock, *op. cit.*, pp. 21-22.

1- The cockpit crew was properly licensed, medically fit and thoroughly trained to conduct the flight. Further, there was no evidence that fatigue may have been a factor in their performance.

2- The Aircraft had a valid Certificate of Airworthiness and had been maintained in accordance to industry standards and FAA regulations.

3- No evidence of any defect or malfunction in the aircraft systems or engines was found that could have been a cause or even a contributing factor to the crash.

4- No evidence of any structural failure or metal fatigue was found that could have been a cause or even a contributing factor to the crash.

5- An IED detonated seconds after take-off, most likely in the forward right area of the B pit and no more than 30 inches from the aircraft's skin, causing an elliptical hole with an outside pucker in a section of the fuselage just aft of the right forward door. This hole was *"assessed to be the result of an object striking the interior of the fuselage at high speed."*

6- The analysis of the Flight Data Recorder revealed little information overall, but sufficient to establish that no stall had occurred, and that a massive failure took place approximately 30 seconds after takeoff. No positive evidence of an explosion could be gleaned from it, nor was there any evidence that could rule an explosion out.

7- The Voice Data Recorder was apparently not useful to make any determination, although contradictory statements from the CASB do not permit us to affirm no information was recorded.

8- The direct explosion of the IED produced a hole in the fuselage, of approximately 18-22 inches in diameter, and disrupted the main cabin floor. Some cracks propagated in the immediate area, though pressure differential was not likely a factor. The direct and indirect forces compromised the integrity of the fuselage, separating the cockpit from the forward fuselage in a matter of seconds. The fire created by the explosion engulfed the passenger cabin immediately above the forward cargo area, causing the death of many passengers before the airplane hit the ground, as indicated by high levels of carboxyhemoglobin and evidence of hydrogen cyanide. The pilots, as the cockpit had been separated almost instantly, did not show signs of COHb and CN in their blood.

9- Cargo or other debris ejected from the forward fuselage collided with the empennage, separating the tail section from the fuselage. Some of this debris was likely aspired into the No 3 engine, and possibly No 4.

10- The plane impacted the terrain between the Trans Canada Highway and Gander Lake producing a large fireball and creating a crater.

Conclusion:

The massive system failure and eventual crash of the airplane was doubtlessly caused by the detonation of an explosive device approximately thirty seconds after lift-off. The IED was likely located towards the front of the forward cargo area, on the right side of the plane. While security was virtually non-existent in Cairo and Cologne it is more likely that the IED was planted in Cologne.

11

The terrorists

'We know that Hitler gave a great deal of thought - as did Lenin, by the way - to Clausewitz's answer to the famous question: 'What is war?'

His answer is well known;

'War is only a continuation of politics with other means'

If these means have been fundamentally changed by the atom bomb, only the special action remains as the clearest expression of 'continuation of politics.' In most cases such an action is more of a matter of politics or economics than actual military science. Like it or not, a new type of soldier has arisen: an organized adventurer. He must have some of the qualities of a guerilla, a man of science and an inventor, of a scholar and psychologist. He can emerge from the water or fall from the sky, can walk peaceably along the streets of the enemy's capital or issue him false orders. In reality war is for him an anachronism. In vain the 'traditional' generals view him with understandable suspicion. He exists and can no longer disappear from the battlefield; he is the authentic secret weapon of his fatherland."[101]

Within hours of the crash, a group calling itself *Islamic Jihad* claimed responsibility in a phone call to the Reuters office in Beirut. The same call was placed to the US Consul-General in Oran, Algeria; and on December 13th, a call

---

[101] Otto Skorzeny, *Maine Kommando Unternehmen*, Munich, 1993, p. 468

placed in Lebanon to the CASB headquarters in Hull (Quebec). The caller stated that Islamic Jihad had acted in collaboration with an *"exiled Egyptian group,"* and that the bomb was supposed to explode at Fort Campbell, but that it exploded in Canada *"because the flight had been delayed."* No one seemed to take into consideration at the time of the call that the fact that the flight had been delayed was not public knowledge.

Over the course of the following weeks, more calls were made to press agencies and US diplomatic facilities. All but one claimed responsibility in the name of *Islamic Jihad*. The other one was in a phone call to an Italian news agency in the name of *al-Gama'a al-Islamiyya*, surely the other *"exiled Egyptian group"* mentioned in the first call. It was not the first time these two groups acted in tandem.

There were, at that time, several groups that went by the same name of *Islamic Jihad*. The association with an *"exiled Egyptian group"* is the key to determine which one it was.

al-Jihad (AKA Islamic Jihad, Egyptian Islamic Jihad)

On September 17th, 1978, after almost two weeks of secret negotiations at Camp David, Israeli Prime Minister Menachem Begin and Egyptian President Anwar el-Sadat signed the *Framework for Peace in the Middle East Agreement* that led to the formal signing of a Peace Treaty in Washington on March 26th, 1979. This is precisely the agreement that led to the formation of the *Multinational Force and Observers* that was to supervise the implementation of the security provisions of the Peace Treaty after Israel returned the Sinai Peninsula to Egypt. In response to the Camp David accords, and soon after their signing, Muhammad 'Abd al-Salam Farraj—a notorious member of the Muslim Brotherhood—founded the *al-jihad* movement.[102] This newcomer gained notoriety on October 6th, 1981, when in collaboration with *al-Gama'a al-Islamiyya* (another *salafi* splinter from the Muslim Brotherhood) carried out the assassination of President Sadat.[103] In the months following the assassination, Farraj was arrested and later executed.[104] Among the leaders of these groups rounded up by Egyptian authorities were other Muslim Brotherhood graduates,

---

[102] Islamic Jihad is an Islamist *salafi* Sunni group. While keeping up with the alphabet soup of Islamic terrorist movements is no easy task, this group is not to be confused with *Palestinian Islamic Jihad*, founded at about the same time by Fathi Shaqaqi and 'Abd al-Aziz Awda, two Palestinian students in Cairo and also members of the Muslim Brotherhood, who—after the Camp David Accords—felt that their Egyptian hosts were not sufficiently committed to the Palestinian cause. While Sunni, they took inspiration from the Shia' revolution in Iran. They sought to establish a Palestinian State in the pre-1948 borders of the Mandate of Palestine and the destruction of the State of Israel, and refused to participate in any diplomatic efforts or—for that matter—in the more recent political process of the Palestinian Authority. According to the US State Department, the group is primarily funded by Iran, and frequently joins Hezbollah in operations against Israel. Their founder, Fahti Shaqaqi, eventually denounced the spiritual leader 'Abd al-Aziz Awda for becoming too "moderate", and marched out of Gaza moving to various places until finally settling in Damascus, Syria, under the protection of Hafez al-Assad. In 1995 he was killed in Malta, presumably by Israeli operatives. There was also a group known as *Islamic Jihad Organization*, although some believe it was the Iranian Revolutionary Guards by other name; *Islamic Jihad of Yemen*, which claimed responsibility for the bombing of the American Embassy in Sana'a in 2008; in 1991, a group calling itself *Turkish Islamic Jihad* claimed responsibility for the bombing of a synagogue in Istanbul and the murder of an Israeli diplomat. Of course, none of these were in existence in 1985, except for the original and their Palestinian cousins.

Confusion between *al-Jihad* and *Palestinian Islamic Jihad* is, not surprisingly, quite common. Even in the dissenting report of the CASB, the writers mix the two, attributing to the latter the calls of the former. They can be forgiven, perhaps, since their area of expertise was not the organizational charts of terrorist groups.

[103] This was done in collaboration with a group of Egyptian Army officers, led by Saadeddin Shazli, which called itself the *Rejection Front for the Liberation of Arab Egypt*, headquartered in Tripoli, Libya, under the protection of Muammar Gaddafi.

[104] April 15th, 1982.

Ayman al-Zawahiri, Abbud al-Zumar and Sayyed Imam al-Sharif.[105] Al-Sharif succeeded Farraj as leader, but it was Zawahiri who secured a large following during his stay in Egyptian jails. The group within *Islamic Jihad* that followed Zawahiri was called *Talaa'al al-Fateh* (Vanguards of Conquest).[106] In 1984, after serving barely three years in prison, al-Zawahiri and Sharif were exiled to Peshawar (Afghanistan) were they later set up the headquarters of *Islamic Jihad*,[107] but not before a brief stay at Benghazi, Libya, where Zawahiri established contact with his handler from Libyan intelligence, Abdelbaset Ali Mohmet al-Megrahi,[108] ostensi-

---

[105] Al-Sharif disappeared for a while in 1991, when al-Zawahiri assumed full control of the group but is now in the maximum security prison of Tora in Egypt.

[106] On November 5th, 1993, the defense lawyer for several militants undergoing trial in Egypt, Montasser Zayyat, stated that al-Zawahiri, who the Egyptians claimed had established *Talaa'al al-Fateh* (also referred to as New Jihad), had applied for asylum in Switzerland in April of that year, and that it had been granted the previous week. Corinne Goetschel, a spokeswoman for the Swiss Justice Ministry, told the press: *"This is not true. There is no one of that name who has applied for political asylum in Switzerland."* She did not speculate over the possibility that al-Zawahiri may have been using a different name. Had she done so, perhaps she would have noticed that al-Zawahiri was issued a Swiss passport under the name *Amin Uthman*.

[107] Another of the leaders, who managed to escape Egyptian prisons during a transfer of prisoners, was Tal'at Fu'ad Quassim, one of the founders of *al-Gama'a al-Islamiyya* who, after spending some time in Afghanistan with al-Zawahiri and the up-and-coming Osama bin Laden, successfully fought extradition to Egypt by obtaining asylum in Denmark. The Danes granted asylum on the grounds that he faced the death penalty in Egypt. He paid the Danes with a number of attacks in Copenhagen and against Danish companies and tourists in Egypt.

[108] Most of the 20 terrorist training camps in Libya were closed by Muammar Gaddafi when he "saw the light" after the fall of Saddam Hussein. Unfortunately, courtesy of the misguided policies of the Clinton State Department, they are now again in full swing. In the 1980's the camps offered training for many of the organizations listed in this book: Red Army Faction, IRA, the Popular Front for the liberation of Palestine, al-Jihad and Abu Nidal, not to mention South American terror groups like Colombia's FARC and Argentina's Montoneros. Gaddafi, a latecomer to the Non-Aligned movement, was quick to subscribe to Nasser and Peron's "Third Way," and supply their terror networks with as much assistance as his limited resources permitted, and then some.

bly a security officer for the Libyan airlines and the only man eventually convicted for the Pan Am 103 bombing.

While in Afghanistan, the group was under the leadership of Sharif[109]—although the nominal leader remained al-Zumar, still cooling his heels in Egypt. They begun to recruit Afghan Arabs and progressively became—if that was possible—more extreme, emphasizing the concept of *takfir*, that is, that non Sunni Muslims are also infidels. It was during this time that al-Zawahiri met Osama bin Laden: *"On August 11, 1988, Dr. Fadl attended a meeting in Peshawar with several senior leaders of al-Jihad, along with Abdullah Azzam, a Palestinian who oversaw the recruitment of Arabs to the cause. They were joined by a protégé of Azzam's, a young Saudi named Osama bin Laden. The Soviets had already announced their intention to withdraw from Afghanistan, and the prospect of victory awakened many old dreams among these men. They were not the same dreams, however. The leaders of al-Jihad, especially Zawahiri, wanted to use their well-trained warriors to overthrow the Egyptian government. Azzam longed to turn the attention of the Arab mujahideen to Palestine. Neither had the money or the resources to pursue such goals. Bin Laden, on the other hand, was rich, and he had his own vision: to create an all-Arab foreign legion that would pursue the retreating Soviets into Central Asia and also fight against the Marxist government that was then in control of South Yemen. According to Montasser al-Zayyat, an Islamist lawyer in Cairo who is Zawahiri's biographer, Fadl proposed supporting bin Laden with members of al-Jihad. Combining the Saudi's money with the Egyptians' expertise, the men who*

---

[109] Sharif took the *nome de guerre* "Dr. Fadl", and while he did not fight, he became a "spiritual leader" of the Jihadists, and used his medical training to treat the wounded. At about this time (1988), he penned a tract, *The Essential Guide for Preparation*, which has become the leading text in the Jihadist movement. Captured in October of 2001 in Ibb and placed in prison at Sana'a, Yemen, he was soon smuggled back to Egypt and has been cooling his heels at Tora maximum security prison since. A rift between him and al-Zawahiri in recent years has some pundits announcing the demise of al-Jihad and al-Qa'ida, but they fail to see the larger context.

met that day formed a new group, called Al Qa'ida. Fadl was part of its inner circle. 'For years after the launching of Al Qa'ida, they would do nothing without consulting me,' boasted Sharif." [110] Thus, *Islamic Jihad* members morphed into *al-Qa'ida* and became bin Laden's primary advisors. As al-Zawahiri's funding in Egypt began to disappear in the 1990s, he was forced to an ever closer arrangement with bin Laden until 1998, when the group was definitively absorbed into *al-Qa'ida* with the issuance of a joint *fatwa* proclaiming *Jihad* against all Westerners and Western interests in the Middle East: *World Islamic Front Against Jews and Crusaders,* penned by Zawahiri. After the attacks on the World Trade Center on September 11th, 2001, and the subsequent killing of Osama bin Laden by US forces on May 2nd, 2011, al-Zawahiri became the sole leader of *al-Qa'ida*, a position he still enjoys.

The leadership of *Islamic Jihad*, other than those already named, included:

Umar 'Abd el-Rahman, also known as *"the blind sheik,"* considered the spiritual leader of the group and who remains in prison in the US after his involvement in the 1993 bombing of the World Trade Center.

Umar 'Abd el-Rahman
United States v. Zacarias Moussaoui
Criminal Case No. 01-455-A
Prosecution Trial Exhibits,
Exhibit NumberAQ00108

---

[110] Lawrence Wright, *The Rebellion Within, an al-Queda Mastermind Questions Terrorism,* The New Yorker, June 2nd, 2008.

Mohammed al-Zawahiri, brother of Aymann and one of the top recruiters and operational commanders of *al-Jihad,* was indicted *in absentia* for his participation in the assassination of Sadat in 1981. He later joined the World Islamic Relief Organization, ostensibly building schools and clinics in Indonesia, Malawi and Bosnia, while recruiting for *al-Jihad,* and joined his brother in Khartoum until the expulsion of *al-Jihad* and *al-Qa'ida* from the Sudan in 1998. Soon after he was arrested by the Albanians and rendered to Egypt, where he spent the next 14 years at the Tora maximum security prison. Released after the fall of Hosni Mubarak, he was rearrested but ultimately freed by the Muslim Brotherhood government of Mohammed Morsi in March of 2012; and was one of the Muslim Brotherhood's leaders who orchestrated the failed attack on the American Embassy in Cairo on September 11th, 2012 (the same day of the *al-Qa'ida* attack on the American diplomatic facility in Benghazi, Libya); and the January 18th, 2013 protests at the French Embassy Cairo—against the return of *"French colonialism on Arab and Islamic peoples"*—and became a key figure of *Ansar al-Sharia* in Egypt. In August of that year, one month after the overthrow of the Muslim Brotherhood government of President Mohammad Morsi, he was rearrested but, alas, was released on March 17th, 2016.

Screen shot of *al-Masra,* online publication of al-Qa'ida in the Arabian Peninsula, celebrating the release of Muhammed al-Zawahiri

This outstanding citizen, most likely one of the planners and organizers of the Arrow Air bombing, continues to work with his brother recruiting and producing propaganda for *al-Qa'ida* and its various offspring: *Ansar al Sharia* in Egypt, Yemen and Libya, *al-Qa'ida* in the Arabian Peninsula and the Islamic Maghreb, etc.

Ahmad Salamah Mabruk, also known as Abu-al-Faraj al-Masri, was a decades-long collaborator of Aymann al-Zawahiri, and a senior member of the al-Nusrah Front. After his arrest following the assassination of Anwar el-Sadat, he was sentenced to seven years in prison. Released in the late 1980s, he made his way first to Afghanistan (1989) and then to Yemen. In the mid-90s he was in Khartoum with the other leaders of *al-Jihad.* In 1996, he and al-Zawahiri were captured by the Russians as they traveled through Dagestan in a mission to find a safe haven for *al-Jihad* and *al-Qa'ida* members in Chechnya. The Russians, under Vladimir Putin's orders, let them go.

Mabruk was captured by the CIA in Azerbaijan in 1998 with help from the local authorities, and rendered to Egypt, where he was later tried and executed. During the trial, he claimed that Osama bin Laden had acquired chemical weapons and was planning to use them against Western targets.

In 1999, *al-Hayah,* a London based Arabic publication reported that the Egyptians considered Mabruk al-Zawahiri's right hand man, and that he was in charge of the *"civilian organization committee"* that kept track of *al-Jihad's* membership. He was supposed to identify Jihadists *"capable of carrying out missions"* under the operative command of Mohammed al-Zawahiri.

He was one of the Jihadists released from Egyptian prisons by Mohammed Morsi (Hillary Clinton's partner in democracy), and became the head of *Ansar al-Shari'a* in

Egypt, recruiting for *al-Qa'ida*. He was frequently spotted at recruiting events with Mohammed al-Zawahiri, who had also been freed by Morsi. After Morsi's fall from power, he run out of Egypt and resurfaced at the head of the al-Nusrah Front and a member of the al-Nusrah Shura Council in Syria.

At the time of his capture in Azerbaijan, his personal computer proved to be a treasure trove of personnel information on the group, including *al-Qa'ida's* organizational charts and *al-Jihad's* roster of operatives, leading to the capture of Ahmed Ibrahim al-Naggar and Ahmed Ismail Osman, who were conducting operations in Europe, and to countless other operatives in the Middle East and around the world, but not before a rather classical dust-up. The CIA initially refused to share the information in the computer with the FBI, though they eventually relented after a *"pointless bureaucratic standoff."[111]*

Ahmed Salamah Mabruk
*Screen shot from al al-Nusrah
propaganda video,
"The Heirs of Glory."*

---

[111] Thomas Joscelyn, *Veteran Egyptian Jihadist now an al-Qa'ida leader in Syria,* in The Long War Journal, March 21st, 2016.

Just as he had little to fear from the Russians in 1996 in Dagestan, he has nothing to fear from them now as he leads *al-Qa'ida* forces in Syria.

***

But what is really *Islamic Jihad*, where did they come from and why was Arrow Air 1285 a target? To shine a light over this subject, we need to go back in time to the fall of the Ottoman Empire.

BOOK II

Jihad,
The Arab *Gotteskampf*

Or

The Rise of
Islamic National Socialism

12
The Beginning

At the end of the First World War, the Ottoman Empire that had ruled the Middle East since the fall of Constantinople in 1453 came to an abrupt end. The Armistice of Mudros of 1918 formally ended the hostilities between the Ottomans and the Allies, but it brought neither peace nor stability. The British were in control of the Ottoman Provinces of Syria, Mesopotamia (Iraq) and Palestine (Jordan); French, Greek and British troops were ready to march into Bulgaria and had the way clear to Istanbul (Constantinople). Mehmet VI, the last Sultan, was in constant fear of being deposed, and the Young Turk government of Even Pasha had already collapsed.

By November of 1919, what was left of the Ottoman armies destroyed by the British in Palestine was reassembling near Aleppo (Syria), under Mustafa Kemal.[112] The Sixth Army, largely intact, was bivouacking and awaiting orders near Mosul (Iraq); a small garrison under General Fakhri Pasha that had been holding out at Medina (Saudi Arabia) had finally surrendered to the Arab tribes; and the troops that Enver Pasha had sent to attack northern Persia

---

[112] Otherwise known as Kemal Atatürk, the father of mother Turkey.

(Iran) would take another six months to return only to disband on arrival. In this chaos, with nationalist groups opposing the Armistice, the Greeks eying the opportunity to lay claim to Anatolia and Smyrna (Izmir), and the Italians ogling Southwestern Anatolia, Kemal Atatürk was elected President of a Grand National Assembly at Ankara—effectively an alternate government—triggering a short but brutal civil war.

The publication soon after of the terms of the Treaty of Sèvres so humiliated the provisional government that people massively went to the side of the National Assembly all but guaranteeing the success of Atatürk's vision of a secular Turkey anchored in Central Anatolia. By April, 1921, a reorganized Turkish Army successfully turned back a major Greek offensive, went on to a decisive victory at Sakarya in 1921 and finally led to the evacuation of all Greek troops by September 1922. Soon After, the Sultanate was abolished, Mehmet marched to exile in San Remo,[113] the Turkish Republic was established with Mustafa Kemal as its first president, and the Treaty of Lausanne (1923) replaced the Treaty of Sèvres essentially re-drawing the map.

These events left the old Vilayets (Provinces) and vassal states of the Ottoman Empire mostly as protectorates of France or of the British Empire.[114] The French took control of Syria, Lebanon, Algiers and Tunis, while the British did the same with Palestine and Trans-Jordan, Mosul, Baghdad, Basra, Hejaz (Saudi Arabia) and a score of tiny emirates around the Gulf. The short-lived League of Nations ratified the mandates and the independence of Yemen and of the Sultanate of Egypt.

---

[113] Beautiful city in northwestern Italy, on the Ligurean coast, then seat of the League of Nations.

[114] See Appendix II on page 263 for a list of these Ottoman divisions.

While the French divided their Syrian Mandate to facilitate military control and create a safe-haven for the Christian Maronites in Lebanon, the British consolidated their mandates into kingdoms under the rule of the sons of Sharif Hussein bin Ali (1853-1931).[115] After the dissolution of the Ottoman Caliphate, bin Ali proclaimed himself Caliph of all the Muslims and king of the Hejaz, while his son Emir Faisal was made king of the newly created kingdom of Iraq and another son, Emir Abdallah, was made king of Jordan as Abdallah I.

By opposing the Balfour declaration that called for Jews to return to Palestine, Sharif Hussein lost favor with the British and thus received no support when ibn Saud challenged him in 1924. Before the end of that year, he was forced to abdicate in favor of a third son, Ali bin Hussein, but scarcely a year later bin Hussein was deposed by *Abdulaziz ibn Abdul Rahman ibn Faisal ibn Turki ibn Abdullah ibn Muhammad Al Saud* (ibn Saud), founder of present day kingdom of Saudi Arabia.

The Hashemites did not fare that well in Iraq either. Enthroned by her Majesty's armies in 1921 (after being the king of Syria for one year), Faisal ruled until his death in 1933 of a heart attack—some claimed it was arsenic poisoning—not before warning England of the brewing political and social climate in the Arab world and recommending limits to Jewish immigration and land purchases. His son Ghazi I succeeded him, but died in 1939 while driving a sports car. He was 26. Faisal's grandson, Faisal II, succeeded his father in 1939, but as he was barely four years old, a regency was instituted until his majority in 1953. Only five

---

[115] Scion to the Hashemite family that had ruled Mecca, Medina and the Hejaz since the 13th Century. Sharif Hussein bin Ali, Emir of Mecca and king of the Arabs, had allied himself with the British during the war in exchange for British support to establish an Arab state from Aleppo to Yemen.

years later, following the model of Nasser's revolution in Egypt, a group of *"Free Officers"* backed by an alliance of the Communist, National Democrat and Ba'ath parties staged a coup. Units of the Iraqi army under Brigadier Abd al-Karim Qasim marched on Baghdad, rushed the Royal family into a courtyard, and mowed their unarmed prisoners with machine guns. Quasim opened the way for the national socialist Ba'ath Party, which ruled Iraq until 2003.

The other son of Sharif Hussein bin Ali, king Abdallah I of Jordan, ruled over the former Emirate of Trans-Jordan from 1946 to 1951. He was assassinated by a Palestinian of the Husseini clan[116] while visiting the Al-Aqsa Mosque in Jerusalem for the funeral of Riad Bey Al Solh, a former Prime Minister of Lebanon gunned down in Amman, Jordan, amidst rumors that he was trying to negotiate a peace agreement between Israel and Jordan. King Abdallah was killed instantly during Friday prayers at one of Islam's most holy sites. Prince Hussein, his grandson, was wounded but, apparently, a medal his grandfather insisted he wear saved his life.[117]

His son Talal bin Abdullah succeeded him as Talal I, but was forced to abdicate a little over a year later in favor of his son, Hussein. Talal, while suffering from schizophrenia, managed in his short reign to have a liberal constitution adopted in 1952, which made the government responsible to the Jordanian Parliament. His son, Hussein,

---

[116] The same Jerusalem clan of Hajj Amin el-Husseini and claimed by Yasser Arafat.

[117] Twenty-one year old terrorist Mustafa Achi was the gunman, in a conspiracy led by Col. Abdullah el-Tell, former Military Governor of Jerusalem, and Musa Abdullah el-Husseini. Perhaps not surprisingly, Col. el-Tell had been a resident of Cairo since 1950, and been in close contact with Amin el-Husseini. For his role in the assassination, he was sentenced to death with three other conspirators. On 6 September 1951, Musa Ali el-Husseini, 'Abid and Zakariyya Ukah, and 'Abd-el-Qadir Farhat were executed by hanging, but el-Tell lived to be pardoned by King Hussein in 1967.

succeeded him but, as he was sixteen years old, a Council of Regency governed in his name until his enthronement in May of 1953. He reigned until his death in 1999, being succeeded by his son, Abdallah II, the current monarch.

In 1958, King Hussein formed the Arab Federation of Iraq and Jordan with his cousin, King Faisal of Iraq, as a response to Nasser's United Arab Republic. The project was short lived, as only six months later king Faisal was deposed and assassinated by national socialists allied with Nasser.

Through the 1960s, King Hussein walked a fine line trying to develop peace arrangements with Israel while maintaining some sort of rapport with the Arab countries, and holding on to his kingdom in a rather hostile environment. Palestinian refugees that fled to Jordan after the 1948 and 1967 wars actually outnumbered Jordanians and Jordan's army was not much to speak of. In September of 1970, following a series of hijackings conducted by the Nazi trained Popular Front for the Liberation of Palestine (NFLP),[118] king Hussein expelled the NFPL and its mother organization, the PLO from Jordan, leading to attacks on Palestinian militant positions that lasted until the end of 1971. Most fled to Lebanon, but Jordan, free from the instability they engendered, was allowed to prosper.

In 1973, while national socialist leaders Anwar el-Sadat of Egypt and Hafez al-Assad of Syria were planning a surprise attack on Israel, King Hussein rejected their plans

---

[118] Five planes, including TWA 741, Swissair 100, El Al 219, Pan Am 93, and BOAC 775 were diverted to a field in Jordan (except for Pan Am 93, diverted to Cairo). After a two week crisis, the hostages were recovered and flown to Rome, where they were met by President Nixon. Ironically, perhaps, on September 11th, 1970, in the midst of the hostage crisis, President Nixon started a new program that included the immediate launch of federal agents to begin serving as sky marshals, and to determine if x-ray devices used by the military could be pressed into civilian service.

and actually warned Israeli Prime Minister Golda Meir by secretly flying to Tel Aviv on September 25ᵗʰ, 1973.

Between 1963 and 1994, king Hussein held over fifty secret meetings with seven Israeli Prime Ministers, and on October 26ᵗʰ of that year, signed the Treaty of Peace between the State of Israel and the Hashemite Kingdom of Jordan. Just a few years later, on February 7ᵗʰ, 1999, the third Hashemite king of Jordan died and was succeeded by Abdallah II, his first son by his second wife, Muna al-Hussein.[119]

With the boundaries of Jordan, Egypt, Syria, Lebanon, Turkey, Saudi Arabia, Iran and the UAE more or less defined, it is time to look at the Mandate in Palestine.

LEAGUE OF NATIONS.

MANDATE FOR PALESTINE,

TOGETHER WITH A

NOTE BY THE SECRETARY - GENERAL
RELATING TO ITS APPLICATION

TO THE

TERRITORY KNOWN AS TRANS-JORDAN,

under the provisions of Article 25.

Presented to Parliament by Command of His Majesty.
December, 1922.

LONDON
PUBLISHED BY HIS MAJESTY'S STATIONERY OFFICE

Price 3d. net.

Cmd 1785.

---

[119] Born Antoinette Avril Gardiner on April 25ᵗʰ, 1941, in Chelmondiston, Co. Suffolk, England, daughter of Walter Percy and Doris Elizabeth (Sutton) Gardiner. According to Islamic culture, she changed her name to Muna al-Hussein upon marriage. Divorced in 1972, he was allowed to retain her title as Princess of Jordan and style as Royal Highness.

13

El-Husseini and von Leers

Amin el-Husseini and Adolf Hitler
Berlin, November 28th, 1941

On November 12nd, 1917, while WWI was still in full swing, the British government expressed support for the establishment of a Jewish national home in Palestine. At the time, of course, Palestine was still a province in the Ottoman Empire, but that did not deter the Foreign Office from making its position clear. On the contrary, we might well call the policy an act of war consistent with British efforts to undermine Ottoman control of the area. The policy was stated by the Foreign Secretary, Lord Arthur James Balfour in a letter to Walter Rostchild, the 2nd Baron Rothschild: *"Dear Lord Rothschild, I have much pleasure in conveying to you on behalf of His Majesty's Government, the following declaration of sympathy with Jewish Zionist aspirations which has been submitted to, and approved by, the Cabinet. His Majesty's Government view with favour the establishment in Palestine of a national home for the Jewish people, and will use their best endeavors to facilitate the achievement of this object, it being clearly understood that nothing shall be done which may prejudice the civil and religious rights of existing non-Jewish communities in Palestine or the rights and political status enjoyed by Jews in any other country. I should be grateful if you would bring this declaration to the knowledge of the Zionist Federation. Yours, Arthur James Balfour."*

Nearly five years later, after the fall of the Ottomans and the occupation of their former provinces by the Allies, the League of Nations granted Great Britain a mandate to administer the Emirate of Transjordan, including the *mutasarrifate* of Jerusalem, the southern parts of the *vilayets* of Syria and Beirut, and the *sanjaks* of Nablus and Acre. The mandate, dated July 24th, 1922, essentially confirmed the occupation that had already taken place and charged Britain with administering the territory—under Ottoman control since the XVIth Century—until such time as it could stand alone.

As we have seen, the Emirate of Jordan was almost immediately transformed into the Hashemite Kingdom of Jordan. The rest remained under British administration. The Mandate also incorporated the Balfour declaration into its preamble: *"Whereas the Principal Allied Powers have also agreed that the Mandatory should be responsible for putting into effect the declaration originally made on November 2nd, 1917, by the Government of His Britannic Majesty, and adopted by the said*

Powers, in favour of the establishment in Palestine of a national home for the Jewish people, it being clearly understood that nothing should be done which might prejudice the civil and religious rights of existing non-Jewish communities in Palestine, or the rights and political status enjoyed by Jews in any other country." The treaty of Lausanne in 1923 ratified the Mandate as drawn in San Remo, which continued in force until the end of WWII.

When the first British High Commissioner of Palestine, Sir Herbert Louis Samuel, 1st Viscount Samuel (1870-1963), arrived in Jerusalem in June of 1920, he was met by gun salutes and words of welcome. He was, after all, the first practicing Jew to serve in the British cabinet, and certainly the first one in a long time to rule over Jerusalem. One of his first acts, perhaps seeking to appease his opponents, was to appoint a relatively unknown cleric, Hajj Amin al-Husseini, as *Grand Mufti*[120] of Jerusalem, in spite of a ten year sentence already pending on him for inciting riots against the Jews.[121] Appeasement never seems to work well, and Lord Samuel probably lived to regret his concessions to national socialists in Palestine probably just as much as Neville Chamberlain should have regretted his own concessions to the National Socialists in Europe.

Lord Samuel's efforts to placate all sides satisfied none, thus: *"He is remembered kindly neither by the majority of Zionist historians, who tend to regard him as one of the originators of the process whereby the Balfour Declaration in favour of Zionism was gradually diluted and ultimately betrayed by Great Britain, nor by Arab nationalists who regard him as a personification of the alliance between Zionism and British imperialism and as one of those*

---

[120] Muslim legal scholar, usually an expert in religious (Shari'a) law. The position of Grand Mufti, created by the British in 1918, designated a cleric in charge of Jerusalem's holy sites, including the al-Aqsa mosque.

[121] Perhaps, the decision was influenced by the fact that his two predecessors, the first Grand Mufti Mohammed Tahir al-Husseini and Kamil al-Husseini were the father and brother, respectively, of Amin al-Husseini.

responsible for the displacement of the Palestinian Arabs from their homeland. In fact, both are mistaken."[122]

By 1925, Lord Samuel returned to England and resumed his political activities there, being elected to Parliament in 1929. From 1931 to 1935 he was leader of the Liberal Party in the House of Commons. In 1937, true to his guns, he allied himself with Neville Chamberlain in support of the Prime Minister's appeasement policy toward Hitler, urging the cancellation of Germany's WWI guilt and a return of its colonies, though he did not accept Chamberlain's offer to join the government in 1938. In 1944, he became the leader of the Liberal Party in the House of Lords, a position he occupied until 1955. It is interesting to note that Lord Samuel's appeasement policies in the 1920s favored the ascent of national socialists in Palestine; in the1930s favored the ascent of the national socialists in Europe, and in the 1950s in Egypt and the Middle East. One is tempted to say with Thomas Jefferson that ignorance is preferable to error. A prisoners of his own ideological prejudices, in over 30 years Lord Samuel learned absolutely nothing.

Amin el-Husseini, the Jew-hating nationalist that Lord Samuel appointed to the highest legal office in Palestine retained that position until 1948, when the king of Jordan—Abdallah I—deposed him and banned him from Jerusalem.

Born in 1893, el-Husseini served in the Ottoman army during the First World War and developed a strong anti-Western philosophy. Not satisfied with making him the highest legal scholar in the land, the High Commissioner soon named him to preside over a newly created *Supreme Muslim Council,* that the appeasement oriented government expected would pave the way for Arab rule in Palestine. El-Husseini took advantage of his position, however, to or-

---

[122] Bernard Wasserstein, *Herbert Samuel and the Palestine Problem,* The English Historical Review, Oxford, 1976, No 91, pp. 753–775.

ganize the Palestinian Arab Party,[123] promoting anti-Jewish riots in 1929 and a full blown rebellion in 1936. During the rebellion, the enthusiasm of the Mufti's paramilitary for the anti-Semitic policies of the Nazis was fueled by weapons, money and ammunition provided by the Fascist regime of Mussolini. The British secured the assistance of Egypt, Syria, Iraq and Saudi Arabia in suppressing the revolt, in exchange for promises of British support for their independence. As the uprising failed, el-Husseini was again condemned and fled to exile in Syria but, bewilderingly, was allowed to keep his title as Grand Mufti.

In 1937, the Mufti met in Damascus with Adolf Eichmann and other emissaries sent by Reinhardt Heydrich— deputy head of the SS under Heinrich Himmler and chief of SS Intelligence and the Nazi security services. This followed an earlier meeting in Jerusalem in 1933 with Heinrich Wolff, the first German Consul-General in Palestine appointed by Hitler. It was clear from these meetings that el-Husseini had strong sympathies for the Nazis, and Heydrich cultivated the new relationship. In 1941, during a German inspired coup in Iraq against the pro-British Government of Prime Minister Nuri al-Sa'id—led by Rashid a'Ali al-Gaylani—el-Husseini went to Baghdad and is-

---

[123] Corinna Metz, *The Way to Statehood: Can the Kosovo Approach be a Role Model for Palestine?*, Bremen, 2014, p. 119: *"Amin al-Husseini founded the Palestinian Arab Party that represented an ideology to which the Istilkal Party as well as all other radical parties accepted a subordinate role. The most important paramilitary subgroup of the new party, named Djihad Al-Mukaddass (Holy war in the Holy Land), trained its Mujaheddin (Holy Fighters) in order to fight the British mandatory power. Its most important protagonist was Sheikh Is ed-Din Al-Kassam who combined the fanatic religious rigorism of the Saudi Arabian Wahabites with the anti-imperialist ideology of the Istiklal party to a social revolutionary doctrine. Hence, the Palestinian national movement obtained its first ideological basis. Although the concept of the Mujaheddin served the Palestinian struggle for self-determination, it was motivated by religion instead of nationalism. In 1935, Al-Kassam invoked the Arab rebellion to fight the British army by using guerrilla tactics. The mountainous area of Samaria served as a base for the Mujaheddin, who were ready to die as martyrs in the Djihad against the British imperialism. When Al-Kassam was assassinated by the British forces, he became the heroic idol of the subsequent anti-British uprising from 1936 to 1939."*

sued a *fatwa* for *jihad* against the British.[124] One of his closest associates there was Kairallah Talfah, an Arab nationalist and officer in Gaylani's army.[125] When British forces occupied Iraq, el-Husseini fled first to Iran and then, with assistance from Mussolini, to Italy, where he was received by
the *Duce*, reaching an agreement: In return for an Axis
recognition of a fascist state in the Arab countries (to include Iraq, Syria, Palestine, and the Transjordan), the Mufti
guaranteed their support in a war against Britain. The Italian Foreign Ministry urged Mussolini to advance one million lire to the Mufti, and el-Husseini drafted a proposed
statement of cooperation: The Arab countries would offer
their support to the Axis powers and the Axis powers
would recognize the right of the Arabs to deal with the
Jews after their own fashion. Mussolini approved the draft

---

[124] Prof. Esther Meir-Glitzenstein, *The Baghdad Pogrom and Zionist Policy*, in Schmuel
Moreh and Zvi Yehuda, editors, *Al-Farhud, The 1941 Pogrom in Iraq*, Magness
Press, Jerusalem, 2010, pp. 186-206: "*Rashid Ali al-Kailani, an anti-British nationalist politician from one of the leading families in Baghdad, carried out a military coup
against the pro-British government in Iraq on April 2, 1941. He was supported by four
high-ranking army officers nicknamed the 'Golden Square,' and by the former Mufti of Jerusalem, Hajj Amin al-Husayni. Since his arrival in Baghdad in October 1939 as a refugee
from the failed Palestinian revolt (1936-1939), al-Husayni had been at the forefront of anti-British activity. Following the coup, the supporters of the deposed pro-British rule, headed
by the Regent, Abd al-Ilah, and foreign minister, Nuri al-Said, fled to Transjordan. In
Iraq, Rashid Ali al-Kailani formed a pro-German government, winning the support of the
Iraqi Army and administration. He hoped an Axis victory in the war would facilitate full
independence for Iraq.*"

Note: *Farhud*, in Arabic, can be loosely translated as riot, or pogrom.

[125] When the British government was restored, Talfah was expelled from the Army
and received a six-year sentence for his role. In 1947, he was freed and returned to his home in Tikrit, north of Baghdad, and reunited with his family,
including his 10-year old nephew, Saddam Hussein, who had been living with
him since infancy, and went on to found the Iraqi Independence Party, that
cooperated with the Free Officers in the coup that ended the monarchy in
1953, and eventually merged into the Ba'ath Party led by his brother-in-law,
Ahmed Hassan al-Bakr. When Saddam Hussein deposed al-Bakr in 1958, he
made his uncle a Brigadier in the Iraqi Army, Major of Baghdad and his father-
in-law, by marrying his oldest daughter, Sajida Talfah, eventually the mother of
the infamous Uday and Qusay Hussein. The world of Islamo-Nazism is rather
small.

and forwarded it to the German embassy in Rome, resulting in an invitation for the Mufti to visit Berlin as an honored guest. He arrived there on November 6th, 1941, and met with Ernst von Weizsäcker, German secretary of state under Foreign Minister Joachim von Ribbentrop. Two weeks later, el-Husseini met with von Ribbentrop, a prelude to his triumphant reception on the following November 28th with Adolf Hitler. During his meeting with *Der Führer,* el-Husseini requested German assistance with Arab independence and Nazi support in the extermination of Palestine's Jews. Hitler promised to aid that liberation movement when the time came, and assured el Husseini that the aim of Nazi Germany was the elimination of all Jews.[126]

SS-Gruppenführer Amin el-Husseini c. 1943
Followed closely by
SS-Brigadeführer und Generalmajor der Waffen-SS Karl-Gustav Sauberzweig,
As they greet the volunteers of the SS-Handschar

---

[126] Ami Isseroff, Peter FitzGerald-Morris, *The Iraq Coup Attempt of 1941, the Mufti, and the Farhud.* El-Husseini's recollection of the meeting is very to the point: *"Our fundamental condition for cooperating with Germany was a free hand to eradicate every last Jew from Palestine and the Arab world. I asked Hitler for an explicit undertaking to allow us to solve the Jewish people in a manner befitting our national and racial aspirations and according to the scientific methods innovated by Germany in the handling of its Jews. The answer I got was: 'The Jews are yours.'"* [See also Appendix I on page 255 for a transcript of the meeting between Hitler and el-Husseini]

In May of 1943, Himmler made al-Husseini a Gruppenführer in the SS,[127] and set him off to recruit Muslim Croats for the 13th Mountain Division (1st Croatian) of the SS-Handschar.[128] The Mufti's brigade took an oath of fidelity to Adolf Hitler and Ante Pavelić,[129] and became infamous for war crimes committed against Serb and Jewish civilians.[130]

It was during this time that el-Husseini became instrumental in the birth of a national socialist movement with Islamic overtones—as furiously opposed to the West as to the presence of Jews in Palestine—that still plagues the world. And he had a lot of help in the early stages from recently unemployed Nazis, including notorious butchers from some of the worst Death Camps, propagandists from the inner circles of Goebbels and operatives from the SS commandos. To these, we must add the perhaps more dangerous "intellectuals" of Nazism. Folks like Ludwig Pankraz Zind or Johann von Leers, who supplied the fledg-

---

[127] Reitlinger, Gerald, *The SS: Alibi of a Nation, 1922–1945*. New York, 1989, p. 199.

[128] Hale, Christopher, *Hitler's Foreign Executioners: Europe's Dirty Secret*, Stroud, Gloucestershire, 2011, p. 264-266

[129] Fascist dictator and Capo of the Ustaše, Pavelić fled to Austria at the end of the war and then to Argentina, where he became a friend and confidant of President Juan D. Perón. He was aided by the Vatican in his escape from Europe, in fact, he arrived in Italy from Austria disguised as a Catholic priest and was given shelter at the Vatican, residing first at Castel Gandolfo and later in a monastery near the Papal summer residence and at the house of a prominent Jesuit in Naples. In 1948, a Croatian priest, Krunoslav Draganović, obtained for him a Red Cross passport in the name of *Pál Aranyos* that upon arrival became Pablo Aranjos. In 1950, former *Abwehr* agent Perón granted amnesty to Pavelić and some 38,000 Ustaše who had joined him in Argentina, at which time he reverted to his old name. After Perón's fall in 1955, he barely survived an assassination attempt and fled again in 1957, this time to Spain, where he died on December 28th, 1959, just a few months after the Fascist regime of Francisco Franco granted him asylum.

[130] Fighting against the Russians in the Baranja region the winter of 1944-45, they fell back in a desperate attempt to surrender to the Allies. Most were captured by British forces. Eventually, thirty-eight officers were extradited to face charges in Yugoslavia and 10 were executed.

ling Islamo-Nazis with a structured—if sickening—rationale through their works, extolling the virtues of national supremacy and social justice while denouncing the evils of liberal individualism, Western imperialism and colonialism, and canvassing Islamic traditions for religious justification. The Mufti conducted his work and developed his relationship with Nazi propagandists from his perch at Berlin's *Islamiche Zentralinstitute,* created by Himmler so that Amin el-Husseini could forge a new generation of Arab leaders that would use Islam as a vehicle to carry National Socialism forward.

Amin el-Husseini and Heinrich Himmler
Auschwitz, c. 1943
Photo: Kurt Aber, Bundesarchive, Bild 10111, Aber, 164-18A

At the end of WWII, the surrender of Germany produced a mass migration of Nazis around the world. Some, considered in possession of intelligence or technological assets, were actively recruited by the Allies (including the Soviets). Others, with more war crimes than assets to their names, were expedited out of Europe through the rat route, mostly out of Genoa to Argentina—with Vatican passports.[131]

---

[131] See, among others, Uki Goñi, *The Real Odessa: How Perón Brought the War Criminals to Argentina,* London, 2002.

The government of Argentina, then controlled by Coronel Juan D. Perón, a Nazi sympathizer and operative agent for the *Abwehr* in Argentina, Bolivia and Paraguay—whose personal secretary and principal financial supporter was Ludwig Freude, the chief of Nazi intelligence in South America—was welcoming to the escapees, who were able to settle quite openly.[132] In most cases, they did not have to adopt a new identity and lived freely under their own names. Adolf Eichmann and Josef Mengele were perhaps the most notorious, but thousands of others were there as well.[133]

In 1955, the fall of General Perón introduced a measure of uncertainty into the ranks of Nazi refugees and many (it is estimated over 3,000) marched into exile again, this time to the land of one of Perón's closest allies in the non-aligned movement, Gamal Abdel Nasser. SS-Sturmbahnführer Dr. Johannes von Leers, an early member of the Nazi party with more than twenty books extolling the virtues of Nazism and the evils of international Jewry, spent ten years in Buenos Aires publishing numerous articles under his own name and became the foremost propagandist for National Socialism in Egypt. More to the point, considering what he called the betrayal of Christian churches, he applied his talents to provide an Islamist bent to National Socialism: *"From Indonesia to Pakistan and Morocco the green banners of freedom and God's justice fly against the iniquities of colonialism…and the powerful figure raises in the desert of the upcoming Mahdi, whom Muslims have been awaiting for centuries."*

---

[132] Ludwig Freude, Perón's handler in the *Abwehr*, acted directly under Lt. Gen. Wilhelm Faupel, Nazi Germany's ambassador to Spain and head of the *Ibero-Amerikanisches Institut* in Berlin who, in turn, was under direct command of Admiral Canaris. Faupel had met Perón in Argentina in the late 1920s, when he was Inspector General of the Argentine Army, and personally recruited him for the *Abwehr*. Eva Perón, according to Faupel, was an intelligent, unscrupulous and beautiful *"zimmerfrau,"* and one of Canaris' favorite agents in South America after *"her work in Brazil."*

[133] Silvano Santander, *Técnica de una traición. Juan D. Perón y Eva Duarte, agentes del nazismo en la Argentina*, Buenos Aires, 1955.

Relatively little known today, von Leers was a *"...A district speaker and leader of the National Socialist Students' League, [who] came to the attention of Goebbels and was assigned to write Party propaganda, producing a stream of twenty-seven books between 1933 and 1945 dealing in popularized form with Nazi ideology. An expert on the Jewish question, on theories of 'blood and soil' and the doctrine of the Germanic master race, von Leers achieved early notoriety with his book, "Juden Sehen dich an", published in 1933 and dedicated to the 'gallant' Julius Streicher."*

Under the guidance of Hajj Amin el-Husseini, von Leers converted to Islam and adopted the name *Omar Amin*, which he explained in a letter to American Nazi Keith Thompson in 1957:[134] *"I myself have embraced Islam and accepted the new forename Omar Amin, Omar according to the great Caliph Omar who was a grim enemy of the Jews, Amin in honor of my friend Hajj Amin el Husseini, the Grand Mufti...The Islamic bloc today is the only spiritual power in the world fighting for a real religion and human values and freedom. Besides that, it is a wonderful religion with a great philosophy and an enormous rich[ness] of wisdom. I think sometimes that if my nation had got[ten] Islam instead of Christianity we should not have had all the traitors we had in World War II, two million women would not have been burnt as 'witches' by the Christian churches, there would have been no Thirty Years' War which destroyed Germany and killed more than half of our nation."*

The Grand Mufti received him personally in Cairo on June 15th, 1956: *"We thank you for coming here to restart the struggle against the powers of darkness of international Zionism."* Soon after, Nasser appointed him Propaganda Advisor at the Information Ministry in Cairo[135] under Hans Appler—former aid to Goebbels and future Minister of Infor-

---

[134] Charles Harold Keith Thompson (1922-2002). The letter, dated November 15th, 1957, is in the H. Keith Thompson Archives of the Hoover Institution. Published in Kevin Coogan, *Dreamer of the Day, Francis Parker Yockey and the Postwar Fascist International,* Autonomedia, 1999, p. 388.

[135] He was also an Advisor to the Arab League on German Affairs.

mation—crafting anti-Jewish propaganda for the Nasser regime. More significantly, von Leers became the author of a new form of National Socialism that combined Mussolini's fascist state with Hitler's anti-Semitism and Amin Husseini's views on Jihad. By 1957, a CIA report noticed his influence: *"Hatem and the Egyptian General Staff [are] closely advised by ex-Nazis. Particularly close to Hatem is FNU von Leers, former assistant to Goebbels."*[136]

While his relationship with Hatem should come as no surprise—after all von Leers was one of Hatem's top advisors— the CIA report goes on to describe the depth of von Leers relations in Nasser's government: *"The relations of German-born Johannes (Umar Amin) von Leers with the UAR government, as advisor to the government on anti-Israel propaganda, have improved since 1957. Since moving to Egypt in 1956 he has become widely known and is apparently considered the first-ranking German in terms of confidence. He has never been officially received by UAR president Jamal 'Abd-al-Nasir, but is persona grata with the following officials:*

1. *Ali Sabri, Minister of State for Presidential Affairs, UAR who has granted him several interviews.*

2. *Anwar al-Sadat, president of the Afro-Asian solidarity Council.*

3. *Muhammad 'Abd-al-Khaliq Hassuna, secretary general of the Arab League.*

4. *Former Grand Mufti of Jerusalem, Haj Amin-al-Husayni, through whom von Leers was initiated into Islam and with whom he wants to make a pilgrimage to Mecca.*

5. *Brigadier General 'Abid –al-Azim Ibrahim Fahmi, Director-General of Investigations Department of UAR Ministry of Interior.*

---

[136] CIA declassified report, January 3rd, 1957. Hatem refers to Abdel Kader Hatem, Nasser's first Minister of Information. He was also the acting Prime Minister under Anwar e-Sadat during the October war in 1973.

6. Sayed Hafez 'Abd-al-Karim, secretary-general of Ministry of Economy and Commerce, UAR (Egyptian Region)" [137]

Prof. Dr. Johannes von Leers
Reichsschulungsleiter des Deutschen Studentenbundes
Berlin, December 31ˢᵗ, 1932
Bundesarchiv, Bild 183-2004-0825-502, Alexander Bengsch, CC-BY-SA 3.0

Von Leers was not working in a vacuum. Albert Speer, the Minister of Armaments and War Production of the IIIrd Reich, already advanced: *"Hitler had been much impressed by a scrap of history he had learned from a delegation of distinguished Arabs. When the Mohammedans attempted to penetrate beyond France*

---

[137] Marco Sennholz, *Johann von Leers: Ein Propagandist des Nationalsozialismus*, Berlin, 2013, pp. 346-347.

into Central Europe during the eighth century... they had been driven back at the Battle of Tours. Had the Arabs won this battle, the world would be Mohammedan today. For theirs was a religion that believed in spreading the faith by the sword and subjugating all nations to that faith. The Germanic peoples would have become the heirs to that religion. Such a creed was perfectly suited to the Germanic temperament...Hitler usually concluded this historical speculation by remarking: 'You see, it's been our misfortune to have the wrong religion. Why didn't we have the religion of the Japanese, who regard sacrifice for the fatherland as the highest good? The Mohammedan religion too would have been much more compatible to us than Christianity. Why did it have to be Christianity with its meekness and flabbiness?"[138]

Far from being merely an opportunistic gesture, Von Leers conversion to Islam was a product of his conviction that only within the framework of Islamic traditions would National Socialism achieve its goals. As he described it: *"...In 1932, I withdrew from the Christian Church after I found that it was a Jewish sect and no path to religion... the Christendom of the West is on the road to decay, and the destiny of its churches is moral disintegration, so that they became the allies of international Zionism and medium of Israeli propaganda."*[139] More, as early as 1934, von Leers vigorously criticized the cruel and destructive violence of Christianity in its conquest of central Europe and the Crusades, while extolling the virtues of Islam's tolerance toward other religions.[140]

Sadly, the very same position was adopted by US President Barak Obama in his speech at the National Prayer Breakfast in February, 2015, *"And lest we get on our high horse and think this is unique to some other place, remember that during*

---

[138] Albert Speer, *Inside the Third Reich: Memoirs by Albert Speer*, trs. Richard and Clara Winston, New York: Macmillan, 1970, p. 96.

[139] Johann von Leers, *Warum ich Muslim wurde*, published in *Mimbar al Islam*, Cairo, February 1967.

[140] Johann von Leers, *Der Kardinal und die Germanen - Eine Auseinandersetzung mit Kardinal Faulhaber*, Hanseatische Verl.-Anst., 1934, pp. 23, 48, 52, 68.

the Crusades and the Inquisition, people committed terrible deeds in the name of Christ," giving us the sorry spectacle of a President of the United States espousing the theories of one of the foremost exegetes of Nazism.[141]

Von Leers fervent zeal for Islam actually alarmed some Egyptian nationalists, who thought that it would bring him closer to the Muslim Brotherhood. And it did. Most of the recruits of the Nazi cadres in Nasser's ministries came from within the ranks of the Muslim Brotherhood, particularly among the students in Cairo University, and while they received military training to become *Fedayeens* or commandoes in the Egyptian Special Forces, they were ready recipients of the Islamic National Socialist ideology to which von Leers dedicated his work. Von Leer's is the intellectual framework that still motivates them and their followers.

This collaboration between Amin el-Husseini and Omar Amin von Leers produced the first of the Jihadist organizations as we know them today. It was, in fact, an advanced version of the Mufti's pro-Nazi organization *Al'Jihad al'muqqadas*, commanded in 1947 by Ali Salameh, a Wehrmacht major that had arrived in Palestine in 1944 as part of Hitler's aid package to the Mufti,[142] and the Arab League's *Jaysh al-Inqadh al-Arabi* (Arab Liberation Army), also led by a Werhrmacht officer, Fawzi al-Quawuqji, made up of a coterie of carryovers from Rommel's Afrikakorps, escapees from war prisoner camps and Albanian and Bosnian Muslims recruited by the Mufti during the war to wage guerrilla warfare on the British forces in Palestine. No one seemed to be troubled that this "Arab nationalists" were no

---

[141] The Washington Post, Washington DC, February 5th, 2015.

[142] Gershon Avner to HIS-AD, 13 April 1948, HA 105/31 as quoted by Benny Morris, *1948*, 121, and Joseph Nevo, *The Arabs of Palestine, 1947-48: Military and Political Activity,* published in *Middle Eastern Studies,* 23, No. 1 (Jan. 1987), p. 35.

more than *"German volunteers [who], as in the old days, have adopted 'Die Fahne Hoch' as their marching song."*[143]

The fourth leg of this table was the Muslim Brotherhood. It was, after all, a leader of the German financed Brotherhood that in 1944 had called for a Jihad against Jews, *"who needed to be destroyed like sick dogs."*[144] With German financing, the Muslim Brotherhood was at the end of WWII an impressive organization with more than a half a million members in Egypt, organized in over 1,500 chapters. And they now embraced Amin el-Husseini as their spiritual leader. It was this support that led the Arab League to appoint the Mufti as the Palestinian Leader, if in name only, in 1946. Upon the Mufti's returned from Paris, he was extolled by the Muslim Brotherhood as a *"hero [who] fought Zionism with the help of Hitler and Germany. Hitler and Germany are gone, but Amin Al-Husseini will continue the struggle."*[145]

The failure of the Allies to prosecute the Mufti in 1945 and the advent of National Socialist regimes in the Arab countries, especially in Egypt, in the early 1950s created the melting pot into which the elements of what we now call—inadequately—*Jihadism*. But we still need to look deeper into its gestation.

---

[143] *Der Spiegel*, 13 March 1948, p. 11.

[144] Thomas Mayer, *Egypt and the Palestine Question: 1936-1945*, Berlin, 1983, p. 191.

[145] Jeffrey Herf, *Nazi Propaganda in the Arab World* , Yale University Press, 2009, p. 244: *Hassan Al-Banna and the Mufti of Palestine*, in *Contents of Secret Bulletin of Al-Ikhwan al-Muslimin dated 11 June 1946*, Cairo, July 23rd, 1946, NACP RG 226 (Office of Strategic Services), Washington Registry SI Intelligence, Field Files, entry 108A, box 15, folder 2.

Wer regieren will, darf es nur zum Wohle des Volkes tun!
General Juan D. Perón[146]

14

The IVth Reich, or the Arab Gotteskampf

Jamāl ʿAbd al-Nāṣīr, better known in the West as Gamal Abdel Nasser (1918-1970) was born in Alexandria and, after a childhood spent with an uncle in Cairo and a few brushes with the British government (he received a blow to the head during a demonstration that left a lifelong scar), entered the Royal Military Academy graduating as a 2nd Lieutenant.

Gamal Abdel Nasser (right) and future Libya strongman Muammar Gaddafi (left)
Cairo, 1967

[146] "Whoever wants to govern can only do it for the benefit of the people." In German in the original, a propaganda pamphlet published by the government of Argentina in 1952: *Ursprung und Entwicklung der argentinischen Sozialgesetzgebung, (Origin and Development of Argentine Social Legislation.)*

In 1948, during the first Arab war against the newly created state of Israel, Nasser was an officer in one of the Egyptian battalions surrounded by the Israelis for weeks in the Fallujah Pocket. He later served in the Sudan, where he met fellow officers *Zakariyya Muhyi al-Din* (Zachariah Mohyeddin), later vice president of the United Arab Republic; *'Abd al-Ḥakim 'Amir* (Abdel Hakim Amir), later field marshal; and Anwar el-Sadat, who succeeded Nasser as president of Egypt in 1970. With them, he formed the *Free Officers* organization, whose membership was known only to Nasser, with the purpose of deposing the Egyptian royal family and ousting the British.[147]

On July 23rd, 1952, Nasser led his *Free Officers* in an almost bloodless coup that deposed king Farouk I. Anwar el-Sadat—the same one who was later recognized with the Nobel Peace Prize—advocated the immediate execution of king Farouk and members of his establishment, but Nasser vetoed the idea and allowed the king to march into exile while establishing a revolutionary government under Major General Muhammad Naguib, but essentially (and secretly) controlled by Nasser. Nasser's control was indeed so secret that no foreign correspondents picked up on it until more than a year later. In 1954, Nasser finally took control by deposing Naguib and appointing himself as Prime Minister. That same year, a Muslim fanatic tried to assassinate him during a mass meeting in Alexandria, and once the would be assassin "confessed" that he did so at the behest of the Muslim Brotherhood, Nasser cracked down on that "ex-

---

[147] There is an interesting parallel between Nasser's formation of the Free Officers as a means of gaining power in Egypt, and General Peron's formation of the GOU (Grupo de Oficiales Unidos) in Argentina ten years earlier. In fact, the strategy is identical for the preparation and execution of the fascist coups in Argentina (1943), Egypt (1952) and Iraq (1958), not to mention their common friendship and close collaboration with the same Nazis.

tremist organization" which had, in fact, played an important role in bringing him to power.

In 1956, Nasser proclaimed a new Egyptian constitution, establishing Egypt a Socialist Arab State, with a one-party system and Islam as the official creed. By then, scores of Nazi propagandists and military advisers recently imported from Argentina and elsewhere were on-hand to assist in shaping the national socialist state. Perhaps not surprisingly, 99.8% of Egyptians ratified the constitution, and 99.948% voted for Nasser as its first President. There is nothing that compares to "free elections" in the realm of the totalitarians.

The similarities between the Arab Socialist Republic of Egypt and the organization of National Socialist Germany were not just a coincidence. Nasser's admiration for Hitler and Nazism was quite public. His brother, Nassiri Nasser, published the first translation of *Mein Kampf* to Arabic in 1939, describing Hitler in his introduction as *"the strongest man in Europe."* And his second in command, Sadat, wrote a fictional letter to Hitler in 1953 in terms that leave little room for speculation about the Nobel laureate's sympathies:

"My dear Hitler,

I congratulate you from the bottom of my heart. Even if you appear to have been defeated, in reality you are the victor. You succeeded in creating dissensions between Churchill, the old man, and his allies, the Sons of Satan. Germany will win because her existence is necessary to preserve the world balance. Germany will be reborn in spite of the Western and Eastern powers. There will be no peace unless Germany once again becomes what she was. The West, as well as the East, will pay for her rehabilitation-whether they like it or not. Both sides will invest a great deal of money and effort in Germany in order to have her on their side, which is of great benefit to Germany. So much for the present and the future. As for the past, I think you made mistakes, like too many battlefronts and the shortsightedness of Ribbentrop vis-a-vis the experienced British diplomacy. But your trust in your country and people will atone for those blunders. We will not be surprised if you appear again in Germany or if a new Hitler rises up in your wake. "[148]

During this time, Nasser secured the assistance of SS-Sturmbannführer Otto Skorzeny and others to promote the migration of Nazis to Cairo. These Nazis did not go there as refugees, but as Ministers of State, presidential counselors and Security Chiefs, to assist in establishing the War, Interior and Propaganda ministries as well as the police departments in Cairo and Alexandria and secret police units and anti-Israeli offices. As part of their duties, they trained young Cairo University students in commando and guerrilla tactics and helped form some of the first so-called Islamic terrorist groups.

Among the trainees was a young engineering student, *Mohammed Yasser Abdel Rahman Abdel Raouf Arafat al-Qudwa Al-Husseini*, better known as Yasser Arafat, born in Cairo, but claiming to be a relative of Hajj Amin el-Husseini. [149] Arafat was also a member of the Muslim Brotherhood and President of the Union of Palestinian Students in Cairo University between 1954 and 1956. After his graduation, he was a Lieutenant in the Egyptian Army during the Suez War. [150] It was during his years at Cairo

---

[148] Andrew G. Bostom & Ibn Warraq, *The Legacy of Islamic Antisemitism: From Sacred Texts to Solemn History*, Prometheus Books, New York, 2008, p. 155. The article was originally published in the Cairo weekly *Al Mussawar* on September 18th, 1953.

[149] A former Romanian intelligence officer claimed that the KGB had invented a background for Arafat with a Jerusalem birth. While some of the facts are still disputed, it is more likely that his Cairo birth certificate is genuine, and that perhaps he was not a member of the same clan as the Mufti, but that he invoked it, and that most accept it is quite telling.

[150] After the war, he went to Kuwait, where he founded Fatah, a terrorist organization with the aim of establishing a Palestinian state in place of Israel and Jor-

University that he received training by Nazi officers Erich Altern, Willy Berner and Otto Skorzeny.[151] Other trainees also sound familiar, including Aymann el-Zawahiri, Abbud al-Zumar, and Sayyed Imam al-Sharif.[152]

Immediately after taking over as President, Nasser secured a secret contract with communist Czechoslovakia for the provision of war materiel, and a public one with the UK and the US for financing a dam up the Nile River in Aswan. But on July 20th, 1956, the US announced the cancellation of the agreement, and the UK followed suit on the 21st. Five days later, Nasser nationalized the Suez Canal, leading to the Suez War. On October 29th, 1956, the Israeli Defense Forces entered the Sinai, and two days later French and English planes bombarded Egyptian military facilities. In a matter of days, the Israelis had occupied the Sinai to Sharm-al-Sheik—the point of origin of the MFO Forces in 1985— and the Egyptian Air Force was thoroughly destroyed by the Anglo-French coalition.

While Nasser's defeat was complete in spite of his German advisors and Soviet support, he managed to look to the Arab world as a national hero and a champion of the anti-imperialists worldwide. In 1958, Egypt and Syria formed the United Arab Republic, which Nasser and Hafez al-Assad expected would grow to include the entire Arab world.[153] That was not to be. Syria withdrew in 1961,[154] and

---

dan. Backed by the Ba'athists in Syria, he launched numerous attacks in Israel, Jordan, Lebanon and Gaza starting in 1964.

[151] See Appendix II for a list of these Nazis in Egypt, including these three.

[152] This three were among the founders of *al-Jihad* while students at Cairo University in 1967. In 1988, al-Zawahiri and al-Sharif became founders of *al-Qa'ida*, still today under the control of al-Zawahiri.

[153] In 1954, Nasser wrote in *Philosophy of the Revolution*, of *heroic and glorious roles which never found heroes to perform them* and outlined his aspiration to be the leader of the 55 million Arabs, then of the 224 million Africans, then of the 420 million followers of Islam. There are those today that insist that modern pan-Islamic

in 1971, one year after the accession to power of Anwar el-Sadat, the UAR ceased to be.

Under Sadat and his Vice-President, Hosni Mubarak, Egypt slowly accepted the reality of the failure of Nasser's pan-Islamic dreams and their inability to achieve victory over the hated Jews by military action—not to mention the dismal failure of their Communist allies' support. Although they certainly did not wise-up before their crushing defeat in 1973. [155] Egyptian *realpolitik* demanded a change of course, and a change of course they had. By 1975, Egypt was abandoning its agreements with the Soviets and seeking an accommodation with the West, even if it meant recognizing Israel. But we cannot stress enough that this sudden move towards the West was born out of necessity rather than any peaceful conviction.

Sadat, the Jew-hating Nazi sympathizer who was telling his army in 1972 that he intended to go to war with Israel with or without Soviet support, had no alternative but to become a reluctant peacemaker for survival's sake. He had, ultimately, no intention of resigning his national social-

---

hegemonic dreams are the invention of latter day terrorist groups. In fact, we can clearly trace its origins to the Socialist Arab state, Gamal Abdel Nasser and Omar Amin von Leers.

[154] During the UAR, Nasser brought to Cairo some Ba'athist officers to prevent them from creating trouble in Damascus. Among them were Hafez al-Assad and Mustafa Tlass. After Syria's departure from the UAR in 1961, Nasser imprisoned Assad, but Tlass managed to escape back to Syria bringing with him Assad's wife and daughter. In 1963, back in Damascus, Assad led a Ba'athist coup against President Nazem al-Kudzi, and became successively, member of the Revolutionary Council, Chief of the Syrian Air Force, and—in 1971—President. At his death in 2000, he was succeeded by his son, Bashir al-Assad.

[155] Egypt and Syria launched a joint attack on Israel on the day of Yom Kippur, October 6th, 1973. By the 24th, the Israelis had completely surrounded Egypt's 3rd Army and were ready to enter the city of Suez. Suddenly, the Egyptians accepted a cease fire. The debacle of the Egyptian Army led to an abandonment of the Soviet Union as Egypt's main ally and to the Camp David Accords in 1978.

ist pan-Islamist dreams, nor did his vice-President Hosni Mubarak. During the few years that Sadat survived the agreements and the many since, the Sadat and then Mubarak regimes continued to support the groups trained by Nazis under Nasser, even when on occasion those groups turned on them. That explains why the assassins of Sadat were eventually allowed to go into exile and continue their campaign of terror, and why, with few exemptions, they continued to operate with Egyptian funding and support, at least until the advent of Mohammed al-Sisi.[156]

Left to right
General **Saad el-Shazli**, Minister of War,
President **Anwar el-Sadat**
and General **Ahmad Ismail Ali**, Chief of Staff
Army headquarters, Cairo, October 15th, 1973
Watching the debacle of their army in the Yom Kippur war.
Anonymous

The demise of Sadat brought to power his vice-President, Hosni Mubarak, who ruled Egypt with an iron

---

[156] The current President of Egypt, al-Sisi seems determined to change course, but only time will tell.

hand from 1981 until his resignation on February 11th, 2011. His fall from grace was a consequence of the only successful US policy in the Middle East in over 70 years, which created what we have come to call the *Arab Spring*. That is, a Democracy movement throughout the Arab lands that rejected the National Socialist regimes that had plagued the Arab countries since the end of WWII and demanded the establishment of democratic governments and individual freedoms. In 2010, for the first time in any-one's memory, masses gathered in the streets of cities from Damascus to Cairo, Tunis and Tripoli not to demand the extermination of the Jews and the hated Americans, but seeking an end to dictatorships and corruption in their own countries. It began in Tunisia on December 17th, 2010, and quickly spread through the land as an inevitable consequence of what was then perceived as the Allied victory in Iraq.

How soon we forget, but in 2009, *al-Qa'ida in Iraq* had been soundly defeated, Saddam Hussein had become but a fainting memory of a bad nightmare, and even opponents of the war, like the newly installed US Vice President Joseph Biden were crowing, one year to the day before Mubarak was forced to resign: *"I'm very optimistic about—about Iraq. I mean, this could be one of the great achievements of this administration…You're going to see a stable government in Iraq that is actually moving toward a representative government."*[157] And in July of that year, during a visit to Baghdad, Vice-President Biden expanded: *"I sound corny, but I think America gets credit here in the region. And I think everybody gets credit, from George Bush to [President Obama]."*[158]

---

[157] Interview with Larry King, CNN, February 11th, 2010.

[158] USA Today, Biden on Democrats: *"Reports of Our Demise Are Premature"*, July 6th, 2010.

How could one of the greatest and most vociferous detractors of the war in Iraq develop the gumption to take credit for its success is for the annals of demagoguery. Nevertheless, he was right in every point except for any credit to himself and his boss.

What he perceived, *the Arab Street* perceived. The emperor's nakedness had been exposed, the self-styled heroes of armed struggle had taken a historical drubbing, Saddam Hussein was in his grave and many expected other dictators to follow him there. Bin Laden, Zawahiri and their cohorts were hiding and desperately trying to survive, never mind carrying on attacks.[159] The graveyard of Jihadists was growing by the day, and the people of the Middle East, the first victims of the Satraps that had ruled their lands for six decades where beginning to see the light at the end of the tunnel. Even in Iran, after thirty-one years under the boot of the Mullahs, people took to the streets, before anyone else, on June 23rd, 2009 sparking a revolution—The Green Movement—that kept the Ayatollahs in check until February 14th, 2010, barely two days after Vice-President Biden's empty rhetoric.

And the US administration betrayed them all.

The Green Movement was allowed to be beaten back into submission without any kind of US assistance at a time when simple statements of support would have sufficed.[160]

---

[159] Alas, the misguided actions of the Democratic Congress under Senators Harry Reid and Speaker Nancy Pelosi after 2004 provided them the oxygen they needed to renew their campaigns of terror, planting the seed of their re-birth after 2008.

[160] Iran's Supreme National Security Council has kept the three leaders of the Green Movement, former Prime Minister Mir Hossein Mousavi, his wife Dr. Zahra Rahnavard, and former Speaker of the *Majles* [parliament] Mehdi Karroub under house arrest; as Ayatollah Khamenei fears the Movement can be re-ignited upon their release.

In Egypt, the imbecility of the Clinton State Department refused to see any danger in the growth of the Muslim Brotherhood as the only organized faction in opposition to Mubarak, embracing the election to the presidency of Mohammed Morsi—a leader of the Muslim Brotherhood and a terrorist in his own right. When Mrs. Clinton was making clear her expectation that bringing the Brotherhood to the table would bring positive changes, Morsi was busy emptying the Egyptian prisons of *al-Qa'ida*, *Hamas* and *Hezbollah* militants to renew attacks on Israel and the West.

After another popular uprising (more than half the entire population of Egypt took to the streets in July 2013), Morsi was deposed by the Egyptian military. In May of 2015, he and other senior Brotherhood officials were condemned to death for the murder and kidnapping of guards, arson and looting during an outbreak at Wadi Natroun prison in January of 2011, colluding with Hamas and Hezbollah militants. In July of 2015, the appellate court ratified the sentence and the Grand Mufti of Egypt gave it his blessing.

In a separate case, Morsi was also sentenced to life in prison for conspiring with foreign organizations to commit acts of terrorism to undermine national security. Prosecutors alleged that the Brotherhood had hatched a plan in 2005 to send "elements" to military training camps run by *Hamas* in Gaza, *Hezbollah* in Lebanon and the Revolutionary Guards in Iran. Upon their return, they joined forces with jihadist groups in Egypt's Sinai Peninsula.[161] Yet, the US administration continued to call for Mohammed Morsi's restitution as President of Egypt! No wonder that in Cairo today, the US is viewed as a pillar of support for the Muslim Brotherhood and *Jihadism*.

---

[161] BBC News, *What's Become of Egypt's Morsi?*, June 16th, 2015.

Further, when the newly elected democratic president of Egypt, Gen. Abdel Fatah el-Sisi addressed Muslim clerics at al-Azhar University on New Year's Day in 2015 he proclaimed: *"I say and repeat again that we are in need of a religious revolution. You, imams, are responsible before Allah. The entire world, I say it again, the entire world is waiting for your next move… because this umma is being torn, it is being destroyed, it is being lost—and it is being lost by our own hands;"* and all we could hear from Washington was crickets.

Apparently, the clerics at the seat of Sunni Islam did hear. A little more than a month later, the Grand Imam of al-Azhar joined the discussion: *"The Muslim Brotherhood, the current American administration's great friend, is the tree whose fruit is the Islamist terrorism embodied by the ISIS, Al-Qaeda, Hamas, Palestinian Islamic Jihad, Al-Nusrah Front, Boko Haram and others…Apparently some of the Sunni Arab States have not yet realized that their own national security, and ability to withstand Iran, depend on how strong Egypt is…It is possible, in fact, that US policy is to weaken the Sunni world seeking to unite under el-Sisi's flag of modernity. With European complicity, the US Administration is trying to defraud the Arabs and turn the Israel-Palestine conflict into a center of Middle Eastern chaos, in order to hide the nuclear deal they are concocting with Iran…The treachery of the US Administration is the reason why Egypt's faith in the United States, which is supposed to defend the Arabs against a nuclear Iran, has effectively evaporated…And now the greatest American insanity of all time: America and Turkey are arming and training Islamist terrorist operatives in Turkey, on the ground that they are 'moderates' opposed to Bashar Assad's regime in Syria. They either ignore or are unaware that there is no such thing as a moderate Islamist terrorist. The other name of the 'moderates' opposing Assad is ISIS…The Muslim Brotherhood, in effect, runs Turkey. According to recent rumors, Turkey is also planning to build a nuclear reactor, 'for research and peaceful purposes.'"*

While it is difficult to agree with the Grand Imam in some of his interpretations of US policy—I think ignorance is more to blame than willfulness—it is not difficult to see what he means. The insistence in incorporating the Muslim Brotherhood into whatever future awaits Egypt while rejecting the leaders that are calling terrorism for what it is in the name of Islam is incomprehensible.

The same can be said of the policies towards Libya, Algiers, Tunisia and, more poignantly, Syria. If there was once a chance to topple the Nazi regime in Damascus and replace it with a more democratic system, the US has blown it out of the water. Perhaps the only parallel that can be drawn is that of the Non-Intervention Club policies towards the Spanish republic in the 1930s. Appeasement of Hitler and mindless refusal to support the fledgling republic from an attack from the Fascist states yielded first the irretrievable polarization of Spanish society, followed by a cruel war that killed hundreds of thousands and displaced millions. Worse, it empowered Hitler, Stalin and Mussolini at the expense of the Spanish people, while providing the Nazis with military bases of operations in Spain and the Canary Islands and a center for intelligence operations against the Americas in Madrid.

Today, the same absurd policy has been applied to Syria, not surprisingly with the same results. Forces that had no support within that country just a few short years ago are now in control of vast swaths of territory. American policies have empowered Assad, Russia and ISIL at the expense of the Syrian people, causing hundreds of thousands of deaths and millions of refugees, taxing the resources of neighboring countries and provoking a crisis that already affects all of Europe as we fast approach a point of no return—if we haven't already. In this light, who can blame the Grand Imam of al-Azhar for displaying a healthy dose of cynicism?

Having betrayed the people of the Middle East, the US continues a policy of appeasement towards terrorist organizations like the Taliban or the Muslim Brotherhood, seeking accommodation through negotiation, allowing Islamists like Recep Tayyip Erdoğan in Turkey and the Ayatollahs in Iran to pursue dangerous expansionist policies in their regions while cutting the legs from under the very democratic movements that we helped create through the War on Terror from 2002 to 2009.

While this insane stance may yet be reversible, we are fast approaching the point in which the possibility of ending Islamic National Socialism and destroying their terrorist organizations may be a footnote to the history of continued attacks on the West. How many more people must die while taking a plane, having a cup of coffee on the streets of Paris, taking a bus in London or a train in Madrid, going to work in New York City or enjoying a night out in Orlando before we wise up to the dangers of Skorzeny's commandoes?

Granted, successfully waging war against Islamic National Socialism it is neither easy nor cheap. But as Thomas Jefferson put it in the vespers of the Barbary Wars, *"any price is preferable to the wages of terror."* Indeed, the cost in lives, treasure and sacrifices endured by our society during the war on terror was high. According to the Department of Defense, the casualties suffered by the US during the wars in Iraq and Afghanistan as of June 29th, 2006, was 4,424 deaths and 31,952 wounded. High as the numbers are, they dwarf in comparison with the victims of terror. In 2015 alone, terrorists killed 28,328 and wounded 35,320 worldwide. Nearly as many Americans were killed in a single act on September 11th, 2001, as have died in over a dozen years of war in the Middle East. If we add the cost to our society in treasure and liberty over the years, it becomes clear that

Jefferson's evaluation of the threat was as right two hundred years ago as it is today.

BEST AVAILABLE COPY

BIR
DST /2896

ATTACHMENT #11   RANDOM NOTES

Real names of seven top ODESSA members: 1) Louis El Haj is Louis Heiden known German newspaperman. Former head of the Reich German News Agency. Has recently translated Hitler's MEIN KAMPF into Arabic - has sold over 1,000,000 copies; 2) Lt. Col. Ben Salam is Sturmbann Fuehrer Bernard Bender. Former head of Special Service Commando in the Ukraine. Wanted for war crimes. Is now head of Nassar's Political Department; 3) Omar Amin von Leers is Johann von Leers - is head of Nassar's Propaganda Department - is head of ODESSA in Cairo; 4) Lt. Col. Hamid Suleiman is SS. (Gruppenleiter)Heinrich Sellman - former Chief of Gestapo in Ulm, Germany. Is now head of Egypt's Secret State Police Department. This Department is Nassar's equivalent of the NAZI SS.; 5) Lt. Col. Naim Iahim is S. S. Hauptstabsarzt Heinrich Willerman - is wanted for sterilization experiments on Jewish women. He is now in charge of Samara Concentration camp in the Western Desert, 120 miles South of Cairo; 6) Col. Na'am Machar is S. S. (Standarten Fuehrer Leopold Gleim. Was head of Gestapo in Poland. Is now head of the entire Secret Police in Egypt. Helped Nassar on his coup d'etat when he seized power; 7) Prof. Ben AMMAN is rocket scientist Wolfgang Pilz - is head of Nassar's secret Project 333 which makes atomic weapons.

Otto Skorzenia is former officer of the German Army now working for Scimbet (Israel's Secret Service). Has given vital information of ODESSA's movements in South America.

ODESSA is responsible for the dealth of Eward Peters, Chancellor Ludwig Erhard's personal bodyguard. It is supposed that he hung himself instead of facing charges for war crimes.

Otto Steft Senior, was one of the officers that along with Fritz Knochlein murdered British soldiers of the Norfolk Regiment who surrended at hamlet of de Paradis. This crime is known as the "Paradis Massacre". Knochlein was tried by British Military Court in 1948, was sentenced to death. But Steft escaped. He is now messenger for ODESSA in South America. Has plates for American dollars. At present is in Brazil due to leave for Paraguay on December 8, 1964. Is rumored he killed Shimbet agent few months ago on the Peruvian-Brazilian border. Has been seen with Dr. Josef Mengele. Last time officially seen was at Rio de la Plata on April 18, 1962 in the company of Federico Schwend and Joseft Mengele.

**Classified memo from James J. Rowley,
Chief, US Secret Service
to
John K. McDonald,
Director, Intelligence Staff, BIR,
May 25th, 1964, declassified in 2006**
Full version in Appendix V

"Bala Misou, bala Mister,
Bissama Allah, oria alard Hitler."
Popular refrain in Egypt during WWII.[162]

15
Hitler's Minions
in
Nasser's *Reich*

By 1957, there were at least 6,249 Nazis working openly in Cairo under Nasser's protection.[163] The *Alemanni*, as they were generically known, lived openly and occupied high positions in the Egyptian government (Ministers of War, Information and Presidential Advisors) as well as in the top ranks of the Egyptian army and police. The rank and file of the Egyptian Army in the 1950s welcomed them, and referred affectionately to Hitler as *abu Ali* (Father Ali). Dr. Noureddine Tarraf, one of Nasser's new ministers, proudly declared: *"Hitler is the man of my life. The German Dictator was an ideal leader. I have always wished to live like him."* Nasser did not need to say much. He simply styled himself *el-Reis*, that is, *Der Führer*.

The popularity of the Nazis in Cairo influenced the country's culture at the time. One of the most popular names for babies was *Hitler*, rivaling more traditional choices like *Muhammad*. Indeed, during the Mubarak regime, the chief of intelligence and head of the Administrative Control

---

[162] Raoul Aglion, *The Fighting French*, New York, 1943, p. 217: *"No more Monsieur, No more Mister, in Heaven Allah, on Earth, Hitler."*

[163] The Montana Standard, Butte, Montana, July 14th, 1957, p.47

Authority was the ominously named Maj. Gen. Hitler Tantawi, who was brought to trial for corruption in 2012. He is a relative of Field Marshall Mohamed Hussein Tantawi Soleiman,[164] and a brother to Mussolini Tantawi.

**Field Marshall Mohammed Hussein Tantawi
and US Secretary of Defense Robert Gates.**
*General Tantawi has been in the Egyptian government since 1991, and is now
Commander-in-Chief of the Egyptian Armed Forces.*

In 2012, General Hitler Tantawi was accused by Cairo attorney Samir Sabri of abusing his positions (chief of intelligence and head of the ACA) for personal gain, securing a large number of valuable properties in exchange for keeping the lid on financial scandals involving senior Mubarak-era officials, including members of the president's family and then housing minister Ibrahim Suleiman. Prosecutor-General Abdel-Meguid Mahmoud referred Sabri's

---

[164] In the Egyptian military since 1956, he participated in the Sinai war of 1956, the Six-Day War of 1967, and the Yom Kippur War of 1973. He was appointed Minister of Defense in 1991, and was believed to be in line for the presidency had the attempt on Mubarak succeeded in 1995. In 2011, he was briefly Deputy Prime Minister and, again, considered a contender for the Presidency.

complaints to the military prosecution, along with 30 complaints received against former head of SCAF and long serving Defense minister Hussein Tantawi, who already faced allegations of manslaughter.[165]

Admiration for Nazi Germany and the influence of Nazi revisionists in Egypt (after all, it was Nazi propagandists who started the Revisionist movement there and elsewhere), has led to singular changes in Hitler's history. Schoolbooks claim that *Der Führer* was not German, but that he began life as an Egyptian village boy under the name of *Muhammad Hadair* who wandered from village to village praying at all the mosques!

The implementation of National Socialist policies during Nasser's regime led to a confiscation program in Egypt modeled after Hitler's. That program took the property of some 800,000 Jews living in the Arab world after World War II.

The German government at the time, far from complaining, congratulated themselves for the businesses generated for the Federal Republic by the goodwill created by German military advisors in Cairo, as some documents from the German Embassy in Cairo in 1957 clearly state. The Israelis, perfectly aware of the danger next door and concerned about the capabilities they might bring to bear, did their best to counter the threat. A letter bomb addressed to a German rocket scientist working in Cairo nearly killed his (also German) secretary. Another device addressed to Dr. Hans Eisele, the butcher of Buchenwald, exploded prematurely killing an Egyptian postman.

Insufficient attention has been paid to this period, and it is imperative that we study it in more detail. In the postwar years, while the Allies were desperately trying to

---

[165] *Al-Ahram Weekly*, Cairo, 20-26 September 2012.

rebuild Europe and Japan, the spawn of Hitler was busy laying the foundation of a new National-Socialist world in South America and then in the Middle East. The results in South America have been almost grotesque, but perhaps the subject of another work. The results in the Middle East include the establishment of somewhat successful models of Nazi states in Syria, Iraq, Egypt, Libya and Algeria (among others), and the creation of fanatical groups whose only objective is the establishment of National-Socialist regimes throughout the Middle East—what some call a modern Caliphate—by any means, including the downing of Arrow 1285 in Gander and countless acts of terrorism and genocide around the world. The abject failure of Democratic governments to recognize—let alone counter—this danger, is a harbinger of yet worse years to follow.

***

Among the Nazis who planted the seeds of Islamo-Fascism in Egypt we can list a few:

Erich Altern, *Kreishauptmann*[166] in Galicia, (Occupied Poland), was a Gestapo agent, Himmler's coordinator in Poland and an "expert" in "Jewish Affairs". After the war, Altern fled to Egypt, converted to Islam and took the name *Ali Bella*. He was an instructor in Palestinian terrorist training camps (PLO) recruited in 1969 by Arafat together with Willy Berner and Johann Schuller (below).[167]

Per Olaf Anderson, Swedish fascist who worked for the Nazis in Finland. Moved to Cairo and handled

---

[166] Regional Chief SD (Himmler's Security Services.)

[167] David G. Dalin, John F. Rothmann, Alan M. Dershowitz, *Icon of Evil: Hitler's Mufti and the Rise of Radical Islam*, New Brunswick, New Jersey, 2009, p. 135. Altern and Berner were not alone. Jean Tireault, secretary of La Nation Européene, a Belgian Nazi organization; Karl van der Put, another Belgian Nazi, recruited for the PLO; and in the 1970s Otto Albrecht, a neo-Nazi, was arrested in Germany with PLO papers and 1.2 million US dollars the PLO gave him to buy weapons.

propaganda missions for the Security Services under Alois Moser (below).

SS-Sturmführer **Hans (Johann) Appler**, an early Nazi, he was since 1928 the District Chief of the NSDAP in Gunzenhausen, Bavaria—Führer der Ortsgruppe Gunzenhausen der NSDAP—just in time to organize the attacks on Jewish cemeteries and synagogues in 1928 and 1929, and remained at that post until 1932, even after being elected to parliament in 1930. From October 1st, 1935, to the end of the war he was Mayor of Gunzenhausen, and at the fall of the Nazis was interned in Ludwigsburg where he was held until 1950.[168] He fled to Egypt, converted to Islam, took the name *Salah Ghaffar*, established a unit for anti-Israeli propaganda, worked for the Islamic Congress and was later Nasser's Minister of Information.[169]

Franz Bartel, Assistant Chief of the Gestapo in Katowice, Poland, an "old fighter" in the early days of the NSDAP. In 1959 he was the Chief of the Office of Jewish Affairs in Nasser's Ministry of Information under Appler.

SS-Standartenführer **Hans Baumann**, one of the officers in charge of the liquidation of the Warsaw Ghetto, became Nasser's Minister of War after spending some time as a military instructor for the FLP (Front for the Liberation of Palestine).

Generalleutnant **Fritz Bayerlein**, commanded the 3rd Panzer Division and the Panzer *Lehr* Division. He was Rommel's *Aide-de-Camp* and briefly commander of the *Deustches Afrikakorps*. He was commander of the 53rd Corps when he surrendered to the Allies only to be released in

---

168 State Archives, Nürnberg.

169 Simon Wiesental Center publication B 162/5656, Bl. 55ff., June 1967. It says he was an officer in Goebbels' *Reichpropagandaministerium*.

1947. Bayerlein wrote numerous books after the war, and died in Würzburg in 1970. He assisted Nasser's Army in the 1950s as a consultant in military affairs.

SS-Obersturmführer **Hans Becher**, officer in the Jewish Affairs division of the Gestapo in Vienna from 1938 to 1944. Between 1940 and 1944, he was detached to the Jewish Department in Belgrade to carry out Eichmann's orders. During his Serbian sojourn, more than 30,000 Jews were murdered and 28,000 deported to concentration camps. He returned to Vienna and was arrested near Salzburg on September 20th, 1945, by the 430th CIC Detachment and placed in the Marcus W. Orr Camp in Glasenbach. He escaped on July 2nd, 1947, possibly with assistance from the *Gehlen* Organization, fled to Egypt and became an instructor for the Cairo and Alexandria Police Departments.

SS-Oberstrumbannführer **Dr. Wilhelm Beissner**, AKA *Jaeger*, Gestapo section Chief in Lodz, Poland and in Zagreb, Croatia. One of the cruelest Gestapo officials, responsible for the deaths of thousands of Jews in Poland as well as many other victims in districts where he had been stationed. After his return to Germany he was promoted to *Sturmbannführer* and became an advisor to the Near East in the RSHA (SS security organization). He made several trips to the Near East in 1939 and 1940. In 1942, was in the Africa Corps with Rommel on a special mission for the Gestapo. In late 1943 or early 1944, he returned to Berlin, was promoted to *Oberstrumbannführer* and was named an "expert" for Switzerland. He was also an SD official in Tunis and liaison with Grand Mufti el-Husseini. After the war, he escaped an American prison camp in Italy (with French help) and went to the French zone in Austria. US informants claimed that he had connections with East Germany, but he was in Egypt *"active with a group of military experts recruited by Skorzeny."* He had known associations with Faisal

Sheik-el-Ard, recruiting agent for the BSHA in East Germany. Sheik-el-Ard was a known German collaborator in Vichy Syria.

SS-Sturmbannführer **Bernhard Bender**, Gestapo officer in Warsaw and head of Special Service Commandoes in the Ukraine. His knowledge of Yiddish allowed him to infiltrate the Jewish underground. After the war moved to Cairo, converted to Islam and took the name *Bashir ben Salem* and became a consultant to the Cairo Police under Nasser. As a *Lt. Col. Ben Salem* in the Egyptian Army, Bender was head of the Political Department of Nasser's Secret Police under Leopold Gleim (below).

Fluent in Arabic, Yiddish and Hebrew, he loved to interrogate prisoners personally at his favorite interrogation center, an old Italian freighter known in Egypt as the "floating hell," berthed on the Nile just outside Cairo. In 1961 he was in the UAR embassy in Lima, Peru, and was allegedly in charge of making the necessary connections with the Communist party in France to circulate counterfeit US currency for the benefit of ODESSA. His contribution to the jurisprudence of Egypt was a Nasser Decree called *"The Final Solution of the Jewish-Zionist Problem Within The Territory of the United Arab Republic."*

Werner Birgel, SS Officer in Leipzig in charge of the deportation of Jews and political prisoners. Converted to Islam and took the name *El-Gamin*. Worked in Nasser's Ministry of Information.

SS-Untersturmführer **Wilhelm Böeckler**, a war criminal wanted in Poland for the liquidation of the Jewish Warsaw ghetto. Converted to Islam and took the name *'Abd el-Karim*. In Egypt since 1949, he was an officer in the Israel Department of the Information Bureau.

SS-Untersturmführer **Wilhelm Boerner**, Brutal guard at Mauthausen concentration camp. Converted to Islam and took the name *Ali ben Kashir*. He was an officer in Nasser's Ministry of the Interior, and a military instructor for the *Fedayeens* of the FPL (Front for the Liberation of Palestine.)[170]

SS-Sturmbannführer **Walter Bollmann**, chief of Nazi intelligence in Britain before the war and active in the anti-Jewish campaigns in the Ukraine during the war, made his way to Cairo and served in Nasser's propaganda ministry under von Leers.

SS-Hauptsturmführer **Alois Brunner** AKA Georg Fisher, an Austrian *Schutzstaffel* and one of the top lieutenants and private secretary of Adolf Eichmann, was in charge of the deportation of Jews in Austria, Czechoslovakia and Greece; and as Chief of the Drancy concentration camp in France he was responsible for sending over 100,000 Jews to the gas chamber.[171] Adolf Eichmann referred to him as his *"best man."* Through the offices of Hajj Amin el-Husseini, who wielded strong influence over the Ba'ath parties of Syria and Iraq, Brunner was granted asylum in Syria and converted to Islam taking the name *Ali Mohammed*. Moved to Damascus and became a consultant for Special Services (secret police), where he was found by French Nazi hunters Beate and and Serge Karlsfeld. According to Efraim Zuroff, director of the Israel Office of

---

[170] El-Reis Nasser announced the group on August 31st, 1955: *"Egypt has decided to dispatch her heroes, the disciples of Pharaoh and the sons of Islam and they will cleanse the land of Palestine....There will be no peace on Israel's border because we demand vengeance, and vengeance is Israel's death."* The term *fedayeen* (men of sacrifice) has been adopted by a slew of terrorists since, including the infamous *Fedayeen Saddam*, a 40,000 odd paramilitary group that conducted guerrilla attacks on coalition forces after the invasion of Iraq in 2003.

[171] Georg M. Hafner, Esther Shapira, *Die Akte Alois Brunner: Warun einer der größten Naziverbrecher noch immer auf freiem Fuß ist*, Hamburg, 2002.

the Simon Wiesenthal Center, he was also an advisor to the Syrian government. Died recently in Damascus in his 90s.

SS-Obergruppenführer **Friedrich Buble**, Director of Egyptian Public Relations Department of the Gestapo, and close Eichmann collaborator. Converted to Islam and took the name *Ben Amman*. In 1952 was a consultant to the Egyptian police.

SS-Sturmführer **Erich Buenz**, "expert" on the "Jewish Question", fled to Cairo, converted to Islam under the name *Ali Allan*, and went to work as an intelligence consultant in the Israel Department under Boeckler.

SA-Obersturmführer **Franz Bünsch**, close collaborator of Goebbels's. Became an officer in the Israel Department of the Ministry of Information in Cairo, working under von Leers in close collaboration with the other graduate of Eichmann's Jewish Department, Alois Brunner.

Wermacht Generalmajor **Otto-Ernst Remer**, was instrumental in putting down the plot of July 20th, 1944, to assassinate Hitler and a prominent postwar Revisionist. At the end of the war he surrendered to the Americans and remained a prisoner of war until 1947.

First Infantry Division officer Stanley Samuelson, the American commander of the camp in which he was held said of him: "*Of the 87 German generals in this camp, General Remer is the only one whom I respect as courageous and honorable.*"[172] After the war, Remer co-founded the *Sozialistiche*

---

[172] With all due respect to Officer Samuelson, he had no idea who he was talking about. Upon his return to Germany, Remer became a prominent member of the Socialist Reich Party, Leaving for Egypt when the party was banned in 1952. In addition to his work in Nasser's ministries, he was a consultant to the Syrian government. In 1987 he was the keynote speaker at the Eighth Conference of the Institute for Historical Review, and in 1988 published his second book *Verschwörung und Verrat um Hitler* (Conspiracy and Treason Around Hitler), to rave reviews by American Nazi Keith Thompson. Indefatigable Nazi, In October 1992 a German court in Schweinfurt sentenced him to 22 months

Reichparterai (SRP) and became an advocate of Holocaust denial. Because of his illegal political activities, the party was banned,[173] and Remer escaped to Egypt where he became an officer in the Israel Department of the Ministry of the Interior and Nasser's military advisor. He worked closely with von Leers. Later he returned to Germany, but was eventually exiled again, this time to Franco's Spain.

In 1962, Remer was hired by Fidel Castro to train the Cuban Revolutionary Army and secure weapons,[174] together with Ernst-Wilhelm Springer, his second at the SRP. Remer died in Marbella in 1997.

---

imprisonment for "popular incitement" and "incitement to racial hatred" because of the anti-Jewish and "Holocaust denial" articles that he published in five issues of his tabloid newsletter, *Remer Depesche*. The judges in the case flatly refused to even consider any of the garbage that Remer's attorneys presented as "evidence".

[173] Founded on October 2nd, 1949 by Remer, Fritz Dorls and Gehrard Krüeger (former leader of the *Deustche Studentenschaft*), although Remer was considered the most important leader, to the point that it was usually referred to as "Remer-Party". The *Sozialistiche Raichsparterai* was the first political party banned by the West German Government in 1952. Nearly all of its members were former members of the *Nationalsozialistische Deustche Arbeiteipartei* (NSDAP, or NAZI Party). With Soviet financing—the Soviets did not support the German Communist Party that they considered "ineffective", but were generous with Remer's party—the SRP maintained that Adenauer was a US puppet and that the legitimate President of Germany was Admiral Karl Dönitz by virtue of his appointment by Hitler. They denied the Holocaust, claimed that the Dachau gas chambers had been built by the Americans after the war, and maintained that should the Soviets decide to invade they would gladly assist them. On October 23rd, 1952, the Constitutional Federal Tribunal finally declared them unconstitutional and banned, prohibiting Remer from participating in any political activity. By then, the party had disbanded and Remer was on his way to Cairo and Havana.

[174] Castro's relations with exiled Nazis are ruefully understated. Two years after hiring Otto Remer, the Cuban government was part of a Nazi conspiracy to flood the US with false dollar bills led by von Leers and financed by Nasser. See Appendix V on page 281.

Otto Remer stomping for the SRP c. 1950, his later employer, Fidel Castro and Remer before the fall of Germany.

SS-Oberstrumbannführer **Joachim Däumling**, AKA *Jochen Dressel,* Chief of the Gestapo in Düsseldorf, head of Division II of the Gestapo in Poland, *Führer* of the *Generalgouvernementsangelegenheiten* in Poland (1941), and *Führer* of the *Einsatzcommandos 10b* in Croatia (1943). Fled to Egypt in 1952, converted to Islam and took the name ***Ibrahim Mustapha,*** becoming a consultant for the Egyptian penitentiary system and an active member of Radio-Cairo (*Radio-Le Caire*). As soon as he arrived in Cairo, he was hired by Nasser to set up the Egyptian secret service along the lines of the *SS-Reichssicherheitshauptamt* (Himmler's Reich Security Main Office or RSHA) which occupied him between 1954 and 1957; he was helped in this noble labor by the former Gestapo chief of Warsaw, who organized the security police.

Däumling returned to Germany in 1957, and became an attorney. On June 26th, 1967, he was arrested along with Bernhard Baatz, Emil Berndorff and others, and accused in the so-called RSHA trial as head of the Council of Poland for numerous war crimes against Polish civilian workers and prisoners of war. However, the court decided that the perpetrators were only Hitler, Himmler and Heydrich, and that for the lesser crimes that could then be imputed to Däumling a statute of limitations had applied on May 8th, 1960; and he was then released. He died in 2007 in Bad Lautenberg, Osterode am Hartz, Germany.

SS-Oberführer **Oskar Dirlewanger**, AKA *the Butcher of Warsaw*, chief of 36th Waffen Grenadier SS Division in Poland and the USSR, and founder of the infamous Dirlewanger Penal Brigade. A notorious criminal before the war known as a sadist and a violent drunk, he was an early member of the NSDP but was expelled and imprisoned in 1934 when he raped a fourteen year old girl. He volunteered to the Fascist Army in Spain's civil war, and returned to Germany where he renewed his rise in the Nazi party.

A mad, sadistic and cruel pedophiliac and necrophiliac, he proved to be a perfect fit for the SS, although some officers protested his arrival. He was too much of a criminal for these fine gentlemen to endure without protestations. *Der Führer* worked out a solution: Dirlewanger recruited some fifty-five like-minded lowlifes into a poacher brigade to hunt members of the Polish resistance. The new outfit, officially named *Wilddiebkommando Oranienburg* (Oranienburg Poacher's Unit), was placed *under control* of the SS (but not *in* the SS, easing the mind of the other officers), and came to be known as the Special Unit Dirlewenger. Of their crimes in Poland there is sufficient record. Some of the apologists of Nazism, including von Leers, saw in the raw criminality of the Dirlewenger brigade a representation of *"pure primitive German men…resisting the law"* in Nietzchean fashion. Even the police chief of the Lublin Ghetto was so distraught by their barbarities, that he insisted they be stopped. Instead, Dirlewenger and his cohort were transferred to Belarus to continue their work. Some say he died in Altshausen on July 7th, 1945, but there is abundant evidence—and sightings—that place him in

Cairo by 1950 assisting in the training of both the military and Palestinian terrorists.

SS-Sturmbannführer **Eugen Eichberger,** Battalion commander in the Dirlewanger brigade. After he fled to Egypt, he joined his old boss Oskar Dirlewanger in Cairo as an intelligence consultant. They tutored the Egyptian guards responsible for Nasser's personal security. Many of the "irregulars" trained by Dirlewanger and Eichenberger conducted dozens of raids in Israel, turning the land bordering the West Bank and the Gaza strip into virtual war zones. About 300 Israelis were killed in those raids. In 1955, the Israelis retaliated by destroying the Egyptian Army headquarters in Gaza.

Nasser then authorized a German trained force of 700 Palestinians they called the *Fedayeen* (men of sacrifice). Otto Skorzeny assisted by securing a 3.5 million dollar deal with Francisco Franco, whereby Spain supplied the *Fedayeen* with mortars, shells and machine guns. The transfer was accomplished through Gerhard Mertins's company in Switzerland (below).

SS-Hauptsturmführer **Dr. Hans Kurt Eisele,** AKA *the Butcher of Buchenwald.*

Chief medical officer in the Buchenwald concentration camp. Convicted for his crimes in Dachau at the first

Dachau trial in 1945 and sentenced to death, he was tried again for crimes in Buchenwald at the second Dachau trial in 1947, with the same results. Eisele had been assigned to the Sachsenhausen concentration camp after he was wounded at the front. At Sachsenhausen, he was known as *the Angel* and the former prisoners gave him a good report. He was later transferred to Dachau where his treatment of the prisoners changed, according to Lt. Col. William D. Denson, who prosecuted him both times.

While at Dachau he was found to be part of a larger conspiracy—a common plan—but no specific crimes could be attributed to him personally, his first sentence was commuted to life in prison in 1948. At Buchenwald, a Class II camp for hard-core Communist political prisoners, Dr. Eisele became known as *the Butcher* for his mistreatment of the inmates. He was found to have murdered prisoners by injection and to have performed *"improper surgeries."* Inexplicably, the War Crimes Review Board commuted that sentence too—to life in prison—in August of 1948, confirming the sentence in the following December.

In the words of Harold Marcuse: *"Two years later in October 1950, another commission recommended remitting the Dachau sentence entirely, and reducing the Buchenwald sentence to ten years with ten days off for each month of good conduct. The recommendation was approved and, and on 19 February 1952, Eisele was released from Landsberg. As far as the new West German government was concerned, Eisele had been captured and imprisoned by the enemy, so that he was eligible for compensation payment (Heimkehrerentschädigung). Eisele used his government award to open a licensed family practice in Munich, where he lived untroubled by his past until 1958, when testimony in the trial of a sadistic Buchenwald guard*[175]

---

[175] The sadistic guard was Martin Sommer, in charge of the bunker, who was convicted in 1958 for the murder of twenty-five prisoners. Sommer's innovation in Buchenwald was to execute prisoners by hanging their arms from a tree.

before a West German court heavily incriminated him. Warned by sympathetic officials that he would be arrested, he personally dropped off a letter to the editor of the Munich Evening News, in which he defended his reputation, and boarded an airplane to Egypt, where he was employed within a network of former Nazis in an army hospital."

Eisele spent the rest of his life in the al-Ma'adi suburb of Cairo, under the name Dr. Karl Debosch (or *khawaga Dabous* by the locals), a medical advisor to the Cairo police. His house was a frequent meeting place for some of the most notorious German exiles, some sporting their new Arab names and others, like *Herr Pils* or *Herr Brandner*, quite happy sticking to their old identities. His children attended the local German school, where some teachers referred to them as *"children of the damned."* While the nuns at St. Borromeo convent up the street swore to his devout Catholicism, he seldom ventured to church. He was, however, observed frequently gazing out of a second story window to the building across the street, the synagogue on Mossery Avenue. He died in 1967, at his house on Mossery Avenue (now Oraby). The one time that the German government requested his extradition, the request was bluntly refused by the Nasser government.

Wermacht General **Wilhelm Farmbacher**, Knight's Cross of the Iron Cross, a General Lieuttnant in the 5th Infantry Division at the time of the invasion of Poland, he was appointed in 1940 commander-in-chief of the 7th *Armeekorps* participating in Operation Barbarossa; in 1942, was made commander of the 25th *Armeekorps* in France, and was latter commander of the Normandy and Brittany army groups. He surrendered to the Americans in Brittany on May 10th, 1945, two days *after* Germany's capitulation, and was held in American and French prison camps until August 10th, 1950. From March 15th, 1952, to August of 1958, he was military advisor to President Nasser and to the central Planning Staff of the Egyptian Army. In the early 1960s he was involved in the German rocket affair in Cairo. He died in 1970 in the small Bavarian city of Garmisch-Partenkirchen.

SS-Standartenführer **Leopold Gleim**, Chief of the Gestapo Department for Jewish Affairs in Poland. Converted to Islam and joined the Egyptian Army, becoming *Lt. Col. Ali Namal el-Nashar,*[176] perhaps in honor of Hassan el-Nashar, one of Nasser's closest friends and confidants. As Lt. Col. el-Nashar, Gleim was a high ranking officer in Nasser's National Security Department in charge of political prisoners the Jewish community, and Chief of the Secret Police which he organized. One of the earliest Nasser collaborators, he assisted in the coup that brought *el-Reis* to power.[177]

SS-Brigadeführer and *Waffen SS-Generalleutnant* **Richard Glücks**, was Chief of Staff to Concentration Camp Inspector Theodor Eicke, until Eicke became Field Commander of the SS Division Totenkopf. On November 15th, 1939, Himmler promoted Glücks to Concentration Camp Inspector, a position he maintained to the end of the war. From picking the Austrian Cavalry barracks at Auschwitz for a camp, to in the end having control of fifteen major camps and five hundred satellite camps with a staff of over 40,000 SS members.

---

[176] Frankfurter Allgemeine Zeitung, *Ulbricht's Protectors in Cairo*, March 1st 1965: *"...Leopold Gleim was an SS officer in Poland. In 1955 he went to Egypt where he now serves, under the name of Col. Namalnashr (sic), as the second man of Nasser's security police. If he were to return to Germany now, he would have to expect a trial because of his activities in Poland..."*

[177] At a luncheon given in his honor at Cairo's Victoria Hall by the League for (East) German-Arab Brotherhood, Gleim described his organization as *"the backbone of Egypt's protective apparatus against the aggressive elements of Zionism and imperialism."*

At the end of the war, he was said to have committed suicide at a naval base but, of course, no body, witnesses or document of any kind were ever found. However, there were persistent rumors in Cairo that Joachim Daümling, the supervisor of Nasser's concentration camps answer to none other than Richard Glücks, alive and well in Egypt.

Hans Gruber, a long time aid to Admiral Canaris in the *Abwehr* (Intelligence Service), moved to Egypt, converted to Islam taking the name *el-Aradji,* and in 1950 was an influential agent in the Arab League, becoming Counsel to the Political Directorate of the League in Damascus, Syria.

Louis Heiden, an SS official under Goebbels, he was an early member of the NSADP, a journalist for the anti-Jewish agency *Welt Dienst*, and Director of the Nazi press agency *Reichsdeustch Pressagentur Berlin*. He was transferred to the Egyptian press office during the war. He converted to Islam and took the name *Luis al-Hajj*. Worked in the Ministry of Information with von Leers, and translated *Mein Kampf*[178] to Arabic, *Kifahi Adolf Hitlar*,[179] to replace an earlier translation by Nassir Nasser, Gamal Abdel Nasser's brother. In his introduction to *Kifahi*, Heiden proclaims: *"National Socialism did not die with the death of its herald. Rather, its seeds multiplied under each star."*

Baron Hermann von Harder, Goebbel's assistant, became an officer in the Propaganda Ministry of Nasser under the supervision of Johann von Leers, playing an important role in the formation of Nasser's anti-Jewish propaganda. Other Goebbels' alumni in the same group included Werner Witschale, Hans Appler and Franz Bünsche.

---

[178] Still a best seller in Egypt, in the first two years of publication sold over 900,000 copies in a country of 13 million people.

[179] The 7th edition, published in Damascus in 1999, continues to be a best seller in Syria.

SS-Hauptsturmführer **Dr. Aribert Heim**, AKA *Dr. Death*, Medical doctor at Mauthausen, known for his grotesque pseudo-medical experiments on Jewish prisoners in Sachsenhausen, Buchenwald and Mauthausen. He was fond of surgical procedures including organ removals without anesthesia, injecting gasoline into prisoners to observe the manner of death, and decapitating Jews with healthy teeth so he could cook the skulls clean to make desk decorations. Born June 28th, 1914 in Radkersburg, Austria, Heim joined the local Nazi party in 1935, three years before the *Anschluss*. He later joined the *Waffen-SS* and was assigned to Mauthausen, a concentration camp near Linz, Austria, as a camp doctor in October and November 1941. While there, witnesses told investigators, he worked closely with SS pharmacist Erich Wasicky on such gruesome experiments as injecting various solutions into Jewish prisoners' hearts to see which killed them the fastest. He escaped to Cairo in 1932, converted to Islam and took the name **Tarek Hussein Farik**, although locals affectionately knew him as *uncle Tarek*. He was a medical doctor for the Egyptian police, and at the time of his death in Cairo in 1992, the German police still had a one million Euro bounty on his head.[180] News of his demise came from a televised interview with his son, Ruediger Heim, although German and Austrian authorities remained skeptical for a number of years.[181]

Franz Hithofer, high ranking Gestapo officer in Vienna, was known to be in Cairo through the 1950s. In 1969 he lived in *al-Fagallah*, a Cairo suburb.[182]

---

[180] Perhaps poetically, the cause of death was cancer of the rectum.

[181] A spokesman for the Austrian Criminal Intelligence Service was quoted as stating that *"The search will remain open until it has been verified that he is dead."* By now, he should surely be.

[182] Werner Brockdorff, *Flught vor Nürnberg*, Munich, Verlag Welsermühl, 1969, p. 116.

SS-Sturmbannführer **Dr. Johannes Von Leers**, a protégé of Alfred Rosenberg and close collaborator of Joseph
Goebbels in charge of anti-Semitic propaganda.[183] An early member of the NSDAP,[184] he authored more than twenty books on the "Jewish Question." He was co-editor of
the weekly *Der Stürmer* together with Julius Streicher, the
only civilian hanged at Nuremberg. Von Leers was a close
friend of Richard Walther Darré,[185] Carl Schmitt, Karl
Hausehoffer and Ernst Jünger. In 1944, he published *Die
verbrechernatur der Juden*, he wrote an introduction to an essay
on ritual murder that states: *"Judaism is hereditary criminality, a
religious syncretism in which faith in demons plays a central role.
Those who fight against Judaism fulfill the work of the Lord and fight
a Holy War."*[186] In 1947 von Leers was still in Germany
working as an English interpreter with false documents, as
recalled by Ernst Jünger in his diary. In 1950, he crossed
into Austria and made his way to Italy following the rat
route from Genoa to Buenos Aires, were he settled under
the protection of General Juan D. Perón.[187] Safe in Argen-

---

[183] Alfred Ashman, *CIA Report dated 26 March 1957*. Leers was an early member of
the NSDAP (number, 143709, August 1st, 1929) and in 1936 joined the
Allgemeine (General) SS (number 276586) receiving the honorary rank of *SS-
Sturmbannführer*. He served in the SS Race Office—*Rasse-und Siedlingshauptamtes;*
the Personnel Office and the Reich Security Main Office—*Reichssicherheitshauptamtes.*

[184] He was responsible for the education (Reichsschulungsleiter) in the League of
National Socialist Students (Nationalsozialistisches Deutsches Studentenbund)
in Berlin, working closely with Fritz Hippler, the Bund's president, and future
director of *Der Ewige Jude*, a famous anti-Semitic documentary.

[185] SS Obergruppenführer, First Director of the Race and Settlement Office (*Rasse-
und Siedlungshauptamt* or RuSHA), and Minister of the Reich for Food and Agri-
culture.

[186] *Gotteskampf* in the original. As we have already stated, *Jihad*.

[187] Perón was a proponent of a *Third Way* (*la Tercera Posición*), as an alternative to
Capitalism and Communism. Himself a veteran of the *Abwehr*, having rendered
valuable services in Argentina, Paraguay and Bolivia (in addition to his wife's
work in Brazil), Perón's *Third Way* was no more than his own version of National Socialism. He formed an unholy alliance with Marshall Tito in Yugosla-

tina, he continued to write anti-Semitic articles and publish books extolling the virtues of Nazism under his own name, and was the chief spokesman for the National Socialist periodical *Wille und Weg*. At the fall of general Perón in 1955, von Leers went again into exile, this time to Cairo, where he was welcomed by Amir el-Husseini: *"We thank you for coming here to restart the struggle against the powers of darkness of international Judaism."* He was joined there by Otto Remer and Walter Rauff. Under the guidance of the Mufti, von Leers converted to Islam, which he stated was "less corrupt" than Christianity, and took the name **Omar Amin,** explaining that he chose Omar for the Caliph who had fought the Jews with such determination, and Amin *"in honor of my friend the Grand Mufti."* In a letter to the Argentine weekly *Pregonando Verdades* in 1960, von Leers explained: *"I am now settled in Egypt, which has become the world's center in the fight against Zionist colonialism that deprives nations of their freedom. Having seen first in Germany and then in Argentina how Christian churches have allied themselves with Zionist Jews, I have converted to Islam, the religion of free men, of the fathers of Liberty and nationalism like Gamal Abdel Nasser and Emir Abdel Krim. I am one with the Arabs in my fight against the tyranny of Israel and the Zionists, and wherever I can be of service against them, I will help with great pleasure."* He went to work in the Ministry of Information, in charge of anti-Israeli propaganda in the Information Department.

---

via and Nasser in Egypt, among others, that came to be known as the Movement of Non-Aligned Countries. In this environment, von Leers was allowed to thrive. Under his own name, he published numerous articles: *Reich und Sonnenordnung* (1955), *Die grünen Banner der Freiheit* (1955), *Volk und Staat* (1955), *Gott geb dem Heil, der bei mir kämpft! Ulrich von Huttens Kampf und unsere Zeit* (1955), *Ein neues Weltzeitalter?* (1956), *Einer wird es sein, in: Die Plattform* (1956), and several articles in *Dinámica Social*, a magazine published by Fascist refugee Carlo Scorza. He also used the nome *de plume* Johannes Uhlen, and under W. von Asenbach, he published *Adolf Hitler. Sein Kampf gegen die Minusseele. Eine Politisch-philosophische Studie aus der Alltagsperspektive*, a notorious anti-Semitic work.

From his perch in Cairo, von Leers promoted the destruction of Judeo-Christianism and the expansion of Islam in Europe to achieve a Euro-Arab union through the adoption of a common religion, while praising the persecution of Jews under Islam as an *"eternal service to the world;"* and proclaiming: *"If there is any hope of liberating the world from Jewish tyranny, then with the help of the Muslims who unwaveringly resist Zionism, colonialism and imperialism."* Even from Argentina, von Leers was already showing his sympathies: *"From Indonesia to Pakistan and Morocco the green banners of freedom and God's justice fly against the iniquities of colonialism…and the powerful figure raises in the desert of the upcoming Mahdi, whom Muslims have been awaiting for centuries."*

He found the *Mahdi* in *el-Reis* (*Der Führer*) Nasser, under whose patronage he was instrumental in developing the ideology that still mobilizes Skorzeny's *"new type of soldier."* Von Leers' house villa on 52 Eleventh Street in the Ma'adi district of Cairo was a central meeting point for Nazis from around the world, and from there he managed a network extending the ratline to Arab countries. No one will ever know how many war criminals he assisted, but we do know of several of the most egregious. In 1950, he arranged for Adolf Eichmann and Karl Klingenfuss's escape to Argentina. In 1952, he expedited Franz Rademacher's to Buenos Aires and again in 1955 to Cairo. In 1958, when the Butcher of Buchenwald, Dr. Hans Eisele, jumped bail, he promptly reappeared in Cairo. Von Leers not only arranged for the trip, but also protected him in Egypt against extradition. Soon after, he arranged the trip to Cairo for former Nazi storm trooper Ludwig Pankras Zind, who immediately went to work for Von Leers and Appler.

SS-Gruppenführer **Fritz Katzman**, after a long and ignominious career in the Third Reich, Katzman was tasked with the liquidation of concentration camps ahead of the Russian advance. In June of 1944, he began gassing prisoners with *Zykon B* in Stutthof, and continued with over one hundred satellite camps, killing over 400,000 Jews. When Germany surrendered he disappeared, although we now know he lived in Darmstadt (in the shade of one of the largest Allied bases, Rhein Main), as Bruno Albrecht. Witnesses have sworn to have seen him in Nasser's camps in the early 1950's. In 1957, he revealed his identity to a priest on his deathbed at a hospital in Darmstadt. Or so the priest claimed.

SS-Gruppenführer **Hartmann Lauterbacher**, one time *Obergebietsführer* of the Hitler Youth and Nazi *Gauletier* of North Hanover. After being tried for crimes in Hamelin and Dachau, he managed to escape in 1948 in circumstances that are still unclear. Arrested in Italy in 1950, he again escaped and in December of that year sailed from Genoa to Buenos Aires following the same route as Adolf Eichmann. He was also wanted in the USSR for crimes against Jews in Ukraine. He made his way to Cairo and became an instructor for anti-Israel Commandos, and later an advisor for the Youth Ministry in Oman. He returned to Germany and died in Bavaria in 1988.

Karl Lüder, chief of the *Hitlerjugend* movement, responsible for crimes against the Jews in Poland. Converted to Islam and changed his name to ***Abd'el Kader*,**[188] surely in honor of his boss, Information Minister Abd'el Kader Hatem. In 1956, Lüder was Director General of the Egyptian Information Department, and went on to become

---

[188] AJR Information, Vol. XIV, October, 1959, London, p. 2, column 2: *"S.S. OFFICERS WITH ALGERIAN REBELS—According to reports in the French press, four former S.S. officers who for several years served with the Egyptian army and trained infiltrators to raid Israeli territory are said to have been seconded by the Egyptians to the rebels in Algeria. The officers are ex-S.S. officer Baumann, a Commander of the Warsaw Ghetto; Willi Berner, alias Ibn Kashir, who was in charge of a concentration camp; Dr. Erich Alten, now Ali Baba, a former Nazi official in Eastern Poland who is credited with a knowledge of Hebrew and Yiddish; and Karl Luder, alias Abdul Kader, a former Hitler Youth Commander."*

Nasser's Deputy Minister for Presidential Affairs and Minister of War.

Waffen-SS Hauptmann **Gerhard Mertins**, German Special Forces commando who participated with Otto Skorzeny in the raid in Grand Sasso to rescue Mussolini. Known associate of pedophile cult leader Paul Schäffer, he received the Knight's Cross of the Iron Cross on December 6th, 1944, and attained the rank of *Fallschirmjäger-Majors*.

After his escape to Egypt in 1951, he joined the team of Wilhelm Farmbacher as military advisor to the Central Planning Office of the Egyptian Army (March 1951-August 1958). In 1955 was head of the Advisory Council for Airborne Troops in the Egyptian Ministry of War and organized an elite Parachute Regiment. Afterwards, he trained paratroopers in Syria, represented German businesses like Mercedes and Siemens, run arms first for the Egyptians and later, according to Manuel Contreras (Chief of the Chilean Secret Police), for the Pinochet regime in Chile after 1973. In 1954, he organized Merex A.G. (Mertins Exports) in Vevey, Switzerland, which he used for many years to funnel weapons from Germany to Egypt.

He was known to have worked for the West German Intelligence Service under the code-name "Uranus" (1956-1962) and with West German complicity diverted American F-86 planes to Pakistan. He also had a working agreement with the Sha's secret police, SAVAK (1965.) After *Der Spiegel* outed his arms deals, he was tried by the German government but was acquitted in 1980, after showing that the BND (German Intelligence Service) had participated in the deals and, therefore, he had acted with the government's sanction. Rather than a prison term, he received five million dollars' compensation. He then went to Mexico and settled in Durango as the owner of a silver mine, but in reality he had created a colony to welcome

Nazis leaving *Colonia Dignidad* in Chile after the fall of Pinochet, and to continue to run his gun smuggling business, this time from Mexico to Central America.

As the Mexican government was notified of Germany's intention of (yet again) demanding his extradition, a Mexican official took Mertins and his son and unceremoniously put him in the first flight from Mexico City to Germany on March 16th, 1983, just as the new German ambassador was arriving. But in 1984, the daily Excelsior in Mexico City, reported that Bonn was asking the Mexican government to reconsider Mertins expulsion! He died in Ft. Lauderdale, Florida, in 1993.

SS-Standartenführer **Rudolf Mildner**, Gestapo Chief in Denmark and in Katowice, Poland. After his deportation of 8,000 Jews from Denmark to Auschwitz was foiled by Danish Resistance fighters, he was transferred out of Denmark and assigned as Inspector of the SiPo and SD in Kassel. Testified at Nüremberg, but disappeared in 1949 to avoid prosecution. Adolf Eichmann claimed to have seen him in Argentina in 1958. Arrived in Egypt in 1963 and became a chief of the Deustcher Rat (German Council) organization.

SS-Gruppenleiter **Alois Moser**, a sinister Sudeten German wanted in USSR for crimes against Jews in Ukraine. He appeared in Cairo in the 1950s and, as reported by *Der Spiegel*, was in charge of training Egyptian youth along the lines of the *Hitlerjugend*, together with his assistant, *SS-Gruppenführer* Friedrich Buble (above). Moser converted to Islam and took the name ***Hassan Nalisman.*** From his Security Service offices at Liberty Square in Cairo, patterned after Goebbels Ministry of Propaganda, he flooded the world with anti-Jewish and anti Western tirades. The Service run *Sawt al-Arab* (the Voice of the Arabs), a broadcast in English and French, run by his fellow

Nazis. At its heyday, the Service run offices in East and West Berlin, Istanbul, Paris, London, Stockholm, Rome and Washington. The Nasser Youth Club, referenced above, was also run by the Security Service, and was part of the *Deutsch-Arabischer Bruderschaftsverb* (German-Arab Brotherhood Society), dedicated to the propagation of Nazi ideals. While Moser was Chairman of the Youth Club, Nasser was its Honorary President and Patron. These propaganda efforts were in addition to and separate from those carried out by the Information Ministry by other Nazis listed here. In his free time, Moser helped in the training of paramilitary groups, especially when it involved his Youth Club members.

Wermacht General **Oskar Münzel**, also a *General der Kampftruppen* in the *Bundeswehr*. Knight's Cross of the Iron Cross. After the war he was a military advisor to President Nasser, but in 1956 returned to Germany and joined the *Bundeswehr*. In 1962 he became a personal military advisor to Chiang Kai-shek assisting in the modernization of the Taiwanese Army as Chief Advisor of the *Ming-the-Gruppe*. He died in Germany in 1992.

General Oskar Müntzel and Chiang Kai-Sheck
Taipei, c. 1962

Georges Oltremare, AKA *Charles Dieudonne*. A Catholic writer from the Swiss Romande, heavily influenced by *Action Française* and Italian Fascism, together with Gonzague de Reynold. Under the Vichy government of France he directed the pro-Nazi magazine *Pilori,* and *Radio Paris.* Exiled to Egypt after the war, he was responsible for the French language broadcast *Sawt al-Arab (La voix des Arabes)* in Radio Cairo, under direction of Alois Moser. Oltremare died in Cairo in 1960.

SS-Fitzher **Daniel Perret-Gentil,** a Swiss journalist and Nazi agent in France, where he worked for the Wermacht intelligence services. In 1948 was sentenced to death by a French war crimes tribunal but, following an all too common pattern, was released in 1955. He followed the ratline to Cairo and became an announcer and eventually French Program Director for Radio Cairo under Alois Moser. He eventually moved to Wiesbaden, Germany.

Joachim Dieter Peschnik, we have not been able to confirm his identity. He is said to be a Nazi exile that changed his name to *el-Said* and resided in Cairo since de 1950s.

Karl Ernst Piester, former SS officer, principal representative of the Arab League in Europe in the late 1950s, he promoted the destruction of Israel, the return of the Arab refugees and, following the old National Socialist aspirations, an alliance between Europe and the Arab countries. After all, he shared Count Hermann Keyserling's impressions: *"From the beginning of the German Revolution, I was impressed by the relationship between National Socialism and Islam,* *and that impression been confirmed and affirmed over time.*"[189] Piester died in 1960.[190]

Franz Rademacher, career diplomat, was selected in 1940 to head the *Judenreferat* in Ribbentrop's Foreign Ministry. As a senior aid to Adolf Eichmann, he was responsible for mass deportations and executions of Serbian Jews and the mass murder of Jews in Holland, Belgium and Croatia. Author of the *Madagascar Plan* that sought to deport all the Jews of Europe to Madagascar. In an expense claim he filed after a trip to Belgrade in 1941, he stated the purpose of that trip was to *"liquidate the Jews."*In 1952, facing trial for the murder of Serbian Jews, he fled to Cairo using the name *Thome Rossel* and was convicted in absentia. In 1962, an Israeli spy, Eli Cohen, delivered an explosive letter to him in a failed assassination attempt. In 1963, he was briefly arrested in Syria—where he was working as a journalist—on charges of espionage, but was released in 1965, after all, he was not really a journalist but was in the employ of the Secret Service with Alois Brunner. He returned to Germany in 1966 and died there in 1973, still facing trial for his crimes.

SS-Standartenführer **Walther Rauff,** was an aide of Reinhard Heydrich in the *Sicherheitsdienst (SD)*, serving later in the *Reichssicherheits-hauptamt* (RSHA). He was the SD Chief in Tunisia. He was one of the creators of the mobile gas chamber, tried in North Africa, and which the Grand Mufti so desperately wanted to use in Palestine. According to MI5 documents released in 2005, "Rauff joined the

---

[189] Hermann von Keyserling, *La Révolution mondiale et la Responsabilité de l'esprit*, Paris, 1934, p. 134.

[190]J. James, *L'historienne Bat Yeor raconte la naissance du "Palestinism,"* Mediapart, October 29th, 2015. A.N. Bat Ye'or is the pen name of Gisèle Littman, who popularized the term *dhimmitude* as the *"specific social condition that resulted from jihad,"* and as the *"state of fear and insecurity"* of *"infidels"* who are required to *"accept a condition of humiliation."*

Reichsmarine (the German Navy) in 1924 as a young cadet. After a period of training as a midshipman he was promoted to Lieutenant in 1936 and given command of a mine-sweeper.

Rauff was a friend of Reinhard Heydrich, who also served in the Navy in the 1920s. Heydrich was hired by SS chief Heinrich Himmler in 1931 to serve as the head of the SS counter-intelligence system, and when Rauff resigned from the Navy in 1937, Heydrich took him under his wing. Rauff was given the job of putting the SS and its security service, the *Sicherheitsdienst*, onto a war footing." The files contain additional information on his favorite contraption: *"As an official of the Criminal Technical Institute of the Reich Security Main Office, Rauff designed gas vans used to murder Jews and persons with disabilities...*[he] *supervised the modification of scores of trucks, with the assistance of a Berlin chassis builder, to divert their exhaust fumes into airtight chambers in the back of the vehicles. The victims were then poisoned and/or asphyxiated from the carbon monoxide accumulating within the truck compartment as the vehicle travelled to a burial site. The trucks could carry between 25 and 60 people at a time."* In 1948, he was recruited by Syrian intelligence where he applied himself to the persecution and torture of Jews enjoying the status of military advisor to President Hosni Zaim. However, he lost his job when Zaim was deposed in 1949.

In December of that year he sailed for Ecuador, later removing to Chile. In 1958 he was recruited by the *Bundesnachrichtendienst*, West Germany's intelligence service to create a spy network in South America, but was let go in 1962. His evaluation described him as an *"untrustworthy character"*, a *"conspirator and intriguer"* and a *"friend of alcohol."* He later confessed to having been in Germany in 1960 and 1962. In 1963, he was arrested in Santiago, and the German Ambassador to Chile, Hans Strack, was ordered to request his extradition.

Strack, a Nazi sympathizer, delayed the request for 14 months, allowing the Chilean court to deny extradition on the basis that his crimes had occurred too long ago according to Chile's statute of limitations.

All subsequent Chilean Governments, including that of Socialist Salvador Allende, continued to deny requests for extradition. The latest request, in 1983, was denied by the regime of Augusto Pinochet, on the grounds that Rauff had been a *"peaceful Chilean citizen"* for over 20 years. When Rauff finally died in 1984, his funeral turned into a Nazi celebration with hundreds of his goose-stepping friends in attendance—including Chilean diplomat Miguel Serrano. He died unrepentant, claiming that his murders were merely the acts of an efficient *"technical administrator."*

SS-Standartenführer Walther Rauff
c. 1945

Prof. Eugen Sänger, head of the Institute of Research on Jet Propulsion in Stuttgart during the war, he first went to France in 1947, where he developed the Veronique rocket, a kind of watered down copy of the V2 (after all, von Braun had gone to greener pastures). After the French interlude, he took his team to Cairo and in 1961 began the process of building ballistic missiles for the UAR. The team included **Wolfgang Pilz**, an engineer at Peenemünde, **Dr. Hans Kleinbachter,** a developer of missile guidance systems, **Dr. Ermin Dadieu,** head of the Chemistry Department, **Dr. Heinz Krug**, also manager of the Jet Propulsion Institute in Stuttgart and straw man in one of the Swiss companies set up to assist in procurement, **Hassan Kamil**, an Egyptian millionaire who set up companies in Switzerland as a *façade* for their operations, **Willy Messerschmitt** and **Ferdinand Bradner,**[191] who were building aircraft engines for Nasser in "factory 36," and served as directors in the straw companies set up for the rocket program.

In a remote area of the Egyptian desert, at a facility code named "Factory 333," 250 of these wonder boys of the 3rd Reich began building missiles for Nasser in 1961. When the German government caught wind of their activities, it ordered Sänger to return, and he was replaced by Wolfgang Pilz. By July of 1962, they had produced 30 missiles, just in time for their unveiling during one of Nasser's military parades. The following month, Mossad intercepted a letter from Pilz to Kamil Azzab, requesting nearly four million Swiss Francs for parts to build 200 Type 2 missiles and 500 Type 5.

Israeli intelligence correctly estimated that Egypt was not spending millions of dollars just to launch conventional explosives. A bomber could do that much cheaper. Isser Harel, the Mossad director who oversaw the capture and transportation to Israel of Adolf Eichmann, was convinced that chemical and even nuclear warheads were in the plans. On September 11th, 1962, Dr. Heinz Krug was kidnapped and later killed in Munich. The disappearance of Dr. Krug

---

[191] Willy Messerschmitt, the father of the deadly plane that bore his name, was hired by General Mahmoud Khalil on November 29th, 1959 to work for Nasser. Ferdinand Bradner, who built the engines for the Messerchmitts, spent a few years in Russia and, after his release was hired by Khalil with the help of a director of Daimler-Benz.

spooked another of the German boys in Cairo, Otto Joklik, who run into the arms of the Mossad and spelled the beans: General Mahmoud Khalil was in charge of two projects, Ibis and Cleopatra, of which Dr. Krug and Pilz were in charge. Ibis was an operation designed to provide Egypt with a radiological weapon designed to spread lethal doses of radiation on impact.

Cleopatra was designed to produce two nuclear bombs, by purchasing 20% enriched uranium in the US or Europe, enriching it to 90% in centrifuges designed in Germany by Dr. Wilhelm Groth, Dr. Jacob Kistemaker and Dr. Gernot Zippe, sufficient to build the bomb. Joklik attempted to buy uranium in the US and, while he failed there, he succeeded in buying Cobalt-60 in Europe, which he had sent to Cairo gynecologist Dr. Khalil, the sister of General Mahmoud Khalil. In late 1962, two parcels addressed to Pilz exploded in his office, killing five employees and disfiguring his German secretary.

On January 11th, 1963, *el-Reis* unleashed chemical weapons in his war in Yemen, adding credibility to the threat. Over the next few months, Mossad conducted operations in Germany and Switzerland, decapitating the missile guidance system team, and fooled Otto Skorzeny into unwittingly collaborating with Mossad, obtaining detailed lists of the German scientists with the help of his fellow SS officers in Cairo, including plans, projects, names, missile blueprints and correspondence spelling their failures with the guidance systems.

In the end, Israel managed to get Germany to recall some and to scare the others. They never finished their missiles, they never resolved their problems with the guidance systems, there was never a question of what kind of warheads they would place on inoperative missiles, and even Willy Messerschmitt's planes were stuck to the ground. Werner von Braun, interviewed in Huntsville, Alabama, after reviewing a list of the projects and scientists involved, concluded that there were *"very slim chances that these second-rate scientists would have ever been able to build effective missiles."*[192] The joke was on *el-Reis*.

Hjalmar Schacht, President of the Reichbank in Nazi Germany, became an advisor to Nasser and a key figure in *el-Reis'* economic policy. As president of a bank in Düsseldorf, he organized a network of German-Arab trade to help Nasser's economy. It should also be noted that Schacht was Otto Skorzeny's father-in-law.

SS-Sturmbannführer **Clemens Carl-Otto Schmalstich**, better known today as a musician, was a committed Nazi, Gestapo liaison officer to French collaborationists and organized transport of Jews from Paris to Auschwitz. In Cairo, he was an intelligence consultant to the Israel department of the Secret Police. He died in Berlin in 1960.

Generalleutnant **Arthur Schmitt**, served as a general under Rommel in the *Africakorps*, where he commanded the *Rückwärtiges Armeegebiet 556* (556th Rear Army Area) for the *Panzzergruppe Afrika*. Earlier, he had been in command of the *Oberfeldzeugstabs 2* in Poland during the earlier stages of the Soviet invasion. In 1944, he was commander of the Axis Division Bardia and, defeated by the South African 2nd Army Division and the New Zealand Divisional Cavalry Regiment, became a prisoner of war. He was awarded the Knight's Cross of the Iron cross in 1942 after his capture.

The Arab League recruited him in 1948 to help form a more effective pan-Arab fighting force. He settled in Cairo, where he was known as *"Mr. Goldstein."* It seems he

---

[192] Michael bar Zohar, Nissim Mishal, *Mossad, The greatest Missions of the Israeli Secret Service*, London, 2012

rubbed some Egyptian generals the wrong way, and in 1950 returned to Germany.

After a trip to the Golan Heights in 1951, Schmitt wrote to an Egyptian colleague that the Arab defeat by Israel had been *"the consequence of Egyptian leaders' inability to take advantage of the early stages of fighting to wipe the state of Israel off the map with a blitzkrieg of two weeks at most."* In 1966, he was a candidate for the Bavarian Parliament elections for the neo-Nazi NPD, campaigning in full Wermacht uniform (including the swastika and Iron Cross). He died in 1972, in Bavaria.

Johann Schuller, Gestapo official, became a supplier of arms to the Palestinian terrorist group Fatah.

SS-Sturmbannführer **Adolf Seipel**, interrogator of the Gestapo in Paris. Converted to Islam and took the name *Ahmed Zuhair.* He run the Security Services of the Interior Ministry in Cairo.[193] Perhaps a relation to Ignaz Seipel, who was Chancellor and Foreign Minister of Austria between the wars, leader of the Christian Socialist party there, and a notorious anti-Semite.

SS-Brigadeführer **Heinrich Sellmann,** Chief of Gestapo in Ulm (Baden-Württemberg, Germany), fled to Egypt, converted to Islam and took the name *Mohammed Suleyman.* Lt. Col. Mohammed Suleyman was a high ranking official at the Ministry of Information in Cairo, as assistant to Lt. Col. al-Nasher (otherwise known as SS-Standartenführer Leopold Gleim), in charge of the Egyptian Special Services and Chief of the Secret Police in 1957.[194] The Special Services were Nasser's equivalent to the Nazi SS.

---

[193] Roy H. Schoeman, *Salvation is From The Jews,* San Francisco, 2003, p. 265.

[194] The Montana Standard, Butte, Montana, July 14th, 1957, p.9, 47.

Ernst-Wilhelm Springer, *Jungvolk* squad leader, he helped organize the Grand Mufti's SS Division during the war. After the war, he became active in the RSP with Generalmajor Otto Remer, as the first Chairman of the Soltau District Association, [195] and when the party was banned in 1952, he joined Remer in Cairo and later settled Damascus, actively engaged in the arms trade. At his arrival in the Middle East, he immediately got to work establishing the Orient Trading Company (OTRACO) in association with Remer, becoming the primary arms supplier for the FLN.[196]

He often worked in combination with Brock & Schnars, and import-export front in Hamburg, co-owned by Dr. Gerhard Krüeger, another one of the founders of the SRP. In the archives of the Kiel High District prosecutor in Schleswig-Holstein, Germany, we find some of the deals made by Springer, like 80,000 tons of firearms and ammunition transported through Yugoslavia to Latakia in Syria. When the Yugoslavian police confiscated the shipment, Syrian minister Salah el-Din el-Bitar intervened directly with Marshall Josip Broz Tito[197] to have it released.

Another shipment involved hundreds of rifles sent to Sheik Quasi Abu Ganem in the then British Protectorate of Aden; or the 3,000 machine guns declared as "electric coffee machines" sent from Europe to the FLN; or the TNT shipment for the FLN in 1959. When Dynamite Nobel AG in Cologne refused to sell, Springer turned to

---

[195] He actually managed to get elected to the Lower Saxony State Parliament (Landtag) from May 6th, 1951, to October 23rd, 1952, when the RSP was banned.

[196] Algerian National Liberation Front.

[197] Josef Broz Tito, strongman of Yugoslavia, was another well known Fascist, friend of Argentina's Perón and Egypt's Nasser, and a steadfast supporter of the Non-aligned movement.

Chemo Impex in Budapest to ship the explosives to Tripoli on a Finnish ship. Springer explained his dedication thus: *"The political attitude of the Arabs and their misery prompted me to work for the North African freedom movement."*[198] Quite the humanitarian, indeed.

According to recently declassified BND (German Intelligence) documents, in 1962, he was recruited by Fidel Castro, together with Otto Ernst Remer, to help the Cuban government purchase 4,000 Belgian machine guns.[199] He survived an assassination attempt in January of 1962, when a plastic bomb exploded under his Mercedes. Allegedly, it had been the work of the French secret organization OAS. This outstanding citizen died of old age, in Germany, on September 19th, 2009.

SS-Sturmbannführer **Otto Skorzeny**, a renowned Nazi commando, he organized and led the rescue of Mussolini from the Grand Sasso in a glider operation and organized the "American Brigades" during the Battle of the Bulge. After the war, he took refuge in Spain under the protection of Francisco Franco. He soon surfaced in Argentina, where he was a personal guard of First Lady Eva Perón, herself a former *Abwehr* agent.[200] Skorzeny became a close friend and confidant of Argentina's ruling couple. General Perón, another *Abwehr* graduate, was committed to his former employers. His personal secretary, Ludwig Freude, was the Abwehr's Chief of Operations for South America, and the man who wrote the checks for Perón's presidential bid—

---

[198] "Die politische Haltung der Araber und ihr Elend veranlaßten mich, für die nordafrikanische Freiheitsbe-wegung tätig zu werden."

[199] John B. Perdue, *What Fidel Castro's Nazi recruits say of the left*, The Washington Times, October 16th, 2012.

[200] In a letter from the German Ambassador in Madrid to the head of intelligence for South America, he describes her as *"one of Canaris' favorite agents, for the good work she did in Rio"*, and as a *"beautiful, intelligent and unscrupulous zimmerfrau."*

other intimates included Martin Bormann and Josef Mengele.

Under Perón's protection, and in close collaboration with Bormann, Skorzeny expanded the ratline and helped hundreds of Nazis to escape justice in Europe for the opportunity to regroup in Argentina. Most did not even bother to change their names and became influential figures in the Argentine Army and Secret Services, with disastrous consequences for the country and the world.

Otto Skorzeny and Adolf Hitler
At the *Wolfeschanze*, after the rescue of Mussolini from the Grand Sasso:
"Skorzeny, you are a man after my own heart.
You have gained the day and crowned our mission with success.
Your Führer thanks you!"

In 1955, as a liberal revolution (*Revolución Libertadora*) deposed Perón in an ultimately futile attempt to end his National Socialist regime, many of the Nazi refugees felt a creeping anxiety that Skorzeny and Omar Ain von Leers helped assuage by assisting them in a new move to Cairo.[201]

---

[201] Upon arriving in Cairo, Skorzeny's friend and mentor Johann von Leers declared: *"Argentina is finished as a superstate. After Peron's fall, the Jews and the clerics, the vultures and the ravens, took over."*

Already in 1953, Skorzeny had visited Nasser—a close friend of Perón's and fellow founder of the Non-aligned Movement—and in collaboration with Bormann and former Wermacht General Reinhardt Gehlen, started the flow of Nazis from Europe to Cairo, soon to be followed by those escaping the demise of Perón in Argentina.

In addition to training the armies of Argentina and Egypt, Skorzeny can be justly credited with developing the terrorist tactics used by such diverse groups as the IRA, PLO, and the Symbionese Liberation Army. He also trained Nasser's Special Forces, paramilitary groups and more to the point of this work, the *Fedayeen* and the early members of *al-Jihad*. Some of his trainees included Arab volunteers trained in commando tactics to use against the British troops stationed in the Suez Canal zone and the *Fedayeen* that launched attacks against Israel from the Gaza strip in 1953 and 1954. One of these was a young engineering student at Cairo University, later a lieutenant in the Egyptian Army, who the world has come to know as Yasser Arafat, with whom he formed a long lasting friendship.

Skorzeny never denounced Hitler or National Socialism; on the contrary, he vigorously propounded the continuation of the struggle by what he termed a *"new soldier"* who, in civilian clothes and below the radar of the enemy, could strike anywhere, at any time, in the most brutal fashion. In his memoirs, published not long before his death in Madrid in 1975, he reminisces about his commando exploits—in Germany and in Egypt—and taunts the Allies: *"The enemy's stubbornness to stick to their decision that Germany must surrender unconditionally, prevented them from using outstanding special troops within the framework of a strategic whole—which would have helped achieve victory seven or eight months earlier."* And ends with a warning: *"In vain the 'traditional' generals view* [the new soldier] *with understandable suspicion. He exists and can no longer disappear from the battlefield; he is the authentic secret weapon of his fatherland."* Forty years later, Skorzeny's Islamic Commandoes continue to rain havoc on the West while "traditional" generals fail to recognize them, and traditional politicians cannot even bring themselves to accept their existence.

Für alle Zeichen der Liebe und Verehrung für meinen
lieben Mann

OTTO SKORZENY

und für die Worte, die sein Wesen und sein außer-
gewöhnliches Leben so lebendig würdigten, sage ich
meinen herzlichen Dank.

Ilse Skorzeny

Madrid, im August 1975
Castellon de la Plana 19

Thank you note sent by Ilse Skorzeny to the
hundreds of sympathizers who mailed her
sympathy cards after his death.

SS-Hauptsturmführer **Franz Paul Stangl,** Commander of the Sobibor death camp. Born in Austria in 1908, he became an early member of the NSDAP, while still considered an illegal organization by the Austrian police. After the *Anschluss,* he was assigned by the *Schutzpolizei* (taken over by the Gestapo) to the *Judenreferat* (Jewish Bureau). In 1940, he volunteered to *Action T-4,* a *"euthanasia program"* that was billed as *"humanitarian, legal and secret."* After serving in various capacities and reorganizing the killing processes at Hartheim and Bernburg, *SS-Reichsführer* Heinrich Himmler named him the first commandant at Sobibor, with the rank of *Obersturmführer.*

Over 100,000 Jews were killed at Sobibor, until the furnaces broke down in October of 1942, soon after Stangl assumed control of Treblinka in September of that year. He is quoted as stating: *"To tell the truth, one did become used to it... they were cargo. I think it started the day I first saw the Totenlager* [extermination area] *in Treblinka. I remember Wirth standing there, next to the pits full of black-blue corpses. It had nothing to do with humanity—it could not have. It was a mass—a mass of rotting flesh. Wirth said 'What shall we do with this garbage?' I think unconsciously that started me thinking of them as cargo... I rarely saw them as individuals. It was always a huge mass. I sometimes stood on the wall and saw them in the 'tube'—they were naked, packed together, running, being driven with whips..."*[202]

Franz Paul Stangle
Left: at Treblinka (in the middle) in 1943
Right, c. 1945

In 1943, he was transferred to Trieste, were he organized the campaign against Yugoslav partisans and Jews, and in 1945 returned to Vienna and was at the *Alpenfestung* (Alpine fortress) at the end of the war. Arrested by the Americans and slotted for trials for genocide at T-4, he was helped to escape by Alois Hudal, a Roman Catholic Bishop and Nazi sympathizer. He made it through the ratline with

---

[202] Yitzhak Arad, *Belzec, Sobibor, Treblinka: The Operation Reinhard Death Camps*, Bloomington: Indiana University Press, 1987, p. 184-86.

a Red Cross Passport issued by the Bishop, and reached Syria. His wife and children joined him there in 1951.

From 1948 to 1952, he was a consultant to Syrian intelligence, and then moved to Brazil, where he worked for Volkswagen in Sao Paulo, still using his own name. Finally extradited to Germany in 1967, he was tried for the deaths of 900,000 prisoners. He admitted to his actions, but famously stated: *"My conscience is clear. I was simply doing my duty..."* He died of heart failure in 1971 in prison at Düsseldorf.[203]

SS-Oberstrumbannführer **Karl (Albert) Thiemann,** joined the NSADP and the SS. Preceded Dr. Joachim Däumling in Poland[204] and was later in Czechoslovakia. Fled to Egypt with Däumling, converted to Islam and took the name ***Amman Qader.*** He was an official in the Information Ministry in Cairo.

SS-Standartenführer **Erich Weinmann** Chief of the SD in Prague. One of the men responsible for the suppression of the Warsaw Ghetto, where 16,000 Jews were massacred and 50,000 sent to death at Treblinka.

Weinmann was said to have died in battle at the end of WWII, but in 1972, the Central Office for the Investigation of Nazi Crimes in Ludwigsburg released a list of 13 names of high ranking Nazis responsible for the murder and deportation of Jews and Czechs. Among them were several Gestapo chiefs in Czechoslovakia, *Obersturmbannführer* Ernst-Joachim Illmer; Deputy Gestapo Commander for Prague, Willhelm Noelle and Dr. Bruno Lettow, who

[203] Guita Sereny, *Into That Darkness: An Examination of Conscience,* London, 1974.

[204] In the 1941 reorganization of the SS the Gestapo, as Office IV, he was put in charge of governmental Affairs in Poland: IV D 2 (Government Affair's, Poland in the Reich): Counsellor Karl Thiemann from July 1941; SS Oberstrumbannführer and Government Counsellor Dr. Joachim Daümling, from July 1943.

directed the Gestapo's activities in Brno. According to Simon Wiesenthal, director of the Vienna Documentation Center, the three were residing in West Germany, neither charged with any crimes nor ostracized, and *"in good economic conditions."* The report revealed that their boss, Erich Weinmann, had not died in any battle, but was in fact alive and well in Alexandria where he became a consultant to the police force.

After the Central Office for Investigation of Nazi Crimes was informed of his whereabouts, his "death certificate" was annulled and, in 1967, his file was reopened. The Czechoslovakian Association of Former Partisans and Anti-Nazi Fighters approached its own government in Prague in 1968, asking that Czechoslovakia demand from Cairo the extradition of Dr. Weinmann as a war criminal. The Communist government in Prague, however, declined to do so out of foreign policy considerations of its own.[205] Losing their lucrative contracts from the *Skoda Werks* was not in the cards.

Celebrating the suppression of the Warsaw uprising in October of 1944 (Left to right) *SS-Standartenführer* **Erich Weinmann**, *SS- Gruppenführer* Heinrich Heinz Reinefarth and *SS-Obergruppenführer* Karl Hermann Frank, Reich Minister for Bohemia and Moravia and General of Police. Frank was hanged in Prague in 1946, Reinefarth died in Germany in 1979.

---

[205] Jewish Telegraphic Agency, *Names of 13 High-ranking Nazis Disclosed; One of Them Now in Egypt*, Bonn, February 4th, 1972.

SS-Hauptstabsarzt **Dr. Heinrich Willermann,** participated in the medical atrocities at Dachau. After the war, he was wanted for his sterilization experiments on Jewish women, but escaped to Cairo and went to work for the Egyptian Secret Police. He converted to Islam and joined the Army, and as ***Lt. Col. Na'im Iahim*** was responsible for the establishment of the Samara concentration camp where, according to numerous testimonies, he pressed-on with the work he started in Dachau.[206]

---

[206] Samara was established in a former Army post in the middle of the desert some 120 miles west of Cairo. It was remodeled based on Nazi concentration camps photos and plans supplied by Willerman. As Paul Meskil describes them in *Hitler Heirs*, New York, 1961, p. 173): "Except for gas chambers and crematories, the U.A.R. camps employ all the old methods of torture and murder. Some of them even have fierce Alsatian dogs trained to tear prisoners apart on command. These dogs, favorite pets of German CC commanders, were unknown in Arabia before the Nazis came.

A report in the files of the United Nations Commission on Human Rights, New York, lists these common "indignities and atrocities" inflicted upon (Nasser's) political prisoners:

Extraction of prisoners' finger and toe nails.

Application of lighted cigarettes to sensitive parts of the body.

[Anal] Insertion of a rubber hose, through which air is pumped until the prisoner loses consciousness.

Tightening a steel ring around the prisoner's head until he blacks out. Scores of prisoners have died or become insane from this widely-practiced torture.

Confining prisoners in cells so small they can neither stand nor lie down.

Binding prisoners' hands and feet so they cannot move and leaving them in complete darkness with cold water dripping continually on their heads or bodies.

Turning "wild dogs" loose on prisoners.

Significantly, all of the tortures named in the U.N. report were in everyday use throughout the Nazi CC system. Although Arab torturers have their own peculiar devices, these particular methods are Germanic, not Arabic."

Not coincidentally, those who survived the Argentine or Chilean secret camps in the 1970s and early 80s would not change a comma. Of course, they were manned by alumni from the same school of evil, as are those in Syria, Iran,

SS-Standartenführer **Dr. Wilhelm Voss**, a prominent member of Himmler's inner circle, he was Chief Executive Officer of the *SS Skoda Werks*. In fact, some tanks manufactured there were named Voss I and Voss II in his honor. At the end of the war managed to hide from the Nüremberg trials and escaped to the Middle East. From 1966 to 1996, he was the first managing director of *Arbeitsgemeinschaft Hamburger Fachvereine eV* and, after founding the Hamburg Port Association, was Chief Executive Officer of the Hamburg Port Authority.

From 1951 to 1956, he lived in villa in the *Ma'adi* district in Cairo from where he run guns to Palestinians in Syria, and was Director of the Egyptian Planning Board and Chief Advisor to the Egyptian Minister of War, General Muhammad Naguib.[207] He was one of three Germans working with the Soviets that arranged an U$S 80,000,000 arms deal between Egypt and Czechoslovakia in 1955.[208] The weapons came, from all places, the *Skoda Werks*. Using his influence in the Ministry of War, Voss aided Ernst Remer to join him in Cairo.[209]

Yemen, Iraq, or, for that matter, Da'esh (ISIS). Samara was not unique. Other camps were modeled after German concentration camps, and the descriptions are the same. Abu Za'abal, known in Egypt as *Maqbarat al-ahya* (Cemetery of the Living)—about ten miles from Islamiya—; *Wa'hat*, in the Western Desert; or *Tora*, in the southwestern Helwan Governorate—this one still operative as a "maximum security prison." Samara, and a few others, was closed in 1971 when Anwar Sadat began his rapprochement with the West. At one time, Nasser kept over 25,000 political prisoners in these camps.

[207] Adrian O'Sullivan, *Nazi Secret Warfare in Occupied Persia*, 2014, Epilogue.

[208] The leader of that group, Fritz Grobba, the top Nazi operative in the Middle East, turned himself and his operation over to the Soviets. Grobba had been Nazi Germany's ambassador to Saudi Arabia and Iraq. General Naguib said of the Cairo Nazis in 1954, that *"they are the only ones in whom we have confidence."*

[209] Martin A. Lee, *The Beast Reawakens: Fascism's Resurgence from Hitler's Spymasters to Today's Neo-Nazi Groups and Right Wing Extremism*, Routledge, 2013, p. 133.

SA-Sturmabteilung[210] **Ludwig Pankraz Zind,** a Nazi storm trooper before and during the war, Zind was a German teacher tried in 1957 in Offenburg for anti-Semitic acts. He declared that the Holocaust had its justification, the basic conception of Nazism had been correct, that his conversation counterparty Lieser *"had better gone up in smoke,"* and called the State of Israel a *"plague spot"* that should be eradicated. Escaped to Egypt in 1958 with the assistance of Johann Von Leers arrived in Cairo as Helmut Volimer, together with the wife of Hans Eisele[211], and immediately found work in Von Leers' Research Institute, and in Appler's Islamic Congress, and converted to Islam taking the name ***Muhammad Saleh.***[212] Soon afterwards, he found a more lucrative position as Geology Professor in the American University in Tripoli. The Libyans happily granted him asylum.

In 1960, he taunted German authorities by returning to Germany and sending postcards with Nazi slogans to the press and government officials while touring Bonn with an American journalist. He intended to go from there to the Olympics in Rome, but the Italian police, perhaps a little more attentive or less complicit that their German counterparts arrested him and sent him back to Germany to begin his prison sentence, and yet he escaped again. He was rearrested in Düsseldorf in 1970, but his sentence was suspended. Nasser and the Suez Canal gave Ludwig Zind a welcome opportunity to reel off a whole catalogue of fixed

---

[210] The SA was a paramilitary organization of the Nazi Party. Taken over by Goering as "auxiliary police".

[211] Her husband, the butcher, had arrived a few months earlier, also courtesy of von Leers.

[212] One of the detainees at Guantanamo Bay gave his name as Abdulrahman Muhammad Saleh Nasser. What a coincidence!

Nazi clichés, ranging from *"the shameful Treaty of Versailles"* to Roosevelt's *"criminal sellout at Yalta."*

Ludwig Pankras Zind
c. 1958

Had Germany only won *"the heroic battle fought under Hitler,"* Zind proclaimed, the world today would be in a different shape. There would be German order and not cold war, Communism, and crime. *"With a German victory we would today enjoy justice and decency, and not suffer under democratic mob rule, corruption, and decadence."* However, not everything was lost; history had not yet come to its end, according to this singular mind: Nasser was proof that the British lion had lost its roar and was ready to die. France was rotting away in chronic disorder, and America was too fat, lazy, and stupid ever to become a soldier nation. Make no mistake, five to ten years hence Germany will again be confronted with the *Schicksalsstunde*—the hour of destiny. For that day the Fatherland must be prepared and the youth must be ready. Look how we have come back from defeat within a dozen years. *"Give us ten years more and we will again be the top nation in the world." "In my opinion far too few Jews went into the gas chambers."*

According to the trial account in the *Frankfurter Allgemeine Zeitung,*[213] Zind proudly stated: *"Without hesitation I*

---

[213] April 10-12th, 1958.

adopted the political concepts of National Socialism and even today I regard these concepts as completely valid." Zind berated the court with long nationalistic tirades. He saw nothing wrong with his statement that Lieser *"should have been gassed too."* Expressions like this, said Zind, *"Have become as common among the great majority of the German people as the curse, 'Go to the devil'."* He died in Germany in 1973.

Alfred Zingler, another assistant of Joseph Goebbels and expert in anti-Semitic propaganda. Arrived in Cairo in the 50s, converted to Islam and took the name **Mahmoud Saleh.** He worked in the Egyptian Information Department where he assisted von Leers in 1955 in the creation of the virulently anti-Semitic Institute for the Study of Zionism in Cairo.

***

There are hundreds more. Karl Hotter, former Gestapo Chief in Oppeln, at the Israel Department; Fritz Roessler, former Nazi leader in Saxony; elected to the Bundestag as Fritz Richter where he served until he was exposed in 1952, fled to Cairo and became a Muslim; Former Gestapo Captains Theodor Dannekera and Heinz Roethke, Eichmann's deputies in Paris, were working for the Syrian Secret Service; Franz Abromeit, Erwin Fleiss, Gerhard Lausegger, Franz Bechte, etc.

UAR militia units were commanded by Antonio Mentigazzi, former Fascist militia leader in Italy, where he was wanted for war crimes; former Wermacht officer, Colonel Kribel, was attached to the Egyptian General Staff. Wermacht and Waffen-SS officers comprised more than fifty per cent of the Syrian Army officer corps in 1955.

Another important group of Nazis was under the protection of France. While one would believe that France had every reason to hate the Nazis, we must not forget that under the Vichy government most of France was neither occupied nor in league with the Allies but was, in fact, an Axis power. It should then come as no surprise that more than 10,000 Nazis went into the *Légion Etrangére* to fight France's colonial wars. Germans outnumbered Frenchmen in the Legion, including hundreds of criminals wanted for wartime atrocities, who remained safe even from such relentless hunters as Israel's secret agents. When the Legion was finally dissolved, they made their way into the Arab countries with ease, into the waiting arms of their *Kameraden.*

Former Vichy bureaucrats went on to become the rulers of post-war France. Valéry Giscard D'Estaing, President from 1974 to 1981, is said to have joined the *Résistance* at age 16, all while his father was being named Grand Officer of the *Légion d'honneur* and receiving *l'Ordre de la Francisque* from the Vichy government, as a token of the esteem in which Marshal Philippe Pétain regarded him. [214]

François Mitterrand, President of France from 1981 to 1995, was a collaborator of Marshal Pétain, both in propaganda efforts through *France, revue de l'etat nouveau,* [215]

---

[214] Pierre Mendés France recalls in *Le chagrin et la pitié,* a 1969 documentary of Marcel Ophüls: *"There is a man who came the next day to see Rochat* [the lawyer of P. Mendes-France], I do not know if Rochat told you this detail, and who said to him: 'I am a *pétainist,* I am indignant by what I saw yesterday, it is abominable, it is a scandal. The Marshal cannot know such things. The Marshal is deceived. It is essential that the Marshal be forewarned and put on notice. I saw that you took the shorthand of the meeting. Can you give me a copy that I will bring to the Marshal himself? Rochat gave him a copy of the shorthand. He went to the Marshal, who naturally had not been informed. And the man who made this move was a councilor of state, whose name was Giscard d'Estaing. He was appointed Grand Officer of the Legion of Honor and was decorated with the Order of the Francisque under the Vichy regime."*

[215] In December of 1942, in the 5th issue of the *Revue,* Noël de Tissot, Secretary General of the *Service d'ordre légionnaire* wrote an article under the title *Our Enemies,* where we read: *"If France is not to perish, it is necessary that last Frenchmen deserving of the name declare a war without mercy to all of those who in France or in foreign lands prepare to open the gates: Jews, Masons, Communists...all of them the same, and all*

as an apologist of SOL (*Service d'Ordre Légionnaire*, a paramilitary group that persecuted "Jews, Masons and Communists"), and as a close associate of René Bousquet, the Chief of Police that rounded-up the Jews in 1942. In 1943, when the demise of Nazi Germany became a distinct possibility, he did as Giscard and joined the *Résistance*.

Jacques René Chirac, President of France from 1995 to 2007, Saddam Hussein's great friend,[216] too young to have played any role in Vichy, was a Communist militant in the late 1950s before he became one of the most corrupt mayors of Paris. His support for the satrap of Iraq is legendary, conducting a relentless campaign against US policies in collaboration with Vladimir Putin (who he called a close personal friend), Hu Jintao and German social democrat Gerhard Schröeder.

---

of them Gaullists." The same issue of the *Revue* sported two more articles, one, *Pèlerinage en Thuringe*, penned by François Mitterrand, where the future President of France condemns the 150 years of mistakes that followed the French Revolution. The third article was by Marshal Pétain.

[216] *Le Canard Enchainé* dubbed him *Jaques Iraq*, calling Ossirac, the site of Iraq's nuclear program, *O'Chirac*. The close relationship between Chirac and Saddam goes back to 1974, when Saddam visited France and spent a weekend at Chirac's home while discussing oil monopolies and the provision to Iraq of two nuclear reactors.

No war is over until the enemy says it's over.
We may think it over, we may declare it over but,
in fact, the enemy gets a vote.

General James Mattis, USMC

16

Back to *al-Jihad*, The Spawn of Islamic Fascism

Aymann al-Zawahiri

Co-founder and leader of *al-Jihad* and *al-Qa'ida* and its many offspring throughout the world, he was one of the leaders of the group that planted the bomb on Arrow Air flight 1285 in 1985, and continues today to spearhead the Islamic National Socialists throughout the world while nincompoops in Washington pat each other in the back celebrating the demise of his figurehead Osama bin Laden.

After the successful assassination of President Sadat, and in spite of the—sometimes quite feeble—efforts of Egyptian authorities to quash the group, *al-Jihad* continued a relentless campaign against Egyptian, Israeli and Western targets, always careful to take credit for their deeds. And they were not alone:

April 18th, 1983:

Bombing of the US Embassy in Beirut, Lebanon. 83 people, including 17 Americans, were killed and 120 wounded when a truck bomb with nearly two tons of explosives blew in front of the building. Among the Americans killed was the CIA's Middle East Director. The attack was claimed by *Islamic Jihad*.

September 29th, 1983:

Gulf Air flight 771, a Boeing 737 flying from Karachi (Pakistan) to Abu Dhabi (United Arab Emirates), blew up over Mino Jemel Ali (UAE), killing all 112 people aboard. The investigation report concluded: *"The aircraft crashed after the crew had issued a brief distress message. It appeared that a bomb had exploded in the cargo compartment, causing a violent fire."* However, on the day of the incident, airport sources declared that *"seems the plane ran into engine trouble shortly before landing."* The engine trouble was a bomb planted in the cargo compartment by a *"Palestinian terrorist group"* that wanted to punish the Emirates for not paying protection money.

October 23rd, 1983:

Truck bomb attack on the Marine Barracks at the Beirut Airport, Lebanon. 241 US personnel were killed, including 220 Marines—the deadliest day for the USMC since Iwo Jima—leading to a fiasco that resulted in the *"strategic withdrawal"* of US Forces from Lebanon in February of 1984. Defense secretary Caspar Weinberger stated at the time that he suspected Hezbollah but, surprisingly, Hezbollah took pains to deny any involvement. *Islamic Jihad,* on the other hand, claimed responsibility in a call to AFP (Agence France Presse), following the same pattern as two years later in the claims for the Arrow Air attack.

October 23rd, 1983:

Truck bomb attack on the French Paratrooper Barracks in the southern suburb of Jnah in Beirut, about two miles away from the Marine Barracks. Fifty-eight French paratroopers were killed. *Islamic Jihad* claimed responsibility, again, in a phone call to AFP.

December 12th, 1983:

A truck bomb attack on the US Embassy in Kuwait was foiled by guards, but there were still five dead and eighty wounded. The attack was carried out by Hezbollah and a Palestinian group, *Da'wa,* both sponsored by Iran. The American and French embassies, the Kuwait airport, the grounds of the Raytheon Corporation, a Kuwait National Petroleum Company oil rig and a government-owned power station were all targeted in synchronized attacks. One of the attackers was Mustapha Badreddine, who after spending several years in a Kuwaiti prison escaped in 1991, when Iraq invaded Kuwait. With support from Iran, he managed to escape to Lebanon, where he was instrumental in the assassination of Prime Minister Rafiq Hariri, and in 2008 became the head of Hezbollah's military and terrorist operations. It was to free him and his 16 accomplices that Hezbollah took hostages in 1984—William Buckley and others, the same ones mentioned in the Arrow Air conspiracies—to exchange them for the seventeen terrorists imprisoned in Kuwait (and not as vengeance for Ollie North's foul-ups). Hezbollah's deputy chief Naim Qassem acknowledged that the freedom of the *Kuwait 17 "was the starting point for the idea of hostages, to impose pressure for the release of prisoners in Israel and elsewhere."* Thirty years later, Hezbollah continues Iran's proxy war on the West, and in recent months have carried out plans in Azerbaijan, Bulgaria, Cyprus, Egypt, Jordan, South Africa, Turkey and Thailand, in addition to their operations in Syria in support of the Assad regime.

September 20th, 1984:

The US Embassy in Beirut was bombed (yes, again). This time, 2 marines and 23 Embassy employees were killed. There were over 50 Lebanese citizens and 21 Americans injured, including the US and British Ambassadors. Again, *Islamic Jihad* claimed responsibility.

December 4th, 1984:

Islamic terrorists hijacked Kuwait Airlines flight 221 and diverted it to Tehran, demanding the release of their 17 comrades in Kuwaiti jails serving terms for attacks against the US and French embassies there in 1983. Two American passengers were killed and thrown on the Tarmac. After six days, Iranian security forces stormed the plane and released the hostages. Some of these hostages claimed that the Iranians were complicit with the hijackers, and that the release had been staged. The seventeen prisoners in Kuwait were members of a Shia' Muslim group that had been operating freely in Iran under the protection of Ayatollah Ruhollah Khomeini.

April 12th, 1985:

A bomb in *El Descanso*—a Madrid restaurant popular among US service members from the nearby US base in Torrejón de Ardoz—killed 18 and injured 84. The bombing was attributed to ETA, a Basque separatist terrorist organization with links to Libya. To this day, no one has been arrested for the attack.

However, in 1992, Baltazar Garzón, a courageous Spanish judge who indicted numerous Latin American dictators for crimes against humanity, interrogated Boumershed Ahmed, a member of the Front for the Liberation of Palestine and associate of Monzer al'Kassar—a notorious Syrian arms dealer—but could not go forward.

In 2004, following the Madrid train bombings, a witness recognized the bomber of *El Descanso* as Mustapha Setmarian Nassar, a Syrian citizen—linked to the head of Spain's al-Qa'ida branch, Abu Dadah—who had obtained Spanish citizenship through marriage. In 2005, Judge Ismael Moreno reopened the case, and Nassar was captured in Quetta, a small town near the border between Pakistan and Afghanistan, but he soon disappeared. In 2009, Judge Garzón requested information from the US to no avail, but Nassar later turned up in a Syrian prison in Aleppo. In 2012, the Syrians released him[217] and he appears to have become "military chief of operations" of ISIL in Syria, although *Dabiq,* a magazine published by ISIL claims he

---

[217] On February 2nd, 2012, *Asad al'Jihad2*, a blogger in *Shumoukh Al-Islam*, a Jihadi forum, announced in his blog that *"I bring you glad tidings. The release of Sheikh Abu Mus'ab Al-Suri has been confirmed on our end, and he is now free, thanks to Allah. I ask Allah to set free the rest of our brothers in Syria and everywhere else..."* On June 22nd, 2012, MEMRI (Middle East Media Research Institute) issued a report on the release of al-Suri. The full text is in Appendix III on page 267.

was, in fact, rejected because of his ties to the Muslim Brotherhood.

It is no surprise that in 1985 Spanish authorities jumped at the opportunity of endorsing the bombing to ETA. The Basque terrorist group was a most convenient scapegoat, and blaming it assisted the government's campaign to eradicate them. But it is also not surprising that, in fact, ETA had nothing to do with this attack in particular, which was part of al-Jihad campaign against the West. The pattern continues to repeat itself.

Over the years, the bomber of *El Descanso* grew to become al-Qa'ida's chief propagandist and is today considered the number four ranking member in that organization. One cannot help but wonder how many lives might have been spared had the Spanish government actually investigated the bombing of a restaurant in Torrejón de Ardoz in 1985 rather than choose the easy way of blaming what was convenient or politically expedient at the time.

**Osama bin Laden and
Mustafa Setmarian Nassar
AKA Abu Musab al'Suri**
1997, interviewing bin Laden for *Al-Ansar,* a Jihadist magazine

June 14th, 1985:

TWA flight 847, en route to Rome, was hijacked and diverted to Algiers, with 8 crewmembers and 145 passengers. A US Navy diver was murdered by the hijackers and his body thrown on the tarmac in Algiers. After 17 days, the US agreed to free 435 Lebanese and Palestinian prisoners, and the hostages were released. The hijacker, Mohamed Ali Hamadei, was a member of Hezbollah. He was arrested in West Germany in 1987, prosecuted, and on May 17th, 1989, condemned to life in prison for murder, hostage taking, assault and hijacking. As usual, life in prison is not really life in prison and, on December 15th, 2005, he was released and allowed to return to Beirut the following day. As the FBI website informs us: *"Hamadei and two of his collaborators—Hassan Izz-Al-Din and Ali Atwa—are at large.* Mohammed Ali Hamadei (aka *Ali Hamadi* and *Castro*) is believed to be living in Lebanon.

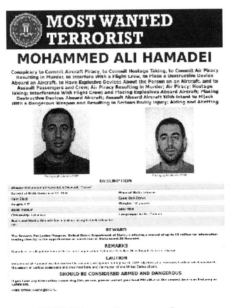

**FBI Wanted poster for
Mohammed Ali Hamadei**
Hijacker of TWA flight 847,
one more beneficiary of Germany's catch and release policy.

August 8th, 1985:

A car bomb exploded outside the headquarters of Rhein Main AFB in Frankfurt, Germany, killing 2 Americans and wounding 20 Americans and Germans. German prosecutors blamed the Red Army Faction (RAF), an apparent heir to the Baader-Meinhof Gang of the 1970s. The same group was blamed four years earlier for a bombing attack at Ramstein AFB, about 80 miles southwest of Rhein Main.[218]

Edward Derejian, a White House spokesman, quickly declared: *"We have no information on the group itself but it is well known that the Red Army Faction and other terrorist groups in Europe are closely coordinating with one another in targeting U.S. military bases."*[219] While the bomb came only six weeks after a similar attack on Frankfurt International Airport, just across the tarmac from this one, the police did not see any connection. On August 2nd, 1986, Eva Haule, a RAF militant, was arrested in Frankfurt in an unrelated raid and eventually sentenced to 15 years prison in 1989 for her role in an unrelated attack on a NATO training center in Oberammergau, but was never formally charged for the Rhein Main bombing. In 2007, however, she was released on parole as she *"no longer presents a threat to society."* The

---

[218] The Red Army faction, like many non-Islamic terrorist groups in Europe at the time, had close ties to the Libyans, and received support from the Libyan government in the form of training at camps in Libya, as well as monetary and logistic support. After the December 1985 attacks on airports at Rome and Vienna (with over 159 casualties among the dead and wounded), Muammar Qaddafi promised continued support for the Red Army Faction in Germany, the *Brigate Rosse* (Red Brigades) in Italy, and the IRA in Northern Ireland, as long as European governments continued their support of his opposition in Libya. It is not a stretch to suppose that the bombings at Rhein Main and Ramstein had been a consequence of this well known association.

[219] The New York Times, August 9th, 1985, *Car Bomb Kills 2 on a US Air Base in West Germany.*

RAF disbanded in 1998, after years of terror. They had close associations with other terrorist organizations in Europe, like *Action Directe* in France, and were frequent guests in terrorist training camps in Eastern Libya.

September 5th, 1985:

Pan Am flight 73 was taken over by terrorists at Karachi airport in Pakistan. After 16 tense hours, the plane was stormed by Pakistani forces resulting in 22 dead and 150 injured. In 2005, after 30 years of silence, the surviving crewmembers spoke to the press. In a statement that I fully understand, Nupoor Abrol, one of these flight attendants said: *"The hijack is far from over for me and my colleagues. Some of us, passengers and crew alike, are still struggling with the skeletons of the past, trying to fix the puzzle of incidents, sequences, people who were involved in the chains of events."* While they had relayed their recollections to the FBI a week after the attack, and again at a Parole hearing for the lead hijacker in 2005, they finally went public in an interview with the BBC in March of 2006. Madhvi Bahuguna, one of the Flight Attendants, said to the interviewer *"Survivors* [of like atrocities] *are living each day with the memories,"* and that she hoped that, in speaking out, *"we can all connect through our survival stories and form a fabric of power and strength going forward."*

The attack was carried out by Zayd Hassan 'Abd al-Latif, Masud al-Safarini,[220] Mohammed Abdul, Khalil Hussain, Daud Mohammed Hafiz, Mohammed Ahmed al-

---

[220] He was released from prison in Pakistan in 2001 (together with the others) after receiving amnesty. He was recaptured by the FBI in Bangkok, on his way to Jordan. In 2003, he was found guilty in a Federal US Court. A plea bargain agreement spared him the death penalty, but the judge imposed three consecutive 160 year sentences, greatly reducing the chance of parole. He disappeared from news reports soon after, and is supposedly still in a maximum security prison in Colorado.

Munawar and Jamal Saeed Abdul Raheem,[221] all members of *Abu Nidal*,[222] a terrorist organization headquartered in Baghdad, under the personal protection of Saddam Hussein, and completely routed by American forces in 2003.

October 7th, 1985:

The Italian cruise ship *Achille Lauro* was hijacked by *Abu Nidal*. A Jewish American passenger on a wheelchair, Leon Klinghoffer, was murdered and thrown overboard. After three days, the Egyptian government offered the terrorists safe passage, securing the release of 700 hostages.

November 23rd, 1985:

Egypt Air flight 648 was hijacked in Malta, with 98 passengers and crewmembers aboard. Five passengers were shot—two of which died—and later 53 more passengers died when the terrorists set off explosives.

The sole survivor of the terrorist gang, Omar Mohammed Ali Rezaq, a Lebanese-born Palestinian (and member of *Abu Nidal*), was apprehended by the FBI in Nigeria on July 15t, 1993. Ali Rezaq had been captured and sentenced to 25 years in Malta, but released in a "general amnesty" after only two years. A few months later, he was arrested in Ghana, but released after a few days. This time

---

[221] Reportedly killed during a US drone strike in the Waziristan region of Afghanistan (principal refuge for al-Qaeda operatives escaping Afghanistan) on January 9th, 2010.

[222] Also known as *Fatah Revolutionary Council*, *Arab Revolutionary Brigades* or *Revolutionary Organization of Socialist Muslims*, was founded by Sabri al-Banna, also known as *Abu Nidal* (Father of the struggle), a former member of the Ba'ath Party and of the PLO. Extremely active in the Middle East and Europe through the 80s and 90s, it has had no known activities since the death of al-Banna and the destruction of its headquarters in Baghdad in 2003, courtesy of the American bombing raids.

the FBI was part of the welcome party in Lagos. They took him into custody but did not arrest him, as American law required that he be "found in the US" in order to be tried in US courts for the hijacking. In October of 1996, he was sentenced to life in prison—the judge regretted that he could not impose life without parole—and to the payment of U$S 264,000 in restitution. His sentence runs out in 2021, if he is not paroled sooner.

December 12th, 1985:

Arrow Air attack in Gander killed 256. *Islamic Jihad* claimed responsibility in phone calls to AFP, Reuters, US diplomatic facilities and the Canadian Aviation Safety Board. Somehow, their claims went unnoticed by investigators. To this day, in spite of the evidence, it is not officially considered a terrorist attack.

April 2nd, 1986

TWA Flight 840 from Los Angeles to Cairo was struck above Greece by a bomb planted beneath a seat. It blasted a hole in the plane's side, leading to the death of four Americans—including an infant sucked through the hole—but the pilot managed to make an emergency landing in Athens. A Palestinian group dubbed *Arab Revolutionary Cells* claimed responsibility, citing a struggle against *"American imperialism."* This group is known to have taken hostage Frank Herbert reed, Director of the Lebanese International School in Beirut, and Joseph James Cicippio, controller of the American University Hospital in Beirut (9/12/1986). On April 17th, 1986, a note in their name was found next to the corpses of two Britons and one American shot at the American University in Beirut. The note stated that the attack was in retaliation for the US bombing of Libya three days earlier.[223] The group used the name of *Sheik Is' ed-Din al-Kazzam,* who in the 1930s combined the fanatical Islamism of the Wahabites with the anti-Imperialism of the *Istiklal* party into a nationalist-socialist doctrine. Al-Kazzam led an Arab uprising in 1935 against the British and, not surprisingly, was vindicated by Hajj Amin el-Husseini during his failed rebellion in 1939. For someone who does not believe in coincidences, it is quite probable that the made-up name (no other attacks before or since were attributed to this "group"), is neither a Palestinian organization nor a purely Libyan intelligence operation but another instance of *al-Jihad* working with both: The choice of a nationalist hero of the pan-Arab National Socialists to name the otherwise inexistent group cannot be happenstance.

April 5th, 1986:

La Belle Discoteque, a disco frequented by American troops in the West Berlin district of Friedenau was bombed. There were three people killed and 230 injured. Of these, two of the dead and 79 of the injured were American servicemen stationed nearby. Although the Germans were not able to pursue the investigation fully until after reunification—when Stasi files were opened—the US conducted retaliatory air raids on Tripoli and Benghazi within two weeks of the bombing.

---

[223] While not much information on this group seems to be available, it appears that it, al-Kazzam Revolutionary cells and the Ezzedine Kazzam revolutionary cells are one and the same. The main operative seems to have been Elias Mansour, working with Abdullah Abd'al Hamid Labib, head of a Fatah dissident group. Mansour was working with Mohammed Rashid—also responsible for a similar bomb on Pan Am flight 830 in 1982. See Mark Ensalaco, *Middle Eastern terrorism: From Black September to September 11,* University of Pennsylvania Press, 2008, p. 170.

December 21st, 1988:

Pan Am flight 103 blew out of the sky over Locker-bie, Scotland killing 270 passengers and crew members, including 35 students from Syracuse University returning home from a study-abroad program and many US service members.

Unlike the Arrow Air plane, Pan Am 103 did not fall in a remote area of Newfoundland but in a populated area of Scotland. An investigation that included some of those whose access had been denied—or whose conclusions had been disregarded—in the Gander case, successfully determined the cause to be a bomb planted in Cologne, Germany in luggage in the forward cargo bay. The bomb was made of Semtex, with a pressure detonator that used pressurization cycles to cause the explosion after the plane had landed and taken off again in London. Indeed, the device was supposed to explode over the Atlantic, erasing evidence of the attack, but it went off prematurely while still over land.

Unlike the Canadian investigation, the Dumfries and Galloway Constabulary worked closely with the FBI resulting in a different conclusion after three years of work: *"The in-flight disintegration of the aircraft was caused by the detonation of an improvised explosive device located in a baggage container positioned on the left side of the forward cargo hold at aircraft station 700."* On November 13th, 1991, indictments were entered against Abdel Basset Mohmet Ali al-Megrahi, a Libyan intelligence officer and the head of security for Libyan Arab Airlines (LAA)[224], and Lamin Khalifah Fhimah, the LAA station manager in Luqa Airport, Malta.

---

[224] A man known to have had extensive relations with the leaders of Islamic Jihad during their sojourn in the terrorist training camps in Libya. On January 31st, 2001, Fhimah was acquitted, and Megrahi convicted to 27 years in prison. Inexplicably, he was released by the Scottish government in April of 2009 "on

March 16th, 1988:

More than 4,000 Kurdish civilians were killed when Saddam Hussein launched a chemical attack on their town. An uprising ensued, resulting in the forced relocation of 1.5 million and the disappearance of over 200,000. US forces uncovered mass graves in 2003 and 2004 related to these events.

***

There were, to be sure, other terrorist incidents during this time. Many. On July 15th, 1983, I was a crewmember on an Arrow DC-10-10 that arrived at Orly airport in the early hours of the morning. After the passengers disembarked and proceeded to the arrivals area, we left for a special section that processed arriving crews. We did not make it far. As we were leaving the jet way with Joe Cameira,[225] an explosion shook the building. I was thrown several feet and landed on my back. A self proclaimed Armenian Secret Army for the Liberation of Armenia (ASALA) had planted a bomb in a piece of luggage destined for a Turkish Airlines flight to Istanbul. The contraption exploded prematurely, in the check-in area, killing five

---

compassionate grounds" to a hero's welcome in Tripoli. He died there, of prostate cancer, in 2012. The case was not without problems of its own, one of the reasons behind Fhimah's acquittal. Vincent Cannistraro, former CIA chief who headed the investigation in Lockerbie, said from the beginning that Mohammed Abu Talb, a terrorist then in jail in Sweden for, of all things, bombing offenses, was behind the Pan Am bombing. Abolhassan Mesbahi, and Iranian intelligence defector, also claimed an Iran–Syria connection. However, the clothing around the bomb came from a shop in Malta, where Islamic Jihad and Libyan intelligence had a tendency to intersect. What many people failed to notice is that until al-Zawahiri's embrace of *takfir*, collaboration between Shia' and Sunni terrorist groups was not unheard of.

[225] Joseph Anthony Cameira, born on June 14th, 1961, the son of José M. and Celeste (Fernandes) Cameira; a good friend who was the FSM on that flight. Tragically, Joe died on January 7th, 1998.

and wounding 56 people as they were standing in line. The lowlife who orchestrated the attack, Waroujan Garbidjian, was arrested on July 20th, 1983, and sentenced to life in prison on March 3rd, 1985. He was, in an all too familiar pattern, released in April 2001. That release came shortly after the French Parliament "recognized" the so-called "genocide" of Armenians in Turkey in 1915, giving the lawyers of Mr. Garbidjian a handy argument for clemency. In 2007, Speaker of the House Nancy Pelosi spearheaded a similar effort in the US Congress, finally defeated when a few Democrats joined the Republicans in opposition to the bill. Neither in France nor in the US was there any reference made to the fact that modern Turkey is not the Ottoman Empire, nor to the atrocities committed by Armenians and Kurds during that singularly bloody conflict.[226]

Between 1983 and 1985 there were countless terrorist attacks in England, France, Germany, the UK and Denmark, not to mention hostage taking in Lebanon and elsewhere. That terrorism was not a consideration from the beginning of the investigation of the Arrow Air flight in 1985 is baffling to the point of being incomprehensible. It was, however, part of a series of willful misstatements that have become the norm to our days.

---

[226] *Archives du ministère des Affaires étrangères, série E, carton 304, dossier 7.* On March 23rd, 1920, Colonel Charles Furlong, an Army intelligence officer and U.S. Delegate to the Paris Peace Conference, elaborated In a letter to President Woodrow Wilson that: *"We hear much, both truth and gross exaggeration of Turkish massacres of Armenians, but little or nothing of the Armenian massacres of Turks. [...] Our opportunity to gain the esteem and respect of the Muslim world [...] will depend much on whether America hears Turkey's untrammeled voice and evidence which she has never succeeded in placing before the Court of Nations."* A year earlier, in several telegrams to the French War Office, General Jules C. Hamelin, commander of the Troupes Françaises du **Levant**, *warned that crimes perpetrated by Armenian soldiers were not less cruel than crimes perpetrated by Turks and Kurds, and that these crimes would in the end damage the image of France in the Muslim world."* He also warned that France should not expect any gratitude from the Armenians. The events in Paris in the 1980s proved him right.

Of course, these attacks did not end in 1985. A list of terrorist incidents perpetrated or sponsored by *al-Jihad* or its successors *al-Qa'ida, AQAP, ISIL AQIM, Ansar al-Sharia, Ansar al-Islam, Ansar al-Sunni, AQI, the al-Nusrah Front,* and dozens of other offspring operating in over ninety countries would fill a book much larger than this one.

And nearly every time, the initial response to their attacks has been willful blindness: *Nothing to see here, folks, move along.* It is always an act of God, workplace violence, gun violence, hate crimes, paranoid schizophrenia or just someone having a bad hair day. Every time, the *savants du jour* will elaborate all kinds of social theories, look the other way and promise that they will make every effort—whatever those efforts are meant to be—to ensure that this *"does not happen again."* And every time it happens again. The perpetrators, when caught, are soon freed on humanitarian grounds, amnesties, prisoner exchanges or, most ominously, as gestures of good will, as imbeciles suggest that keeping those prisoners under lock and key would serve as a *"recruiting tool for Jihadists."*

However, it does not take an expert to figure out that, in war, prisoners should not to be freed until the war is over and they pose no more danger. Just imagine if someone had demanded that the Soviets free their Wermacht prisoners two months after the Battle of Stalingrad; or that the US release their Japanese prisoners at the end of the Battle of Iwo Jima. Painfully ridiculous as these arguments are, that is precisely what we are doing, only to see them return to the battlefield and cause renewed carnage among our service men and women and, indeed, our civilians.

The sheer idiocy of approaching what is not only a war, but a war that has been waged against us without quarter for almost seventy years as if it were common crimes has done nothing but provide the enemy with a forum for their propaganda efforts, and free their operatives for renewed attacks. The consistency in downplaying their successes has only rendered our people defenseless and unprepared for the next wave. The plain stupidity of affording their masters equal rank in our diplomatic dealings only empowers them and reduces our ability to counter their actions, much less anticipate them.

As late as January 2011, referring to events in Egypt, the ineffable Hillary Clinton, then US Secretary of State, declared:

"Today we learned the Muslim Brotherhood decided to participate, which suggests they at least are now involved in the dialogue that we have encouraged...We're going to wait and see how this develops, but we've been very clear about what we expect."

What exactly did Mme. Secretary expect the grandmother of terrorist organizations to bring to what table is not yet clear, nor do I believe will it ever be. But in embracing the Muslim Brotherhood as a partner in diplomacy and worse, in giving their minions a voice in our institutions as consultants and advisers to our Government, we not only empower them beyond their means and dreams, but weaken our real allies. Mrs. Clinton can be as clear as she pretends to be, but the Muslim Brotherhood's objectives are not to have tea with the likes of her while trying to find a comfortable arrangement: It is to continue to wage war on the West until there is nothing left of the principles that sustain us. And they are very near.

We will get back to this, but as I look back to the last 30 years, I already see changes in our way of life that are not just regrettable, but perhaps the death rattle of our open society.

17

Closure

Since the bombing of Arrow Air, more than 30,000 Americans have died in terrorist attacks, and dozens of thousands more were maimed or wounded. The total victims of terrorism worldwide since 1981 have a sobering effect:[227]

Year	Killed	Wounded
1981	240	751
1982	230	750
1983	650	1,252
1984	260	998
1985	826	1,217
1986	576	1,708
1987	633	2,272
1988	658	1,131
1989	407	427
1990	200	677
1991	102	242
1992	93	693
1993	109	1,393
1994	314	663
1995	165	6,291

---

[227] US State Department. For 1981-2004, *Patterns of Global Terrorism;* 2005-2015 *Country Reports on Terrorism*, except for 2004, calculated on the basis of news articles.

1996	311	2,652
1997	221	693
1998	741	5,952
1999	233	706
2000	405	791
2001	3,572	1,083
2002	725	2,013
2003	625	3,646
2004	3,024	9,935
2005	14,602	24,705
2006	20,487	38,413
2007	22,719	44,095
2008	15,708	33,885
2009	15,310	32,651
2010	13,186	30,665
2011	12,533	25,903
2012	11,098	21,652
2013	17,891	32,577
2014	32,727	34,791
2015	28,328	35,320
Total	**220,209**	**402,593**

Of these, 89,136 dead and 189,034 wounded correspond to the 28 years between 1981 and 2008, and 131,073 dead and 213,559 wounded for the first seven years of the Obama administration. And this numbers do not include the hundreds of thousands of victims of the wars in Syria and Iraq against ISIL. The wages of appeasement are staggering and yet, the refusal to come to terms with the nature of Islamic National Socialist terrorism can only result in increasing casualties at home and abroad. Indeed, 2016 promises to be a banner year for Jihadists.

The failure of successive administrations to grapple with the nature of our common enemy, coupled with the

politically motivated conflation of National Socialist Islamism with Islam at large—as if the innocence of the latter
somehow diminishes the criminality of the former—has
created an environment of mistrust and fear that paralyzes
our military, intelligence and policy planning. Should anyone raise his voice to decry the dangers posed by Jihadists,
he should be prepared to withstand accusations of bigotry,
racism and worse, and as our leaders retreat for fear of
branding, the hordes only get stronger.

In the past seven years, thanks to the pusillanimity
brought about by this fear, Al-Qa'ida has morphed into
ISIL (Da'esh), the al-Nusrah Front, Ansar al-Sharia in all of
its manifestations, al-Qa'ida in Yemen, al-Qa'ida in the
Arabian Peninsula, al-Qa'ida in the Islamic Maghreb and a
few dozen more groups, while continuing to recruit disen-
franchised Muslims in the West to do their bidding through
the internet and print media in a vast propaganda campaign
carried out under the protection of our civil liberties, in our
cities, with our resources.

At the same time, the same venal politicians who
shamelessly used disasters like the Arrow Air bombing to
advance their petty interests continue to use their pulpits to
transform the war against Islamic Fascism into immigrant
witch hunts or some other similar nonsense that, in fact,
creates an environment of perceived persecution where
there was none, sending the youth that could have otherwise provided valuable support to eradicate the scourge of
Islamo-Fascism into despair, and—in some cases—into the
welcoming arms of our—and their—enemies.

On September 20th, 2001, President Bush in his ad-
dress to Congress stated that *"Our war on terror begins with al-
Qa'ida, but it does not end there. It will not end until every terrorist
group of global reach has been found, stopped, and defeated;"* and on
July 12th, 2004, added *"The appeal of justice and liberty, in the*

end, is greater than the appeal of hatred and tyranny in any form."
He was right, on both counts. Unfortunately, the war on
terror was transmuted into the fallacy *"bin Laden is dead and
al-Qa'ida is on the run,"* repeated *ad nauseam* during the 2012
election campaign, and the justice of his statement on the
appeal of Justice and Liberty was diluted by those who,
claiming to fight racism, cannot but act on the soft bigotry
of their own beliefs. To them, modern day Fascists by any
other name, tyranny is a natural form of government for
the Arab countries, promoting Liberty in their lands is folly,
and encouraging Justice a fool's errand.

The transmutation is not by chance. In an effort to
show their open mindedness after decades of ignorance,
some policymakers embraced the wrong partners to show
their support for Muslims they had never bothered to know
in the first place. Lacking any knowledge, they embraced
associations like CAIR (Council on American Islamic Relations), whose leaders have long had a comfortable relationship with Islamic terrorists. CAIR's Executive Director,
Nihad Awad, was shown to have participated in planning
meetings with the Holy Land Foundation that resulted in
more than 12 million dollars being sent to Hamas to finance terrorism,[228] as well as in meetings of the Muslim
Brotherhood's Palestine Committee in 1993.[229] In 2014,
the United Arab Emirates listed CAIR as a terrorist organization.[230] And yet, CAIR's campaign to ban the use of the

---

[228] Dallas Morning News, *FBI: CAIR is a Front Group, and Holy Land Foundation
tapped Hamas Clerics for Fundraisers,* October 2008, Dallas News Online. Five officers of the Holy Land Foundation were eventually convicted and sentenced
to up to 65 year in prison.

[229] Scott W. Johnson, *Coming Clear about CAIR,* The National Review, August 27th,
2007.

[230] WAM, Emirates News Agency, UAE Cabinet Approves List of Designated Terrorist Organizations, Groups, Dhabi, November 15th, 2014. For a complete list
of these organizations, see Appendix IV, on page 275.

word *jihadist* in references to Islamo-Fascist terrorism finds sympathy in the halls of Congress and in intellectual circles, and CAIR members are appointed even to the White House to serve as advisors!—for instance, Zaki Barzinji, grandson of the Muslim Brotherhood point man in America, Jamal Barzinji, and a Brotherhood militant in his own right, was appointed liaison to the Muslim American community under the White House's Office of Public Engagement, after serving as Deputy Director of Intergovernmental Affairs for Gov. Terry McAuliffe of Virginia.

It is ironic, perhaps, that with millions of law-abiding Muslims in the US, indeed, of Muslim Patriots who have freely given their blood in our armed forces advancing the cause of Liberty, it is among the purveyors of Islamic National Socialism that the Obama administration and some politicians have found their points of reference. It is tragic that, in so doing, they contribute to further alienate the very Muslim population they claim to embrace. As Arab American journalist Ray Hanania so eloquently put it on occasion of the election of Donald J. Trump to the Presidency of the United States: *"The bottom line is that Trump's election is a slap on the face of American media which feeds on anti-Arab, anti-Muslim racism more than Donald Trump ever did."*[231] And so they do. Under the guise of righteous indignation for imaginary affronts, subtly they plant the seed of discord.

The same can be said of the empty rhetoric about open borders. As Kemal Atatürk remarked in his memoirs: *"Poor Wilson, he did not understand that lines which are not defended by the bayonet, by force, by honor and dignity, cannot be defended*

---

[231] Ali Younes, *Mixed reaction to Trump from prominent Muslim Americans: How do Muslim Americans feel about Trumps presidential victory?* Al-Jazeera, November 10th, 2016.

by any other principle."[232] In the strange world of social demo-cratic political correctness in which we live, to speak of controlling our borders is indulging in the unforgivable sin of immigrant bashing. But Atatürk was right. Vigilance in our borders is a necessity today more than at any other time in our history, and all the empty talk of modern-day Chamberlains will not change that fact

***

At the end of Chapter 15, I mentioned that *"as I look back to the last 30 years, I already see changes in our way of life that are not just regrettable, but perhaps the death rattle of our open socie-ty."* While I understand that this may sound alarmist, it is in fact the necessary conclusion to the changes I have seen.

In the early 1980s, before I went to work for Arrow Air, I was a tour guide for a tour operator in Corona, Queens, taking groups of mostly aspiring US citizens to Washington DC. I loved my work to the point that when I was hired as a Consultant to the Administrator of the Unit-ed Nations Development Programme in 1982, I continued to take my groups to DC on weekends.

We usually left New York on late Friday afternoons, arriving at a hotel on Dupont Circle five hours later. On Saturday, I would take the group first to the Capitol. The bus stopped in front of the building, at the foot of the stairs leading to the main door. A Capitol police officer would greet me and wave me in. There were Capitol guides, but usually they were quite busy on weekends, and the guard would simply say *"go ahead, you know the building better than anyone."* We'd visit the Rotunda, the Statuary Hall

---

[232] Jean Deny, *Souvenirs du Gâzi Moustafa Kemâl Pacha*, Revue des Etudes Islamiques I, 1927, p. 174. (Originally published in *Hakimiyeti Milliye*, Ankara, and *Milliyet*, Istanbul, March 13th to April 12th, 1926.)

(whisper spot and all), the hallways of the first floor lined with the statues that could not be placed in the Hall, the House Chamber upstairs, passing through the glancing eyes of Justice John Marshall atop the West Grand Staircase.

You can imagine the faces of my charges as we entered the Hall of the House, a mixture of delight and disbelief. None of them had come as close to the seat of government in their own countries as they were now experiencing. But that was the beginning. After lunch, we'd go to the People's House. Entering through a visitors gate in the East Side, and after passing through metal detectors, we would go upstairs to the East Room, and on to the Green Room, the Blue Room (I had to explain that that was not the Oval Office), the Red Room and the State Dining Room, before finishing the tour walking downstairs from the Cross Hall to the Entrance Hall. Usually, I was leading the group without assistance, having memorized the discourse of the official guides.

On at least three occasions we had an unexpected surprise. As we were walking into a wonderfully decorated Red Room just before Christmas in 1982, a grandfatherly figure was comfortably sitting in a sofa opposite the windows. President Reagan, I came to know, was very fond of surprising visitors by walking in unannounced. He gently and attentively talked to everyone who was not stunned out of their ability to speak.

Entrance to all public buildings, memorials and monuments was free and unimpeded. No more. Streets have been closed, pedestrian walkways diverted, entry limited and sometimes closed altogether. A tour of the White House now requires a minimum of 21 days notice, can only be obtained through a member of Congress, and in very limited numbers. Cameras and strollers are prohibited, and ID requirements are stringent. So much for the People's

House. The Capitol is not much better. Same day passes are theoretically available but very unlikely. Tours must be booked through a Representative, Senator or online, and one can only visit as part of a staff-led tour. Cameras are allowed in the building, but not in the House Chambers or the Senate floor. There goes the souvenir picture.

Try to enter a Federal Building or, for that matter, the lobby of the Woolworth Building in New York, an architectural masterpiece no longer enjoyable by the public.

As the incompetence of our leaders and the sheer imbecility of our policies continue to enlarge the threat of Islamic terrorism, we have lost freedom of movement and contact with our government institutions to a degree unimaginable thirty years ago. What was once a legitimate source of American pride is now the specular reflection of our failures.

Having to endure something barely short of a colonoscopy to access air travel, or an interpellation and demand for forms of identification not required to vote in most states to enter any public building but the post office is not only an inconvenience, it alienates the citizens from their government. Thirty years ago there was no such antagonism. The government *was* the people. Government buildings were People's Houses, and access was unrestricted beyond the imagination of the citizens of other lands. Now, as government officials retreat behind barricades, guard posts, jaw-like security barriers, chains, cement blocks, armed guards and all sorts of ineffective and ultimately useless security mirages, the concept of *them* and *us* takes hold and all sorts of people throughout the political spectrum begin to sound as if their government were an alien power.

It is in this sense that I fear the terrorists are winning. Rather than confront the problem at its source, we are bombarded with false security, alienation and the slow destruction of our open society. Sadly, the policies of the Obama administration in the Middle East have provided Jihadists with territory control and training camps in Libya, Sudan, Syria, Iraq, Yemen, and a dozen other countries, where they are preparing the next wave of commandoes. These resources will inevitably dry-up, but the thousands upon thousands of trainees will then spread like a cancer through the world and force renewed retrenchment and loss of Liberty for the rest of us, while our own Social Democrats, perennial architects of failure, will continue to speak of their crimes as if they were no more than petty larceny, and react accordingly.

There might be a reason for their apparent blindness: while not all Social Democrats are necessarily Fascists, all Fascists are by definition Social Democrats first. And our garden variety "Progressives," schooled in the Fascism of Henry A. Wallace, Vito Marcantonio and Elliott Roosevelt, might find it difficult to recognize an enemy that sounds just like they do and make the same demands that are dear to their own hearts. After all, what could possibly be wrong with fighting against colonialism and imperialism and for social justice and the improvement of the downtrodden and forgotten masses? What can possibly be wrong with the idea that the state has a role regimenting trade, business and industry? How can they be wrong who are willing to sacrifice their lives for such a noble cause? And so they fail to act. Their empathy is placed on the suffering Jihadists and not on their victims, and the cycle goes on indefinitely.

On February 17th, 2015, Marie Harf, State Department spokeswoman, took pains to describe this view on MSNBC's Hardball: *"We're killing a lot of them, and we're going to keep killing more of them...We cannot kill our way into this war...We need in the medium to longer term to go after the root causes that leads people to join these groups, whether it's lack of opportunity for jobs...We can work with countries around the world to help improve their governance, we can help them build their economies so they can have job opportunities for these people."* It is easy to mock the woman, but in all fairness, she was just stating the official US policy. Maybe we could question her integrity, instead: any person of character should have resigned rather than become the medium for such imbecility. Following the example of Susan Rice,[233] she did not resign. Instead, she was promoted to Senior Advisor for Strategic Communications to US Secretary of State John Kerry, leaving no doubt that she expressed the Obama administration's views. According to the Kerry State Department, rather than send soldiers to Europe in WWII, we should have devised a jobs program for the poor SA troopers in Germany.

Yet, maybe there is still hope, a mere possibility that we will wake up to the fact that we are not facing unemployed waiters or a crime wave, but a war. A war started over 70 years ago in the sands of the Middle East as the unrepentant Nazis and their counterparts in the Arab world created the scourge of Islamic National Socialism. Perhaps, we still have time to deploy the necessary political, diplomatic, intelligence and military resources to wipe this threat from the face of the Earth, and I fervently hope we will. For if we fail to do so, the most beautiful experiment in self government ever imagined will die a most ignominious death at the hands of the most brutish barbarians any civilization has ever faced, as our Republic joins the victims of Arrow Air in the graveyard of the forgotten.

---

[233] The hapless US Ambassador to the United Nations that tried vainly to convince us all in 2012 that the al-Qa'ida in the Islamic Maghreb attack on the US diplomatic facility in Benghazi and the mob organized by Mohammed al-Zawahiri against the US embassy in Cairo were "spontaneous demonstrations" brought about by some offensive video nobody ever saw.

***

If I could ever meet the moron who came up with the notion of *closure*, I would probably backhand slap him or her without the benefit of a word. There is no such thing as *closure*. We learn to live with wounds that never close. In the early hours of December 12th, 1985, a part of me died leaving a vacuum that time has not and, I fear, will not ever fill.

Life does go on and we wade through it, but all it takes is a smell, a sound, an image, a few notes of a song or a gentle breeze to trigger memories we thought we had successfully buried in the deepest recesses of our minds. Other times, the sight of devastation following terrorist attacks serves not only as an unwelcomed mnemonic, but as a realization that others have just become members with us in a fraternity none of us ever wanted to join. Thirty years is a long time and yet not nearly long enough.

On December 12th, 2016, we will move deeper into the fourth decade since Arrow Air 1285 was lost in Gander. Maybe we will finally have the courage to look into it with honesty and attempt, if nothing else, to dress the festering wound. Maybe the perpetrators will be caught, if they are not dead already. Maybe we'll get to know what was in those FBI files that Congress could not read in 1990. Maybe someone in Congress will grow a pair and look into this with their full oversight powers. Maybe. But I am not holding my breath.

South Boston, VA
December 12th, 2016

Appendices

Appendix I

HMSO
Documents on German Foreign Policy 1918-1945
Series D, Vol. XIII, London, 1964.

Official German record of the meeting between Adolf Hitler and the Grand Mufti of Jerusalem, Hajj Amin el-Husseini, on November 28ᵗʰ, 1941, at the Reich Chancellery in Berlin.

GRAND MUFTI:

The Grand Mufti began by thanking the Fuhrer for the great honor he had bestowed by receiving him. He wished to seize the opportunity to convey to the Fuhrer of the Greater German Reich, admired by the entire Arab world, his thanks of the sympathy which he had always shown for the Arab and especially the Palestinian cause, and to which he had given clear expression in his public speeches.

The Arab countries were firmly convinced that Germany would win the war and that the Arab cause would then prosper. The Arabs were Germany's natural friends because they had the same enemies as had Germany, namely the English, the Jews and the Communists. Therefore they were prepared to cooperate with Germany with all their hearts and stood ready to participate in the war, not only negatively by the commission of acts of sabotage and the instigation of revolutions, but also positively by the formation of an Arab Legion.

The Arabs could be more useful to Germany as allies than might be apparent at first glance, both for geographical reasons and because of the suffering inflicted upon them by the English and the Jews. Furthermore, they had had close relations with all Muslim nations, of which they could make use in behalf of the common cause. The Arab Legion would be quite easy to raise. An appeal by the Mufti to the Arab countries and the prisoners of Arab, Algerian, Tunisian and Moroccan nationality in Germany would produce a great number of volunteers eager to fight. Of Germany's victory the Arab world was firmly convinced, not only because the Reich possessed a large army, brave soldiers and military leaders of genius, but also because the Almighty could never award the victory to an unjust cause.

'The Arabs could be more useful to Germany as allies than might be apparent at first glance, both for geographical reasons and because of the suffering inflicted upon them by the English and the Jews'

In this struggle, the Arabs were striving for the independence and unity of Palestine, Syria and Iraq. They had the fullest confidence in the Fuhrer and looked to his hand for the balm on their wounds, which had been inflicted upon them by the enemies of Germany.

The Mufti then mentioned the letter he had received from Germany, which stated that Germany was holding no Arab territories and understood and recognized the aspirations to independence and freedom of the Arabs, just as she supported the elimination of the Jewish national home.

A public declaration in this sense would be very useful for its propagandistic effect on the Arab peoples at this moment. It would rouse the Arabs from their momentary lethargy and give them new courage. It would also ease the Mufti's work of secretly organizing the Arabs against the moment when they could strike. At the same time, he could give the assurance that the Arabs would in strict discipline patiently wait for the right moment and only strike upon an order from Berlin.

With regard to the events in Iraq, the Mufti observed that the Arabs in that country certainly had by no means been incited by Germany to attack England, but solely had acted in reaction to a direct English assault upon their honor.

The Turks, he believed, would welcome the establishment of an Arab government in the neighboring territories because they would prefer weaker Arab to strong European governments in the neighboring countries and, being themselves a nation of 7 million, they had moreover nothing to fear from the 1,700,000 Arabs inhabiting Syria, Transjordan, Iraq and Palestine.

France likewise would have no objections to the unification plan because it had conceded independence to Syria as early as 1936 and had given her approval to the unification of Iraq and Syria under King Faisal as early as 1933.

In these circumstances he was renewing his request that the Fuhrer make a public declaration so that the Arabs would not lose hope, which is so powerful a force in the life of nations. With such hope in their hearts the Arabs, as he had said, were willing to wait. They were not pressing for immediate realization for their aspirations; they could easily wait half a year or a whole year. But if they were not inspired with such a hope by a declaration of this sort, it could be expected that the English would be the gainers from it.

HITLER:

The Fuhrer replied that Germany's fundamental attitude on these questions, as the Mufti himself had already stated, was clear. Germany stood for uncompromising war against the Jews. That naturally included active opposition to the Jewish national home in Palestine, which was nothing other than a center, in the form of a state, for the exercise of destructive influence by Jewish interests. Germany was also aware that the assertion that the Jews were carrying out the functions of economic pioneers in Palestine was a lie. The work there was done only by the Arabs, not by the Jews. Germany was resolved, step by step, to ask one European nation after the other to solve its Jewish problem, and at the proper time to direct a similar appeal to non-European nations as well.

Germany was at the present time engaged in a life and death struggle with two citadels of Jewish power: Great Britain and Soviet Russia. Theoretically there was a difference between England's capitalism and Soviet Russia's communism; actually, however, the Jews in both countries were pursuing a common goal. This was the decisive struggle; on the political plane, it presented itself in the main as a conflict between Germany and England, but ideologically it was a battle between National Socialism and the Jews. It went without saying that Germany would furnish positive and practical aid to the Arabs involved in the same struggle, because platonic promises were useless in a war for survival or destruction in which the Jews were able to mobilize all of England's power for their ends.

Germany was resolved, step by step, to ask one European nation after the other to solve its Jewish problem, and at the proper time to direct a similar appeal to non-European nations as well'

The aid to the Arabs would have to be material aid. Of how little help sympathies alone were in such a battle had been demonstrated plainly by the operation in Iraq, where circumstances had not permitted the rendering of really effective, practical aid. In spite of all the sympathies, German aid had not been sufficient and Iraq was overcome by the power of Britain, that is, the guardian of the Jews.

The Mufti could not but be aware, however, that the outcome of the struggle going on at present would also decide the fate of the Arab world. The Fuhrer therefore had to think and speak coolly and deliberately, as a rational man and primarily as a soldier, as the leader of the German and allied armies. Everything of a nature to help in this titanic battle for the common cause, and thus also for the Arabs, would have to be done. Anything however, that might contribute to weakening the military situation must be put aside, no matter how unpopular this move might be.

Germany was now engaged in very severe battles to force the gateway to the northern Caucasus region. The difficulties were mainly with regard to maintaining the supply, which was most difficult as a result of the destruction of railroads and highways as well as the oncoming winter. If at such a moment, the Fuhrer were to raise the problem of Syria in a declaration, those elements in France which were under de Gaulle's influence would receive new strength. They would interpret the Fuhrer's declaration as an intention to break up France's colonial empire and appeal to their fellow countrymen that they should rather make common cause with the English to try to save what still could be saved. A German declaration regarding Syria would in France be understood to refer to the French colonies in general, and that would at the present time create new troubles in Western Europe, which means that a portion of the German armed forces would be immobilized in the west and no longer be available for the campaign in the east.

The Fuhrer then made the following statement to the Mufti, enjoining him to lock it in the uttermost depths of his heart:

1.   He (the Fuhrer) would carry on the battle to the total destruction of the Judeo-Communist empire in Europe.

2. At some moment which was impossible to set exactly today but which in any event was not distant, the German armies would in the course of this struggle reach the southern exit from Caucasia.

3. As soon as this had happened, the Fuhrer would on his own give the Arab world the assurance that its hour of liberation had arrived. Germany's objective would then be solely the destruction of the Jewish element residing in the Arab sphere under the protection of British power. In that hour the Mufti would be the most authoritative spokesman for the Arab world. It would then be his task to set off the Arab operations, which he had secretly prepared. When that time had come, Germany could also be indifferent to French reaction to such a declaration.

Once Germany had forced open the road to Iran and Iraq through Rostov; it would be also the beginning of the end of the British World Empire. He (the Fuhrer) hoped that the coming year would make it possible for Germany to thrust open the Caucasian gate to the Middle East. For the good of their common cause, it would be better if the Arab proclamation were put off for a few more months than if Germany were to create difficulties for herself without being able thereby to help the Arabs.

He (the Fuhrer) fully appreciated the eagerness of the Arabs for a public declaration of the sort requested by the Grand Mufti. But he would beg him to consider that he (the Fuhrer) himself was the Chief of State of the German Reich for five long years during which he was unable to make to his own homeland the announcement of its liberation. He had to wait with that until the announcement could be made on the basis of a situation brought about by the force of arms that the Anschluss had been carried out.

The moment that Germany's tank divisions and air squadrons had made their appearance south of the Caucasus, the public appeal requested by the Grand Mufti could go out to the Arab world.

GRAND MUFTI:

The Grand Mufti replied that it was his view that everything would come to pass just as the Fuhrer had indicated. He was fully reassured and satisfied by the words which he had heard from the Chief of the German State. He asked, however, whether it would not be possible, secretly at least, to enter into an agreement with Germany of the kind he had just outlined for the Fuhrer.

HITLER:

The Fuhrer replied that he had just now given the Grand Mufti precisely that confidential declaration.

GRAND MUFTI:

The Grand Mufti thanked him for it and stated in conclusion that he was taking his leave from the Fuhrer in full confidence and with reiterated thanks for the interest shown in the Arab cause.

Appendix II

The Ottoman Empire in 1917

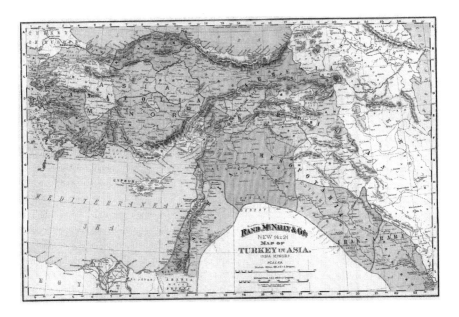

Vilayets (Provinces)

- Vilayet of Constantinople
- Vilayet of Adrianople
- Vilayet of Adana
- Vilayet of Angora
- Vilayet of Aidin

- Vilayet of Beirut
- Vilayet of Aleppo
- Vilayet of Bursa
- Vilayet of Diarbekr
- Vilayet of Syria
- Vilayet of Sivas
- Vilayet of Trebizond
- Vilayet of Kastamuni
- Vilayet of Konia
- Vilayet of Mamuret ul-Aziz
- Vilayet of Mosul

Independent Sanjaks (Districts)

- Sanjak of Eskishehir
- Sanjak of Urfa
- Sanjak of Izmid
- Sanjak of Ichili
- Sanjak of Boli
- Sanjak of Teke
- Sanjak of Janyk
- Sanjak of Chatalja
- Sanjak of Zor
- Sanjak of Kara Hissar Sahib
- Sanjak of Karasi
- Sanjak of Dardanelles
- Sanjak of Kaisari
- Sanjak of Kutahia
- Sanjak of Marash
- Sanjak of Menteshe
- Sanjak of Nidge

Vassal states and autonomies

- Eastern Rumelia (Rumeli-i Şarkî); autonomous vilayet (1878–1885); unified with Bulgaria in 1885.
- Benghazi (Bingazi Sancağı): autonomous sanjak. Formerly a part of the vilayet of Tripoli, but after 1875 dependent directly on the ministry of the interior at Constantinople.
- Biga (Biga Sancağı) (also Kale-i Sultaniye), autonomous sanjak.
- Çatalca (Çatalca Sancağı), autonomous sanjak.
- Cyprus (Kıbrıs Adası), island with special status.
- Egypt (Mısır Hidivliği), autonomous khedivate.
- Izmit (İzmid Sancağı), autonomous sanjak.
- Jerusalem (Kudüs-i Şerif Mutasarrıflığı), independent mutasarrifate, directly linked to the Minister of the Interior.
- Mecca (Mekke Şerifliği), autonomous sharifate.
- Mount Lebanon (Cebel-i Lübnan Mutasarrıflığı), autonomous sanjak or mutasarrifate, dependent directly on the Porte.
- Samos (Sisam Beyliği), principality, island with special status.
- Tunis (Tunus Eyaleti), autonomous eyalet, ruled by hereditary beys.

Appendix III

The Release of Top Al-Qa'ida Military Strategist/Ideologue Abu Mus'ab 'Al-Suri from Syrian Prison – A Looming Threat
MEMRI, February 8th, 2012

The assassination of Osama bin Laden on May 2nd, 2011, provided another opportunity for Al-Suri's philosophy to gain in stature within Al-Qa'ida's ranks. As professor of defense analysis at the United States Naval Postgraduate School Dr. John Arquilla wrote in *Foreign Policy* magazine on May 10th, 2011, *"Al-Suri, who likely plotted the 2004 Madrid bombing that caused the fall of the Spanish government and the withdrawal of Spanish troops from Iraq, has been in custody for over five years. His name is scarcely known to the mass publics of the world, and to surprisingly few in the military. But his ideas, articulated at great length—clocking in at some 1,600 pages—in his e-book "The Global Islamic Resistance Call," seem to have carried the day in setting Al-Qa'ida's new course. He and bin Laden used to spar over this approach, in which links to the core were to be almost completely severed in favor of local cells' freedom to chart their own courses and plan their own violent campaigns."*

The release of the June 3rd, 2011 official Al-Qa'ida media wing *Al-Sahab* video titled *"Do Not Rely on Others, Take [the Task] Upon Yourself"* provides further evidence that Al-Suri's doctrine will be a part of Al-Qaida's future plans. In the video, Al-Qa'ida Central's leaders all focused on the topic of *al-jihad al-fardi* (individual jihad), namely, jihad operations performed by a single individual or by a small group, which was one of Al-Suri's main principles. Abu Yahya Al-Libi explained the concept of individual jihad, defining it as *"a single person or small group of mujahideen carry out a military operation according to the laws of the shari'a...a one-man operation in the midst of the infidels' territory may be much more effective—in terms of precision and choice of target—than dozens of operations on the battlefield."*

Attiyat Allah Al-Libi praised individual jihad as *"one way of penetrating the enemy's ranks; [such operations] constitute an attack by a single individual against a great and numerous enemy...this enemy has clear weak spots, and his interests are spread across our lands, his lands, and the whole world—and they are important targets that can be reached with relative ease..."*

Anwar Al-Awlaki's statement focused on Major Nidal Hasan, the sole suspect in the 2009 Fort Hood shooting which killed 13 people and wounded 30 more. According to Al-Awlaki, Hasan serves as a model for followers of Al-Qaeda in the West dedicated to individual jihad explains, *"What he [i.e. Nidal Hasan] did was a heroic act—a magnificent operation...I support what he [i.e. Nidal Hasan] did, and call upon anyone who belongs to Islam, [or] claims to belong to Islam, and [while] he serves in the U.S. Army, to follow the footsteps of Nidal Hasan. The example of Nidal Hasan is magnificent, we ask almighty Allah to make it the beginning of many [other] Muslims [who decide] to follow in its footsteps."*

Adam Gadahn also called on members of Al-Qa'ida abroad to return *"to the countries of the Crusades,"* i.e. the West, as well as for Western-born followers to embrace individual jihad and launch attacks from their homeland. *"Muslims in the West have to remember that they are perfectly placed to play an important and decisive part in the jihad against the Zionists and the Crusaders, and to do major damage to the enemies of Islam...The way to show one's appreciation and thanks for this blessing is to rush to discharge one's duty to his ummah, and fight on its behalf, with everything at his disposal. And in the West, you've got a lot at your disposal."*

Interestingly, Gadahn also refers to Al-Qaeda leaders in jail, who many believe will spend their lives in prison, but who could go free in the future. *"I'd like to add this note of reassurance and encouragement. If it's Allah's will that you be captured, then it's not the end of the world, and it doesn't necessarily mean that you are going to spend the rest of your life in prison. In fact, let me tell you something. Over these past few years, I've seen the release of many, many mujahideen whom I'd never even dreamed would regain their freedom, yet are, as I speak, now back home with their families or back on the frontlines, fighting the enemies."* Following the recent events and instability in Syria, Al-Suri may become one such example.

Al-Qaeda Military Strategist Abu Mus'ab Al-Suri's Teachings on Fourth-Generation Warfare (4GW), Individual Jihad and the Future of Al-Qaeda

By Steven Stalinsky, Executive Director,
MEMRI – Middle East Media Research Institute[234]

Introduction

On July 1, 2010, Al-Qaeda in the Arabian Peninsula (AQAP) released the first edition of its English-language online magazine *Inspire*. The magazine, a slickly produced propaganda document, represents an effort to engage the English-language world and to recruit English-speaking Muslims to join the cause of jihad.

Inspire's primary message to its readers is that they too can be part of Al-Qa'ida and its mission, but from the comfort of their own home. Instead of traveling thousands

---

[234] http://cjlab.memri.org/uncategorized/the-release-of-top-al-qaeda-military-strategistideologue-abu-musab-al-suri-from-syrian-prison-a-looming-threat/

of miles to join the jihad, the reader need only turn on their computer and visit websites to receive training —i.e. viewing videos and listening to sermons of their favorite leaders, and learning to handle weapons, explosives and even planning attacks. For example, a Q&A section in the most recent edition of Inspire includes an unnamed Muslim living in the West asking for guidance regarding the best way to join jihad and reach the jihad fronts. The magazine's answer to him, and to all readers, is: *"[B]ased on your ability, you choose the target [in your home area]. Your pool of targets is large, so make sure to think of all of the available options. An example of something local, easy, and effective is attacking an army recruiting center, nightclub, highway, or busy shopping mall."*

Five issues of *Inspire* have now been released. They include multiple article series focusing on different aspects of jihad of vital interest to Al-Qaeda recruits and potentials recruits. One series, *"The Jihad Experience,"* by Abu Mus'ab Al-Suri, has appeared in four of the magazine's issues, and *Inspire* No 5 offers a preview of the next chapter, to be published in the upcoming *Inspire* No 6.

Abu Mus'ab Al-Suri—General Background

Abu Mus'ab Al-Suri, 53, is one of Al-Qaeda's most prominent ideologues and strategists. Born Mustafa bin 'Abd Al-Qader Setmariam Nassar, he has multiple aliases, among them 'Umar 'Abd Al-Hakim. As a member of the Syrian branch of the Muslim Brotherhood, he was exiled from Syria in 1982 after the clash between the Syrian Muslim Brotherhood and president Hafez Al-Assad.

His past in the ranks of the jihad includes close ties to Abdullah Azzam, Osama bin Laden, Mullah Omar, and Abu Musab al-Zarqawi, to name a few. At various times, he has been affiliated with, or officially a member of, the Muslim Brotherhood, the GIA (Armed Islamic Group of Algeria), the Taliban, and Al-Qaeda.

Al-Suri is also known as a trailblazer in jihadist media. In 1997, he was a founder of the media company called the Islamic Conflict Studies Bureau. Al-Suri and the Islamic Conflict Studies Bureau are believed to be responsible for delivering Al-Qaeda videotapes to foreign news media. He is also known for having arranged multiple interviews for Osama bin Laden with the Western media while he resided in Britain. He was an editor of *Al-Ansar* magazine, which promoted the insurgency in Algeria and was aligned with the Armed Islamic Group of Algeria, and, according to his wife, Helena Moreno, had "worked in the Taliban Ministry of Information as a consultant."

The U.S. government's *wanted*
and *captured* posters for Al-Suri

The U.S. National Counterterrorism Center's 2011 calendar lists Al-Suri as an *"Al-Qaeda propagandist and trainer, indicted in Spain for his role in the Madrid train bombings in 2004, and [who] was arrested in Pakistan."* A February 15, 2011 posting on the jihadi forum Shumukh Al-Islam revealed that Al-Suri is being held at a Syrian military intelligence prison in Damascus. The post stated that Al-Suri was brought to a Damascus prison on February 7, 2011. This follows a June 11, 2009 report in the London daily *Al-Sharq Al-Awsat*, also stating that Al-Suri was being held by Syria, and that it was his defense lawyers who had revealed his whereabouts – which had been unknown since his 2005 arrest in Quetta,

Pakistan. According to sources, Al-Suri had been imprisoned in Guantanamo between 2005 and 2011. Prior to that, the U.S. government offered a $5 million reward for information leading to his arrest. His wanted poster was subsequently removed from the State Department's Reward for Justice website, in 2005.

Al-Suri
A Model for Followers of Al-Qaeda in the West

For numerous reasons, Al-Suri can be seen as a model for jihadists in the West. First, as a fair-skinned, blue-eyed redhead, it is easy for him to blend in to European or American surroundings (in fact, one of his aliases is El Rubio—*"the blond one"* in Spanish). He has Spanish citizenship, and his wife, Helena Moreno, is a Spanish convert to Islam. Al-Suri has lived in several Western countries and understands Western culture. He was involved with *Da'wa*—Islamic outreach to non-Muslims in an attempt to convert them – and his wife has described him as someone "who wanted to build bridges and open dialogue with non-Muslims." She also explained that she was an atheist when she met him but that a few weeks later she converted to Islam and they were married.

Al-Suri's Blueprint for the
Next Generation of Al-Qaeda

From 2001, when the U.S. put a bounty on him, until his capture in 2005, Al-Suri wrote prolifically, including thousands of pages detailing his philosophy for a post 9/11 world. In 2004, he published online the 1,600-page *"The Global Islamic Resistance Call,"* which laid the foundations for the current generation of followers of Al-Qaeda in the West who would be willing to engage in jihadi activities without leaving their home countries, and with little or no contact with the organization. His book provided steps to launch jihad without the need to attend a training camp; indeed, he was one of the first to grasp the Internet's potential for replacing the training camp. *"The Global Islamic Resistance Call"* (which was republished in Inspire magazine and can be found later in this report) outlines strategies for future jihadists, with an emphasis on unorganized cells and leaderless Jihad. Portions of his lectures also showed up on the Internet and were circulated by jihadists on DVD for the past few years.

Even after his arrest, multiple attacks in the West were attributed to Al-Suri. While no direct evidence has emerged to formally connect him to the 2004 train bombings in Madrid or the 2006 train bombings in London, many counterterrorism officials referred to him as a guiding force behind them. Lone-wolf attacks, such as those by Fort Hood shooter Nidal Hasan and Roshonara Choudry, who stabbed a British MP, are in line with Al-Suri's teachings.

Al-Suri has been described in the media as *"one of the most important contrarians and theorist-practitioners in the history of Al-Qaeda. If bin Laden's lieutenant, Ayman Al-Zawahiri, is analogous to V.I. Lenin, Al-Suri is the jihadist Leon Trotsky: eager to pick a doctrinal fight and inject a reformist current into Al-Qaeda's operations."*

In a message attributed to Al-Suri and posted online after his capture, he boasted: *"I have in me a joy stronger than the joy of the farmer who sees the harvest of his fruits after a long planting and efforts and patience throughout decades of building."*

Teaching Lessons On Jihad
To Young Al-Qaeda Followers in the Classroom

Al-Suri taught and trained Al-Qaeda members in Afghanistan in the year 2000. His main strategy was to educate a younger generation of Al-Qaeda followers in the methods for building successful, autonomous cells for *"in-*

dividualized terrorism." He set up his own training camp and a series of videos from his lectures there can be found on leading jihadist websites. In the lectures, he can be seen pointing to maps and drawing out diagrams, his vision for Al-Qaeda becoming *"local cells in each country with little or no contact with an overall organization, but fighting for a common cause and under a common banner, in the name of jihad."*

In the videos, he is seen explaining to his students how to return to their own countries and set up their own cells. *"Don't make them more than 10 people,"* he said: *"You shouldn't expand or form too many [cells]"*...*"Form a cell with six people that you know, [even if] they don't know each other; in case you are caught they are all caught."* These small groups have been credited with helping Al-Qaeda expand and form a larger worldwide movement.

The full report can be read at:

http://cjlab.memri.org/uncategorized/the-release-of-top-al-qaeda-military-strategistideologue-abu-musab-al-suri-from-syrian-prison-a-looming-threat/

Appendix IV

UAE Cabinet approves list of designated terrorist organizations, groups

DHABI, 15th November 2014 (WAM-Emirates News Agency) — The UAE Cabinet has approved a list of designated terrorist organizations and groups in implementation of Fel Law No. 7 for 2014 on combating terrorist crimes, issued by President His Highness Sheikh Khalifa bin Zayed Al Nahyan, and the Cabinet's own resolution on the designation of terrorist organizations that provided for the publication of the lists in the media for the purposes of transparency and to raise awareness in society about these organizations.

The following is the list of organizations designated as terrorist that has been approved by the Cabinet:

The UAE Muslim Brotherhood.

Al-Islah (or Da'wat Al-Islah).

Fatah al-Islam (Lebanon).

Associazione Musulmani Italiani (Association of Italian Muslims).

Khalaya Al-Jihad Al-Emirati (Emirati Jihadist Cells).

Osbat al-Ansar (the League of the Followers) in Lebanon.

The Finnish Islamic Association (Suomen Islam-seurakunta).

Alkarama organization.

Al-Qaeda in the Land of the Islamic Maghreb (AQIM or Tanzim al-Qaidah fi Bilad al-Maghrib al-Islami).

The Muslim Association of Sweden (Sveriges muslimska forbund, SMF)

Hizb al-Ummah (The Nation's Party) in the Gulf and the Arabian Peninsula

Ansar al-Sharia in Libya (ASL, Partisans of Islamic Law).

Det Islamske Forbundet i Norge (Islamic Association in Norway).

Al-Qaeda.

Ansar al-Sharia in Tunisia (AST, Partisans of Sharia) in Tunisia.

Islamic Relief UK.

Dae'sh (ISIL).

Harakat al-Shabaab al-Mujahideen (HSM) in Somalia (Mujahideen Youth Movement)

The Cordoba Foundation (TCF) in Britain.

Al-Qaeda in the Arabian Peninsula (AQAP).

Boko Haraam (Jama'atu Ahlis Sunna Lidda'Awati Wal-Jihad) in Nigeria.

Islamic Relief Worldwide (IRW) of the Global Muslim Brotherhood.

Jama'at Ansar al-Shari'a (Partisans of Sharia) in Yemen.

Al-Mourabitoun (The Sentinels) group in Mali.

Tehrik-i-Taliban Pakistan (Taliban Movement of Pakistan).

The Muslim Brotherhood (MB) organization and groups.

Ansar al-Dine (Defenders of the faith) movement in Mali.

Abu Dhar al-Ghifari Battalion in Syria.

Jama'a Islamia in Egypt (AKA al-Gama'at al-Islamiyya, The Islamic Group, IG).

The Haqqani Network in Pakistan.

Al-Tawheed Brigade (Brigade of Unity, or Monotheism) in Syria.

Ansar Bait al-Maqdis (ABM, Supporters of the Holy House or Jerusalem) and now rebranded as Wilayat Sinai (Province or state in the Sinai).

Lashkar-e-Taiba (Soldiers, or Army of the Pure, or of the Righteous).

Al-Tawhid wal-Eman battalion (Battalion of Unity, or Monotheism, and Faith) in Syria.

Ajnad Misr (Soldiers of Egypt) group.

The East Turkistan Islamic Movement in Pakistan (ETIM), AKA the Turkistan Islamic Party (TIP), Turkistan Islamic Movement (TIM).

Katibat al-Khadra in Syria (The Green Battalion).

Majlis Shura al-Mujahideen Fi Aknaf Bayt al-Maqdis (the Mujahedeen Shura Council in the Environs of Jerusalem, or MSC).

Jaish-e-Mohammed (The Army of Muhammad).

Abu Bakr Al Siddiq Brigade in Syria.

The Houthi Movement in Yemen.

Jaish-e-Mohammed (The Army of Muhammad) in Pakistan and India.

Talha Ibn 'Ubaid-Allah Compnay in Syria.

Hezbollah al-Hijaz in Saudi Arabia.

Al Mujahideen Al Honoud in Kashmir, India (The Indian Mujahideen, IM).

Al Sarim Al Battar Brigade in Syria.

Hezbollah in the Gulf Cooperation Council.

Islamic Emirate of the Caucasus (Caucasus Emirate or Kavkaz and Chechen jihadists).

The Abdullah bin Mubarak Brigade in Syria.

Al-Qaeda in Iran.

The Islamic Movement of Uzbekistan (IMU).

Qawafil al-Shuhada (Caravans of the Martyrs).

The Badr Organization in Iraq.

Abu Sayyaf Organization in the Philippines.

Abu Omar Brigade in Syria.

Asa'ib Ahl al-Haq in Iraq (The Leagues of the Righteous).

Council on American-Islamic Relations (CAIR)

Ahrar Shammar Brigade in Syria (Brigade of the free men of the Shammar Tribe).

Hezbollah Brigades in Iraq.

CANVAS organization in Belgrade, Serbia.

The Sarya al-Jabal Brigade in Syria.

Liwa Abu al-Fadl al-Abbas in Syria.

The Muslim American Society (MAS).

Al Shahba' Brigade in Syria.

Liwa al-Youm al-Maw'oud in Iraq (Brigade of Judgment Day).

International Union of Muslim Scholars (IUMS).

Al Ka'kaa' Brigade in Syria.

Liwa Ammar bin Yasser (Ammar bin Yasser Brigade).

Ansar al-Islam in Iraq.

Federation of Islamic Organizations in Europe.

Sufyan al-Thawri Brigade.

Ansar al-Islam Group in Iraq (Partisans of Islam).

Union of Islamic Organizations of France (L'Union des Organisations Islamiques de France, UOIF).

Ebad ar-Rahman Brigade (Brigade of Soldiers of Allah) in Syria.

Jabhat al-Nusrah (Al-Nusrah Front) in Syria.

Muslim Association of Britain (MAB).

Omar Ibn al-Khattab Battalion in Syria.

Harakat Ahrar ash-Sham Al Islami (Islamic Movement of the Free Men of the Levant).

Islamic Society of Germany (Islamische Gemeinschaft Deutschland).

Al-Shayma' Battalion in Syria.

Jaysh al-Islam in Palestine (The Army of Islam in Palestine)

The Islamic Society in Denmark (Det Islamiske Trossamfund, DIT).

Katibat al-Haqq (Brigade of the Righteous).

The Abdullah Azzam Brigades.

The League of Muslims in Belgium (La Ligue des Musulmans de Belgique, LMB)

Appendix V

Classified memo from

James J. Rowley,
Chief, US Secret Service

To

John K. McDonald,
Director, Intelligence Staff, BIR

May 25th, 1964

Declassified in 2006

Cia.gov/library/readingroom/docs/SCHVEND, FRITS_0093.pdf

Gander

BEST AVAILABLE COPY

CONFIDENTIAL

~~DIR~~ 9P
(DST /2896

MAY 2 0 1965

TO : Mr. James J. Rowley, Chief
U. S. Secret Service,
Treasury Department,
Washington, D. C.

FROM : John K. MacDonald,
Director, Intelligence Staff,
Bureau of Intelligence and Research.

SUBJECT: Counterfeit U. S. Currency: Peru

The enclosed copy of a memorandum, with attachments, from
the Regional Security Officer at the American Embassy, Lima,
dated April 29, 1965, is furnished for your information and
whatever action you may wish to take.

Enclosure:

As stated (with 11 attachments to reference;
attachments 1, 18, and 11 to all others)

cc: The Honorable
J. Edgar Hoover, Director,
Federal Bureau of Investigation

The Deputy Director, Plans,
Central Intelligence Agency, attn:

DECLASSIFIED AND RELEASED BY
CENTRAL INTELLIGENCE AGENCY
SOURCES METHODS EXEMPTION 3B2B
NAZI WAR CRIMES DISCLOSURE ACT
DATE 2001 2006

MICROFILMED
NOV 1 0 1970
DOC. MICRO. SER.

MICROFILMED
JUN 4 1965
DOC. MICRO. SER.

CONFIDENTIAL

GROUP 1
Excluded from automatic
downgrading and declassification

IATT H/W

CS COPY

58-500

EXEMPTIONS Section 3(b)
(2)(A) Privacy
(2)(B) Methods/Sources ☑
(2)(G) Foreign Relations

FOR COORDINATION WITH STATE

NAZI WAR CRIMES DISCLOSURE ACT

282

BEST AVAILABLE COPY

6

OPTIONAL FORM NO. 10
MAY 1962 EDITION
GSA. GEN. REG. NO. 27

UNITED STATES GOVERNMENT

Excluded from ~ ~grading
and d....

Memorandum   CONFIDENTIAL

TO : Chief, Foreign Operations   DATE: April 29, 1965

FROM : Regional Security Officer - LIMA

SUBJECT: Cesar DUARTE, Jr.

The Subject first approached me soon after my arrival
at this post in 1962. He identified himself as a special
assistant to the then Chief of the Guardia Civil-National
and further stated that he had duel citizenship,—Peruvian
and American. He claimed to possess an American passport
and, in fact, was a very active member of the American
Legion Post in Lima, Peru. In describing his background
to me he appeared to be the type individual that could
very readily surpass the truth and, I am inclined to believe did so not only during this first interview but also
on many subsequent occasions. Nevertheless, information
he has furnished on a number of occasions did check out
and was of use. Unfortunately, because of his somewhat
overbearing nature, he has been able to disenchant a
number of officers in this Embassy of which, the Army
Attaché, Colonel John Benson, is one. Rather than cutting
him off completely, the Reporting Officer has been able
to keep his relationship with the Subject at arms length,
so to speak, and yet friendly enough to continue to receive
information from him.

At the present time, the Subject is no longer affiliated
with the Guardia Civil - the Chief, General Quia, having
been replaced, nevertheless, coming from a "good" family,
he retains contacts with a number of functionaries including
President Belaunde himself.

Several months ago, the Subject called the Reporting
Officer and reported in greater detail than was discrete
over the telephone of his personal investigations into the
Nazi underground movement that is presently in operation
throughout South America. He claimed the organization name
to be ODESSA, founded by Martin Bormann in Buenos Aires,
Argentina in 1947 is presently financed and headquartered
in Cairo, Egypt. Of special interest to him was the alleged
possession by this organization of counterfeit $10, $20,
$50 and $100 plates. He claimed these plates were originally
made for "Operation Bernhardt" during World War II

CONFIDENTIAL

Buy U.S. Savings Bonds Regularly on the Payroll Savings Plan

283

CONFIDENTIAL

headed by Federico Schwend who presently resides in Peru.
Furthermore, he insists that Schwend is still an active
NAZI as are several others which he named.

Attached is a statement he dictated to the RSO secretary and attachments. These documents, a copy of which
has been forwarded to CAS-Lima, are forwarded to you for
appropriate follow-up action if you deem it necessary.
Treasury may be interested.

Incidentally, the Subject claimed to have been on
the Los Angeles Police Force for a short period of time
as well as having acted in Hollywood in one (or several)
movies.

Attachments:

1. Statement of Cesar Ugarte, Jr.
2. Clipping "El Comercio" - Lima, Peru - April 12, 1965
3. Teletype news releases
4. Lima 13 (ANSA) News release
5. Aide Memoire - Press Conference
6. Letter from Dr. Teodoro Binder to Señor Dn.
   Marcelo Onganía, dated January 12, 1965
7. Letter from Mr. Roland Steinmetz to Senor
   Don José Antonio Encinas P., Director of
   "Expreso", undated.
8. Newspaper article "Correo" - Lima, Peru - January
   16, 1965
9. Newspaper article "Correo" - Lima, Peru - January
   17, 1965.
10. Typewritten copy of random notes
11. Typewritten copy of random notes

LRColombo:rvc

2

284

Appendices

BEST AVAILABLE COPY

STATEMENT OF CESAR UGARTE, JR.

From the time of my appointment as technical advisor for Public Relations to the Commanding General of the Guardia Civil y Policia of Peru in October 1961 - having been appointed by the then President of Peru, Manuel Prado - until my resignation on September 1, 1964, I received secret telephone calls from a confidential source with whom, to this writing, I have never had physical contact. My contact would get in touch with me by telephone whenever he would have any information of importance either for the Peruvian Government or the United States Government.

To the best of my knowledge, my source has never given me any false information, thus, I have no reason to doubt the information contained in this statement. I believe that he is either Venezuelan, Cuban or Panamanian because of his Spanish accent. By different tricks on my part I have come to know that he speaks fluent German, English and Italian. I strongly suspect that he is a member of the German Secret Organization called ODESSA which was established in 1947 in Buenos Aires by Hitler's former secretary Martin Bormann.

Since the Fall of Peron's Regime ODESSA has found refuge in Nasser's Government in Egypt and is reported to have a total of 3,087 NAZI members in this organization under the payroll of the Egyptian Government.

The first information I received that the ODESSA Organization was backing up the Communists with money was given to me at 7:03 PM on July 23, 1964. The information was the following: Counterfeit plates made for Operation Bernhardt during World War II which was headed by Federico Schwend were at present in Sao Paulo, Brazil. These plates are in the denomination of $10, $20, $50 and $100. My informant's information was that some high former NAZI war criminal now under the payroll of the Egyptian Government was due in Peru some time near the end of the year 1964. This information proved correct when Johann von LEERS arrived in Peru on December 3, 1964 with an Egyptian passport using the name of Omar Amin von LEERS under the pretext of buying $100,000 of queer bills. Von Leers had an interview with Federico Schwend at the United Arab Republic Embassy in Miraflores, Lima, Peru at 8 PM December 4, 1964. On

3

- 4 -

December 9 von Leers left for Sao Paulo, Brazil and from
there back to Cairo, Egypt. On January 28, 1965 my informant, during a pre-arranged telephone call, informed
this writer that Lima was going to be flooded with queer
US dollar bills sometime before July. This information
was passed on to US Embassy officials on the same day it
was received. Counterfeit bills did, in fact, appear in
Lima. On April 6, at 7:22 PM I received a hurried telephone call from my informant quoting the following sentence:
"Next port of entry Republic of France". I gathered from
this that the Communists, with the help of the former German, von Leers, will introduce over a million dollars
queer dollar bills in France. (NOTE: It is interesting
to note that if this statement is true, it could play a
part in the present French Government's policy of selling
dollars for gold.)

The present head of ODESSA Organization in South
America is Federico Schwend who entered Peru in 1947 with
an Italian passport. At the present time this passport
is in an Italian Embassy safe in Lima. Once Schwend was
given a German passport by the German Embassy in Lima in
1948 he paid out the sum of $4 million soles to certain
Peruvian officials in power at the time.
(Lt. Colonel) Ben Balam, who in reality is (Sturmbann
Fuehrer) Bernard Bender, former head of Special Service
Commando in the Ukraine, is now head of Nassar's Political Department. The above named Subject is to make the
necessary connections in France with the Communist Party
to release US counterfeit monies. At present he is stay-
ing at the UAR Embassy.

Special courier, Otto Steft, Jr. of Austrian nationality, was formerly leader of the Hitler Youth Group and
until 1961 was a purser for Canadian Pacific Airlines.

Richard Kohlweg is co-owner of Versailles, a combination dining and counter service located at Plaza San
Martin, telephone number 82449, Lima, Peru. He is married
to a Peruvian citizen who was formerly employed by the
First National City Bank of New York, Lima, Peru. Her
name is unknown to me at the present time. Kohlweg is
suspected as being the Number 4 man in the ODESSA Organization in Peru whose duties are to help distribute counterfeit US bills.

The case of Dr. Teodoro Binder who is also a member
of the ODESSA Organization and suspected as being its main
contact in the Peruvian jungles was brought to light on
Thursday, January 1, 1965 at a conference whereby Dr.
Zuzunago Flórez defended Dr. Binder. To my knowledge,
Marcelo Ongania, at present Manager of ANSA, Italian
news agency in Peru, is the only newspaper man+who has made
a full inquiry into the background of Dr. Binder. Attached herewith are teletype news releases from the above
named news agency and also a copy of the speech made by
Dr. Zuzunaga at the press conference. It is proven that
Dr. Binder entered Peru with a false passport along with
his wife. The following are the translated questions which
Ongania asked at the press conference:

1. Where is the letter of presentation written
    by a Miss Meyer addressed to a Miss Maria
    Luisa Giddemeister?

2. Where does this Miss Meyer live now - what
    part of Germany?

3. Binder gave a talk on Vitbzche at the German
    Club and ended by giving a summary on German
    War criminals. At the press conference Binder
    claimed to have helped the United States Govern-
    ment capture three war criminals.

4. Which passport did he use when he came to Peru?

5. With which passport did his wife enter Peru?

6. Did he serve in the German Army?

7. Where did he stay in Brazil?

8. Why did he not medically operate?

9. Are you a friend of Hans Schaeffer? (Schaeffer
    at present lives behind the home of Federico
    Schwend at Kilometer 17 Central Highway in
    Santa Clara. Schaeffer's former address was
    Rue Roch, Paris, Gestapo Headquarters.)

10. Are you also a friend of Federico Schwend?

5

- 4 -

11. Who is Becker? (Becker for 9 months was
    Dr. Binder's personal guest at the former's
    hospital in Pucallpa, Peru.)

12. With what kind of documents did you live
    in Brazil?

13. What were your relationships with a Miss
    Colitim in a hospital in Hamburg. This
    woman claims that she knows you under the
    name of Ollendorfer.

According to Ongania's newspaper investigation, Dr. Binder
was a member of the Hitler Youth Group, never studied to
be a doctor and served in the German Army from 1941 to
1945 when said Subject escaped to Zurich, Switzerland,

Upon being given information that the next port of
entry for the counterfeit US dollar bills will be the
Republic of France, Lt. Col, Henry Dufour, French Military Attache, French Embassy, Lima, Peru left for the
Island of Martinque to hold a conference with a high official of the French Military Intelligence. He left Lima,
Peru on April 2, scheduled to arrive in Bogota, Colombia
on April 9 and returning to Lima on April 13. Further information supplied by the undersign to Mr. Rode, Assistant
to the French Attache in Lima is to be forwarded to Bogota,
Colombia in time to be given to Colonel Dufour. This information will include: Approximate date of arrival in
France of Lt. Colonel Ben Salam with Egyptian diplomatic
passport. Salam is to make contact with the French Communist Party. It is reported that as yet, not confirmed,
that he is to distribute with the help of the French Communist Party the sum of $2 million counterfeit US dollar
bills, denomination of $10, $20, $50 and $100 which includes US travelers checks.

6

ATTACHMENT #10   RANDOM NOTES

    ODESSA's latest planned escape was for HANS WALTER ZECH-NENNTWHICH, Ex-Capt. SS. This man was up for trail for the mass murder of 5,200 Polish Jews at PINSK. His escape to Egypt from BRUNSWICK PRISON.

    ODESSA - its initials are for Organization DER ENEMALIGEN S. S. ANGEHORIGEN (organization of former members of the SS.

    This Organization is also known as the "Spider's Web".

    Head of ODESSA in Spain is former SS Colonel Otto "Scarface" SKORZENY of resc (?) Mussoline fame.

    Of the 2,000 odd ex-members of Hitler's SS Gestapo & SD members I list some of the most important on the wanted list and also active members of ODESSA: at present in Lima is OMAR AMIN VON LEERS who is Johann (or Jahannes) von Leers - has made contact with Federico Schwend for the buying of queer dollar bills. The amount to be bought will be that of the equivalent of $100,000 read monies. The price set is at 47 on the dollar - the plates made for "Operation Berhardt" of $10, $20, $50 and $100 are now in Sao Paulo, Brazil.

    This queer monies are said to be sent to Cuba and then to find its way to the US. The $100,000 in this writing is being given by the Egyptian Government.

    One of ODESSA's main contact here is Baron Von Sothen at present second to the German Ambassador in Peru. At present he is now in Rio de Janeiro apparently on a month's vacation with wife and children - it is known the Baron von Sothen is still an ardent NAZI.

    My informant has told this writer that the one man who can give any clue of who has the plates now is Federico Schwend. Schwend has been seen coming out of the United Arab Embassy in Miraflores four times in the past six months - after von Leers left ODESSA's office in Buenos Aires; (after the Fall of Peron) Schwend has taken over as #1 as ODESSA's man in South America. I have not been able to find out under what name von leers in traveling under. He is due to return to Europe and the Far East via Brazil day after tomorrow. I have no reason what so ever to doubt my source of information for it has been proven XXM true in the past. I know not who he is for he gets in touch by phone at no given date only when he has vital information. I have been promised, if at all possible a queer bill.

DIR ~~443~~

DST 12896

ATTACHMENT #1

RANDOM NOTES

8

Real names of seven top ODESSA members: 1) Louis El Haj is Louis Heiden known German newspaperman. Former head of the Reich German News Agency. Has recently translated Hitler's MEIN KAMPF into Arabic - has sold over 1,000,000 copies; 2) Lt. Col. Ben Salam is sturmbann Fuehrer Bernard Bender. Former head of Special Service Commando in the Ukraine. Wanted for war crimes. Is now head of Nassar's Political Department; 3) Omar Amin von Leers is Johann von Leers - is head of Nassar's Propaganda Department - is head of ODESSA in Cairo; 4) Lt. Col. Hamid Suleiman is S. S. (Gruppenleiter) Heinrich Sellman - former Chief of Gestapo in Ulm, Germany. Is now head of Egypt's Secret State Police Department. This Department is Nassar's equivalent of the NAZI S. S.; 5) Lt. Col. Naim Iahim is S. S. Hauptstabsarzt Heinrich Willerman - is wanted for sterilization experiments on Jewish woman. He is now in charge of Samara Concentration camp in the Western Desert, 120 miles South of Cairo; 6) Col. Na'am El Wachar is S. S. (Standarten Fuehrer) Leopold Gleim. Was head of Gestapo in Poland. Is now head of the entire Secret Police in Egypt. Helped Nassar on his coup d'etat when he seized power; 7) Prof. Ben AMMAN is rocket scientist Wolfgang Pilz - is head of Nassar's secret Project 333 which makes atomic weapons. (He is a non-ODESSA member.)

(Otto Skorzia is former officer of the German Army now working for Scimbet (Israel's Secret Service). Has given vital information of ODESSA's movements in South America.)

ODESSA is responsible for the death of Eward Peters, Chancellor Ludwig Erhard's personal bodyguard. It is supposed that he hung himself instead of facing charges for war crimes.

Otto Steft Senior, was one of the officers that along with Fritz Knochlein murdered British soldiers of the Norfolk Regiment who surrended at hamlet of de Paradis. This crime is known as the "Paradis Massacre". Knochlein was tried by British Military Court in 1948, was sentenced to death. But Steft escaped. He is now messenger for ODESSA in South America. Has plates for American dollars. At present is in Brazil due to leave for Paraguay on December 8, 1964. Is rumored he killed Shimbet agent few months ago on the Peruvian-Brazilian border. Has been seen with Dr. Josef Mengele. Last time officially seen was at Rio de la Plata on April 18, 1962 in the company of Federico Schwend and Josef Mengele.

Bibliography

Bibliography

In addition to hundreds of newspaper and magazine articles, declassified documents and studies, most of which are listed in the footnotes, the following sources were used:

Books

Raoul Aglion, *The Fighting French,* New York, 1943

'Abd al-Fattāh Muhammad al-Awaysī, *The Muslim Brothers and the Palestine Question, 1928-1947,* London, 1998

Amin al-Husayni, *Facts or Truths about the Palestine Problem,* Cairo, 1954

Touraj Atabaki, Erik Jan Zucher, eds., *Men of Order: Modernisation in Turkey and Iran, 1918-1942,* London, 2004

Falih Rifki Atay, *19 Mayis,* Ankara, 1944

Falik Rifki Atay, *Atatürk'ün Bana Anlattiklari,* Istanbul, 1955

Capt. T. C. Badcock, *A Broken Arrow, The Story of the Arrow Air Disaster in Gander – Newfoundland,* St. John's Newfoundland, 1988

Randall C. Baselt, Robert H. Cravey, *Disposition of Toxic Drugs and Chemicals in Man,* Year Book Medical Pub., 1989

Nicholas Bethell, *Das Palästina Dreieck: Juden und Araber im Kampf um das britische Mandat 1935 bis 1948,* Frankfurt, 1979

Ian Black, Benny Morris, *Israel's Secret Wars: A History of Israel's Intelligence Services,* New York, 1991

Richard Breitman and Norman J.W. Goda, *Hitler's Shadow: Nazi War Criminals, U.S. Intelligence, and the Cold War,* Washington DC, 2010

Werner Brockdorff, *Flught vor Nürnberg,* Munich, Verlag Welsermühl, 1969, p. 116.

Jorge Camarasa, *Los Nazis en la Argentina,* Buenos Aires, 1992

Neil Caplan, *Futile Diplomacy, Vol. II: Arab-Zionist Negotiations and the End of the Mandate,* London, 1986)

John Roy Carlson (Arthur Avedis Boghos Derounian), *Cairo to Damascus,* New York, 1951

Hillel Cohen, *Army of Shadows: Palestinian Collaboration with Zionism, 1917-1948,* University of California Press, 2008

Kevin Coogan, *Dreamer of the Day; Francis Parker Yockey and the Postwar Fascist International,* Brooklyn, 1999

Martin Cüppers, et. al. (Hrsg.), *Naziverbrechen: Täter, Taten, Bewältigungsversuche,* Darmstadt, 2013

David G. Dalin, John F. Rothmann, Alan M. Dershowitz, *Icon of Evil: Hitler's Mufti and the Rise of Radical Islam,* New Brunswick, New Jersey, 2009

Norbert Ehrenfeld, *The Nuremberg Legacy; How the Nazi War Crimes Trials Changed the Course of History,* New York, 2007

Zvi Elpeleg, *Through the Eyes of the Mufti: The Essays of Haj Amin,* London, 2009)

Les Filotas, *Improbable Cause, Deceit and Dissent in the Investigation of America's Worst Military Air Disaster,* Toronto, 1991

Klaus Gensicke, *Der Mufti von Jerusalem und die National-sozialisten. Eine politische Biographie Amin el-Husseinis,* Darmstadt, 2007

Sander L. Gilman and Steven T. Katz, eds., *Anti-Semitism in Times of Crisis,* New York University Press, 1991

Jeffrey Herf, *Nazi Propaganda in the Arab World,* Yale University Press, 2009

Adolf Hitler, *Hitler's Table Talk: His Private Conversations,* London, 1953

Gerhard Hoepp, *Mufti-Papiere,* Berlin, 2004

Joseph Howard, *Operation Damocles: Israel's Secret War Against Hitler's Scientists, 1951-1967,* New York, London, 2013

Eberhard Jäkel, *Hitlers Weltanschauung: Entwurf einer Herrschaft* Tübingen, 1969 (translated as *Hitler's World View: A Blueprint for Power,* Middletown, CT, 1972)

Efraim Karsh, *Palestine Betrayed* , Yale University Press, 2010

Hermann von Keyserling, *La Révolution mondiale et la Responsabilité de l'esprit,* Paris, 1934

Elie Kedourie and Sylvia G. Haim, *Zionism and Arabism in Palestine and Israel,* London, 1982

Walter Laqueur and Barry Rubin, *The Israel-Arab Reader,* New York, 2001

Jennie Lebel, *The Mufti of Jerusalem Haj-Amin el-Husseini and National-Socialism,* Belgrade, 2007

Johann von Leers, *Brennpunkte der Weltpolitik,* Stuttgart, 1941

Meir Litvak and Esther Webman, *From Empathy to Denial: Arab Responses to the Holocaust,* London, 2009

Wolfgang Lotz, *Fünftausend für Lotz: Der Bericht des Israelischen Meisterspions Wolfgang Lotz,* Munich, 1973

Halford J. Mackinder, *Democratic Ideals and Reality*, New York, 1962

Klaus-Michael Mallmann and Martin Cüppers, *Halbmond und Hakenkreuz. Das Dritte Reich, die Araber und Palästina*, Darmstadt, 2006

Klaus-Michael Mallmann and Martin Cüppers, *Nazi Palestine: The Plan for the Extermination of the Jews in Palestine*, Washington, DC, 2010

Thomas Mayer, *Egypt and the Palestine Question: 1936-1945*, Berlin, 1983

Corinna Metz, *The Way to Statehood: Can the Kosovo Approach be a Role Model for Palestine?*, Bremen, 2014

Benny Morris, *1948: A History of the First Arab-Israeli War*, Yale University Press, 2008

David Motadel, *Islam and Nazi Germany's War*, Harvard University Press, 2014

David Patterson, *A Genealogy of Evil: Anti-Semitism from Nazism to Islamic Jihad*, Cambridge University Press, 2011

Henry Picker, *Hitlers Tischgeschpraeche im Führerhauptquartier*, Stuttgart, 1977

Karla Poewe, *New Religions and the Nazis*, New York, 2006

Barry Rubin and Wolfgang G. Schwanitz, *Nazis, Islamists, and the Making of the Modern Middle East*, Yale University Press, 2014

Anwar Sadat, *In Search of Identity: An Autobiography*, New York, 1978

Silvano Santander, *Técnica de una traición. Juan D. Perón y Eva Duarte, agentes del nazismo en la Argentina*, Buenos Aires, 1955

E. Sasson, *Baderekh el Hashalom: Igrot Vesihot* [On the Way to Peace: Letters and Discussions] (Hebrew) (Tel Aviv: Am Oved, 1978

Joseph B. Schechtman, *The Mufti and the Fuehrer,* New York, 1965

David Th. Schiller, *Palästinenser zwischen Terrorismus und Diplomatie,* München, 1982

Niclas Sennerteg, *Hakkorset och halvmånen: Nazister i Mellanöstern,* Stockholm, 2014

Marco Sennholz, *Johann von Leers: Ein Propagandist des Nationalsozialismus,* Berlin, 2013

Christopher Simpson, *Blowback: America's Recruitment of Nazis and Its Effects on the Cold War,* New York, 1988

Albert Speer, *Inside the Third Reich: Memoirs by Albert Speer,* New York, 1970

William Stevenson, *The Bormann Brotherhood,* New York, 1973

Holm Sundhaussen, *"Jugoslawien,"* in *Dimension des Völkermords: Die Zahl der jüdischen Opfer des Nationalsozialismus,* ed. Wolfgang Benz, Munich, 1991

Pierre-André Taguieff, *Rising from the Muck: The New Anti-Semitism in Europe,* Chicago, 2004

David Tal, *War in Palestine 1948: Strategy and Diplomacy,* London, 2004

H. R. Trevor-Roper, *Last Days of Hitler,* New York: Collier Books, 1986

US Department of State, *Blue Book on Argentina, History of the Nazi-Argentine Plot Against the Freedom and Peace of the World,* Memorandum of the United States Government, Washington, DC, February 1946

Simon Wiesenthal, *Großmufti: Großagent der Achse,* Salzburg-Wien, 1947

Michael Wildt, *Generation of the Unbound; The Leadership of the Reich Security Office (Generation des Unbedingten; Das Führungskorps des Reichssicherheitshauptamtes),* Jerusalem, 2002

Robert S. Wistrich, *Who's Who in Nazi Germany,* London,, 1995

Robert S. Wistrich, *Anti-Judaism, Antisemitism, Delegitimizing Israel,* University of Nebraska Press, 2016

Michael bar Zohar, *J'ai risqué ma vie: Isser Hadel le n° 1 des services secrets Israéliens,* Paris, 1971

Michael bar Zohar, Nissim Mishal, *Mossad, The greatest Missions of the Israeli Secret Service,* London, 2016

Michael ben Zohar Randall C. Baselt, Robert H. Cravey, eds., *Introduction to Forensic Toxicology,* Biomedical Publications, 1981

Medical Studies

Canfield DV, Chaturvedi AK, Dubowski KM, *Carboxyhemoglobin and blood cyanide concentrations in relation to aviation accidents,* Civil Aerospace Medical Institute, Federal Aviation Administration, Oklahoma City, OK

Abstract:

INTRODUCTION: It is important in aviation accident investigations to determine if a fire occurred during flight or after the crash and to establish the source(s) of the toxic gases.

METHODS: Bio-specimens from aviation accident fatalities are submitted to CAMI for analyses. In blood, CO is analyzed as carboxyhemoglobin (COHb) and hydrogen cyanide as cyanide (CN-). Analytical data were stored in a database, and this database was searched for the period of 1990-2002 for the presence of COHb and CN in the submitted cases.

RESULTS: Out of 5945 cases, there were 223 (4%) cases wherein COHb was > or = 10%. Of the 223 cases, fire was reported with 201, no fire with 21, and undetermined fire status with 1. CN concentrations were at or above 0.25 microg x ml(-1) in 103 of the 201 fire-related cases. None of the 21 non-fire cases had CN-, but nicotine was detected in 9 of the cases. All non-fire cases with COHb > 30% (four cases) were associated with exhaust leaks. Of the 223 cases, COHb-CN- fractional toxic concentration (FTC) was lethal only in 31 cases with elevated CN levels.

CONCLUSIONS: The presence of COHb and CN in elevated concentrations in the blood of victims found by autopsy to have died on impact would indicate an in-flight fire. In the absence of fire and CN-, the elevated COHb concentrations would suggest an exhaust leak, particularly at COHb > 30%. The findings of this study also suggest that, in addition to COHb, CN plays a detrimental role in fire-associated aviation accident fatalities.

Chaturvedi AK, Smith DR, Canfield DV. *Blood carbon monoxide and hydrogen cyanide concentrations in the fatalities of fire and non-fire associated civil aviation accidents, 1991-1998,* Toxicology and Accident Research Laboratory (AAM-610), Aeromedical Research Division, Federal Aviation Administration, US Department of Transportation, Civil Aeromedical Institute, Oklahoma City, OK

Abstract:

Blood samples submitted to the Civil Aeromedical Institute (CAMI) from aviation accident fatalities are analyzed for carbon monoxide (CO), as carboxyhemoglobin (COHb), and hydrogen cyanide, as cyanide (CN(-)). These analyses are performed to establish possible exposure of victims to smoke from in-flight/post-crash fires or to CO from faulty exhaust/heating systems. The presence of both gases in blood would suggest that the victim was alive and inhaled smoke. If only COHb is elevated, the accident (or a death) could be the result of CO contamination of the interior. Information pertaining to blood levels of these gases in aviation fatalities, in relation to the associated accidents, is scattered or not available, particularly with regard to toxicity. Therefore, considering that COHb> or =10% and CN(-)> or =0.25 microg/ml are sufficient to produce some degree of toxicological effects, the necessary information was extracted from the CAMI database. Samples from 3857 fatalities of 2837 aviation accidents, occurring during 1991-1998, were received; 1012 accidents, encompassing 1571 (41%) fatalities, were fire associated, whereas 1820 accidents were non-fire related. The remaining five accidents were of unknown fire status. There were fewer fire *related fatalities and associated accidents in the (COHb> or =10% and CN(-)> or =0.25 microg/ml) category than that in the (COHb<10% and CN(-)<0.25 microg/ml) category. No in-flight fire was documented in the former category, but in-flight fires were reported in 14 accidents (18 fatalities) in the latter category. No non-fire accident fatality was found wherein levels of both gases were determined to be at or above the stated levels. There were 15 non-fire accidents with 17 fatalities wherein only COHb (10-69%) was elevated. The present study suggests that aviation fire accidents/fatalities were fewer than aviation non-fire accidents/fatalities and confirms that aviation accidents related to in-flight fires and CO-contaminated interiors are rare.*

Stamyr K, Thelander G, Ernstgård L, Ahlner J, Johanson G, *Swedish forensic data 1992-2009 suggest hydrogen cyanide as an important cause of death in fire victims,* Work Environment Toxicology, Institute of Environmental Medicine, Karolinska Institutet, Stockholm, Sweden.

Abstract

Between 60 and 80% of all deaths related to fire are attributed to toxic fumes. Carbon monoxide (CO) is commonly thought to be the major cause. However, hydrogen cyanide (HCN) is also formed. Still, the exact contribution of HCN to fire-related fatalities is unknown. The aim of the study was to investigate the impact of HCN in relation to CO as a cause of death in fire victims. Data on carboxyhemoglobin (COHb) and blood cyanide from deceased fire victims in the period 1992-2009 were collected from two Swedish nationwide forensic databases (ToxBase and RättsBase). The databases contain data on COHb and/or cyanide from 2303 fire victims, whereof 816 on both COHb and cyanide. Nonparametric statistical tests were used. Seventeen percent of the victims had lethal or life-threatening blood cyanide levels (>1 µg/g) and 32% had lethal COHb levels (>50% COHb). Over 31% had cyanide levels above 0.5 µg/g, an indication of significant HCN exposure. The percentages may be underestimates, as cyanide is quickly eliminated in blood also after death. Our results support the notion that HCN contributes more to the cause of death among fire victims than previously thought.

Grabowska T, Nowicka J, Kulikowska J, Kabiesz-Neniczka S., *Assessment of exposure to hydrogen cyanide in fire fatalities in the aspects of endogenous hydrogen cyanide production as a result of putrefaction processes in the deceased,* Z Katedry i Zakładu Medycyny

Sadowej i Toksykologii Sadowo-Lekarskiej, Slaskiego Uniwersytetu Medycznego w Katowicach, Katowice.

Abstract

On account of endogenous hydrogen cyanide (HCN) production in the deceased, it is not easy to assess exposure to HCN in people who died in fire involving closed rooms (flats, garages, cellars, etc). In the paper, the authors present the results of blood determinations of hydrogen cyanide in fatalities of explosions and fires occurring in coal-mines, as well as fires in closed rooms. It has been demonstrated that the time of exposure to a high temperature and the temperature itself hamper autolysis processes that lead to production of endogenous HCN in fire fatalities.

Newspapers

Boston Globe, Boston, Massachusetts
Los Angeles Times, Los Angeles, California
The Chicago Tribune, Chicago, Illinois
New York Times, New York, New York
San Francisco Chronicle, San Francisco, California
The Herald, Miami, Florida
The Plain Dealer, Cleveland, Ohio
The Sun Sentinel, Fort Lauderdale, Florida
Times Picayune, New Orleans, Louisiana
Washington Post, Washington, DC

Other

SS Officer's Service Records, Berlin Document Center Series 6400, National Archives, Washington, DC.
The SS Officers' Service Records consist of personnel dossiers for more than 61,000 SS officers with the rank of SS-Untersturmführer (second lieutenant) and above, arranged alphabetically by surname. These constitute personnel files maintained by the SS-Personalhauptamt (SS Personnel Main Office) in Berlin, later supplemented by the BDC with records from other collections. Included are individuals who belonged to the Allgemeine-SS (general SS), Waffen-SS (the military branch of the SS), Sicherheitsdienst (SS security service), and SS and police security formations, including the Gestapo (secret state police). Waffen-SS officers include many non-Germans of various European nationalities. The date span of records contained in the dossiers extends from 1932 to as late as March 1945. The

collapse of Germany in 1945, however, precluded the regular maintenance of records, and therefore not all SS officers can be verified.

Argentina, Government, Amt für internationale argentinische Veröffentlichungen, *Ursprung und Entwicklung der argentinischen Sozialgesetzgebung,* Buenos Aires, 1952 (Origin and Development of Argentine Social Legislation, produced by the Argentine Office for International Publications during the Nazi regime of General Perón. Original in German)

Made in the USA
San Bernardino, CA
07 January 2018